D1600992

Leisure and cultural conflict in twentieth-century Britain

MANCHESTER
1824

Manchester University Press

STUDIES IN POPULAR CULTURE

General editor: Professor Jeffrey Richards

Leisure and cultural conflict in twentieth-century Britain

Edited by
BRETT BEBBER

Manchester University Press
Manchester and New York

distributed in the United States exclusively by Palgrave Macmillan

Copyright © Manchester University Press 2012

While copyright in the volume as a whole is vested in Manchester University Press, copyright in individual chapters belongs to their respective authors, and no chapter may be reproduced wholly or in part without the express permission in writing of both author and publisher.

Published by Manchester University Press
Oxford Road, Manchester M13 9NR, UK
and Room 400, 175 Fifth Avenue, New York, NY 10010, USA
www.manchesteruniversitypress.co.uk

Distributed in the United States exclusively by
Palgrave Macmillan, 175 Fifth Avenue, New York,
NY 10010, USA

Distributed in Canada exclusively by
UBC Press, University of British Columbia, 2029 West Mall,
Vancouver, BC, Canada V6T 1Z2

British Library Cataloguing-in-Publication Data
A catalogue record for this book is available from the British Library

Library of Congress Cataloging-in-Publication Data applied for

ISBN   978 0 7190 8704 2 hardback

First published 2012

The publisher has no responsibility for the persistence or accuracy of URLs for any external or third-party internet websites referred to in this book, and does not guarantee that any content on such websites is, or will remain, accurate or appropriate.

Typeset in Adobe Garamond with Gill Sans display by
Special Edition Pre-press Services, www.special-edition.co.uk
Printed in Great Britain by CPI Antony Rowe Ltd, Chippenham, Wiltshire

STUDIES IN POPULAR CULTURE

There has in recent years been an explosion of interest in culture and cultural studies. The impetus has come from two directions and out of two different traditions. On the one hand, cultural history has grown out of social history to become a distinct and identifiable school of historical investigation. On the other hand, cultural studies has grown out of English literature and has concerned itself to a large extent with contemporary issues. Nevertheless, there is a shared project, its aim, to elucidate the meanings and values implicit and explicit in the art, literature, learning, institutions and everyday behaviour within a given society. Both the cultural historian and the cultural studies scholar seek to explore the ways in which a culture is imagined, represented and received, how it interacts with social processes, how it contributes to individual and collective identities and world views, to stability and change, to social, political and economic activities and programmes. This series aims to provide an arena for the cross-fertilisation of the discipline, so that the work of the cultural historian can take advantage of the most useful and illuminating of the theoretical developments and the cultural studies scholars can extend the purely historical underpinnings of their investigations. The ultimate objective of the series is to provide a range of books which will explain in a readable and accessible way where we are now socially and culturally and how we got to where we are. This should enable people to be better informed, promote an interdisciplinary approach to cultural issues and encourage deeper thought about the issues, attitudes and institutions of popular culture.

Jeffrey Richards

Contents

List of figures

Series editor's introduction

This impressive collection of essays has been written to a specific revisionist agenda. It aims to remove the subject of leisure from the periphery to the mainstream of social and cultural history and to do so by stressing that leisure is not just a mass distraction uniformly consumed but is subject to differential responses dictated by age, gender, race and class. The collection is also bound together into a cohesive whole by its adherence to three shaping themes: the idea of contestation and conflict within the culture, the imposition of regulation by the authorities and the relationship of leisure to national identity.

The collection opens with a magisterial overview by Jeffrey Hill of the historiography of leisure from the critiques of mass culture by such early commentators as E. P. Thompson, Richard Hoggart and J. B. Priestley through the work of Marxists, feminists, postmodernists and empiricists to argue for a move away from overly rigid approaches and to identify unexplored areas and unanswered questions in the history of leisure. Cécile Doustaly, who brings the collection to a close, is similarly critical of the existing historiography of women's leisure, rejecting the idea of women as a homogeneous group, and, while recognising that leisure both reflects and validates gender divisions, argues that women have found greater opportunities for freedom and opposition within the culture.

The other essays turn the spotlight on different leisure activities. Alison Abra examines the 1920s dance craze and the contest between dance professionals and the dancing public over what the national dance should be, a conflict crystallised in attitudes to the Charleston. Brad Beaven challenges the notion of working-class audiences as passive consumers of cinema, citing differences of age, class and gender in shaping individual responses, and investigating audience behaviour and motivation for attendance at the cinema which was not always primarily to see the film. Sandra Dawson charts the promotion of circus between 1920 and 1945 as an essential element in a democratic and unified English identity and national heritage. Kelly Boyd argues persuasively that the ubiquity of westerns on British television screens in the 1950s was not an example of Americanisation of the culture but should be seen as part of a shared transatlantic culture, which reflected the 'special relationship' but allowed British audiences to interpret the films and programmes as parables of good versus evil and examinations of adventurous masculinity rather than propaganda for the American way of life. Brett Bebber examines the efforts of successive governments, recognising the significance of football to the national identity, to regulate the violence of football crowds by introducing new policing policies, sponsoring architectural improvements and invoking family values as the justification for reform. Chad Martin analyses the failure of successive attempts to decriminalise cannabis since the 1960s, linking it to the demonisation of the 'Permissive Society' of that 'swinging' decade in the succeeding years. Extensive primary research, fresh thinking and fluently argued interpretations characterise this stimulating, readable and welcome new collection.

Jeffrey Richards

List of contributors

Allison Abra is in the Faculty of Arts at the University of Manitoba. She is the winner of the 2009 Twentieth-Century British History Prize for her article, 'Doing the Lambeth Walk: Novelty Dances and the British Nation', published in *Twentieth Century British History*.

Brad Beaven is principal lecturer in social history at the University of Portsmouth. His most recent book is entitled *Leisure, Citizenship and Working-Class Men in Britain, 1850–1945* (Manchester University Press, 2005).

Brett Bebber is assistant professor of history at Old Dominion University. He is the author of *Violence and Racism in Football: Politics and Cultural Conflict in British Society, 1968–98* (Pickering and Chatto, 2012).

Kelly Boyd is senior fellow at the Institute for Historical Research, London. She is the author of *Manliness and the Boys' Story Paper in Britain: A Cultural History, 1855–1940* (Palgrave, 2003) and co-editor with Rohan McWilliam of *The Victorian Studies Reader* (Routledge, 2007).

Sandra Trudgen Dawson is instructor of history at Northern Illinois University. She is the winner of the 2006 Twentieth Century British History Prize for her article, 'Working Class Consumers and the Campaign for Holidays with Pay', published in *Twentieth Century British History*. Her book, *Packaging Pleasure: Holiday Camps in Twentieth Century Britain* (Manchester University Press, 2011) is a cultural and social history of the holiday camp industry.

Cécile Doustaly is lecturer in British Studies and a member of the CICC (Civilisations et Identités Culturelles Comparées des Sociétés Européennes et Occidentales) at the University of Cergy-Pontoise, Greater Paris.

Jeffrey Hill is professor of history at De Montfort University and the former director of the International Centre for Sport History and Culture. He is the author of several books and articles. Among his most recent publications are *Sport and the Literary Imagination* (Peter Lang, 2006), and *Sport, Leisure and Culture in Twentieth-Century Britain* (Palgrave, 2002).

Chad Martin is assistant professor of history at Indianapolis University. He studies post-war British countercultural and subcultural movements, as well as music.

Contextualising leisure history

BRETT BEBBER

What are the links between leisure and British society? How does leisure reflect and contribute to broader patterns of cultural and social change in Britain? The history of leisure is not merely the analysis of play, recreation or free time, nor only the study of pleasures experienced as individuals or collectives. Forms of leisure in twentieth-century Britain, as elsewhere, were part and parcel of cultural change, shaped by ongoing processes of social negotiation and cultural contestation. In neglecting close attention to the political and social contexts from which forms of leisure emerged and developed, historians risk separating their analysis of leisure and how people enjoyed them from the structural and material circumstances in which people lived. Likewise, as British historians build broader narratives of cultural history in the twentieth century, the activities and amusements of historical actors cannot be ignored. Yet, amidst renewed calls for historicisation and contextualization, not only in leisure histories but also throughout the discipline generally, the multiple ways in which leisure and culture intersect, overlap, and become mutually constitutive still need careful analysis.

Historians hoping to stitch the fabric of cultural history with patterns of continuity and change often build their arguments on constituent forms of culture, including art, architecture, music, style, religion, counterculture, history and leisure, among others. Weaving the threads together by forging linkages between analysis of these forms and broader transitions in politics and society, however, often proves exceedingly difficult. This analytical problem reflects an institutional one. As Jeffrey Hill points out in this volume, histories of British leisure have often been marginalised and separated from conventional cultural histories, relegated to some secondary place outside the 'mainstream'. Fashioning various connections between leisure and culture, between the histories of leisure and social and cultural history generally, comprises the central challenge facing the field of leisure history.

Most leisure historians now recognise, of course, that leisure activities were not formed in a vacuum. They were products of desire and ingenuity, formed within the contours of cultural debates that indicated people's longing not only to partake of entertainment and recreation but also to create their leisure. Nor were forms of leisure static or given: they were created over time and through social dialogues that reflect contemporary political and cultural tensions. Leisure was also conditioned by the dominant struggles for power that hierarchised difference in any given society. Race, class, gender, sex and generation all delineated and fractured the experiences of leisure and forced social groups to remake their recreation within delimited boundaries. These power relationships also configured identities and mentalities, shaping the way people think about themselves and their recreations. Moreover, leisure evolved and responded to the ways in which partakers imbued leisurely activities with their own goals, ideals and expectations. Like other forms of popular culture, leisure was not only reflective of struggles for social power but also productive of them. In sum, leisure was clearly implicated in the making of British culture.

This volume aims to demonstrate how debates within select forms of leisure not only reproduced broader discursive disputes but also constituted challenges to the broader British social and cultural landscape in the twentieth century. The articles here emphasise the contextualisation of their objects of study, understanding manifestations of leisure within the multiple contemporary social milieus where they both thrived and declined. In doing so, they stress that illuminating the social anxieties and political ideals surrounding the development of particular varieties of leisure helped to shape their development and consumption. No cultural forms were merely top-down phenomena: they may have reflected effete expressions of 'high culture', especially as social elites governed many spaces where leisure was carried out, but they nearly always also suggested the touch of their consumers. Most forms of leisure and mass entertainment were both created and consumed by a wide variety of historical actors. Forms of leisure thus not only echoed cultural trends and reflected dominant British values but also became prime engines of social contestation and cultural negotiation in twentieth-century Britain.

The articles in this collection examine moments in the development of a wide range of leisurely activities, including cinema, the circus, dance, television, football, drug culture and women's leisure. They do not represent a total history of twentieth-century leisure in Britain, nor do they weave the whole sum of multiple threads of historical research into the history of leisure and popular culture. However, in emphasising the figurative role of context, as well as the demand to historicise prominent moments in the history of leisure, they do complement each other in the exploration of three main themes.

First, the theme of contestation and conflict appears in several of these studies, revealing how forms of leisure were often forged from debates about their proper (or improper) form. Participants and consumers not only demanded changes to what was on offer but also became subject to impositions from political authorities and legal parameters. Conflict often determined the shape of leisure, a result of the struggles between participants and providers. In many cases, these differences resonated with widespread cultural debates about British values and British society.

Second, regulation constitutes a primary theme in twentieth-century leisure. The extensive proliferation of leisure activities after the First World War brought with it new questions about how leisure should be experienced, provided and overseen. These questions both mirrored and differed from earlier Victorian concerns about impropriety and free time. But they also reflected the ongoing processes of modernisation and standardisation, revealing how impulses to remake and purportedly improve leisure experiences unfolded. Of course, not everyone could agree on how leisure should be provided or regulated, as many of these articles demonstrate. Regulation was further complicated when the state assumed the responsibility of providing leisure for its citizens in the post-war period. As state agencies attempted to both direct and meet the demands of leisure-seekers, they participated in processes of manipulating and developing leisure provision and management.

Finally, because of their common focus on British leisure, exploring the theme of 'Britishness' in forms of leisure is patently unavoidable. Emphasising the importance of Britishness in shaping leisure, as well as how it imbued partakers with national and imperial identities, reveals how many Britons viewed leisure as an extension of British values. In many of these articles, questions of propriety and socially acceptable conduct, riddled with class-based and racialised language, demonstrate the degree to which leisure and British identity overlapped. For many, regulating and standardising leisure, along with challenging existing modes of leisure control, were matters of both personal and national importance. In addition, ensuring activities were 'appropriately British' helped many to evoke meaning from leisure. As many historians have pointed out, 'Britishness' and national identities of the four nations were not always congruent. Though challenged by constituent national identities, Britishness often loomed above and beyond them, making up a consciousness that defined itself against other continental counterparts.[1] A Protestant, English national identity tended to dominate the creation of Britishness, imposing itself on the other 'peripheral' nations, though they did assert themselves more prominently in the post-war period.[2] Nonetheless, Britishness became an adaptable and flexible identity that most Britons lived, experienced and accepted as common sense, often in leisure activities.[3]

The chapters have been organised chronologically to stress their historicisation, beginning with an introductory article on theory, methodology and historiography. Jeffrey Hill appropriately addresses the problem of contextualisation, along with a whole host of other theoretical issues, in his thinkpiece on British leisure studies. Hill identifies two dominant and overlapping themes in previous leisure histories: social control and mass culture. Born of early Marxist social histories, these themes illuminated how historical actors and historians alike worried about the compromising effects of leisure. In addition, because leisure was increasingly packaged and marketed in the twentieth century, early analysts fretted about the loss of popular pastimes and voluntarism. More recent studies have incorporated the postmodern or cultural turn in historiography generally, stressing the importance of meaning and identity in leisure experiences, to challenge the emphasis on leisure's ill effects on the body politic. Hill also identifies new directions that emphasise the importance of consumption, heritage and history studies, and the formative aspects of gender in shaping leisure experiences. He concludes that in engaging a broad array of topics and methodologies, historians have exploded original concerns about social control and now attempt to answer a multitude of questions that defy any attempt at an aggregate history of leisure.

Taking the First World War as one bookend in periodising the twentieth century, leisure historians have noted that the end of the war led to an increase in public leisure as Europe recovered from the tragedies of global conflict. As Allison Abra describes it, a veritable dancing craze emerged in bourgeois Britain and gave rise to a wide range of enthusiastic participants. Modern ballroom dancing quickly became subjected to various forms of regulation, including accreditation for teachers and standardisation of the dancing style. Using dance publications and ephemera, Abra shows that just as modern ballroom dancing emerged as a popular form of leisure, organisers and teachers aimed to ensure that its English qualities were maintained and codified. A series of ballroom dancing conferences initiated debates about the professionalisation of British dance and helped to determine the form and steps of acceptable dancing practice. Their role was to determine the acceptable conventions of dance within boundaries of gentility and propriety that determined the English dancing aesthetic, and then to disseminate these decisions to the public through classes, exhibitions, competitions and print culture. However, Abra also demonstrates that the interests and preferences of dancing professionals did not always coincide with everyday practitioners. She argues that the public's attachment to the Charleston style conflicted with professionals' emphasis on the tango, forcing both groups to accommodate changes to practice and regulation. The entire debate reveals that popular dancing in Britain did not evolve through a top-down imposition of professionals to public, but rather that both played an active role in the production of the nation's dance culture. In the end, the development of dance reveals a dialectical relationship between the producers and consumers of popular culture, elucidating the processes of negotiation between professional will and public inclinations in British leisure.

Another international leisure activity, going to the cinema, emerged in decidedly different ways in Britain as well. Brad Beaven's chapter on interwar cinema challenges dominant historical perceptions of working-class film audiences and the experiences of cinema-going. Historians have too often assumed that audiences for any type of popular culture are uncritical or static in their reception of the fare on offer. This is due, in part, to researchers who have followed the lead of cinema studies in privileging the films themselves as sources. Here, Beaven uses contemporary surveys and memories of working-class men and women who regularly attended the cinema to show that others have overstressed the impact of films. In first analysing two dominant trends in historical studies of film, Beaven elucidates how previous examinations focused on film as propaganda for both British national sacrifice and the saliency of empire. Yet, while films certainly projected messages of social acquiescence and imperial majesty, cinema-goers rarely accepted these messages uncritically, often attending the cinema for purposes other than the film itself. As in football matches and musical concerts later in the century, the rowdy behaviours of working-class neighbourhoods were recreated in cinemas, which came to serve not only as venues for cheap entertainment but also as sites of community interaction, routine socialisation, and romantic pursuits. Moral critics intent on protecting British gentility and morality attacked the cinema for its degenerative and pacifying effects on British citizens, especially when houses showed American films but could not determine the decorum of working-class men and women.

Beaven not only reworks questions of consumption and reception of forms of popular culture in interwar Britain but also interrogates oversimplified reckonings of the presence of social divisions amongst cinema-goers that colour our perceptions of popular interwar leisure. Gender and generation certainly affected cinema attendance. Youths and women looking for relief from every-day domestic drudgery attended cinemas more frequently than older men still captivated by other forms of popular leisure. But from the beginning the cinema became an arena for social interaction across gender and genera-tion, especially at showings on nights and weekends when most did not work. Beaven also argues that accessibility of cinema-going to the working poor did not necessarily make it a form of popular leisure devoid of class distinctions. Cinema companies maintained social stratification through priced seating and sectioning, allowing working-class men and women to create their own social habits and cinema experiences within their areas of the picture houses. Reassessing these experiences reveals that despite moral anxieties from middle-class Britons, constant regulation from authorities, and inculcation of domi-nant imperial and national values through film, working-class men and women enjoyed cinema on their own terms.

Sandra Dawson's research on the circus also traces how older forms of mass leisure were replaced by new varieties of recreation and pleasure-seeking. The revival of the British circus in the interwar period has scarcely been explored. Because historians have focused either on the medieval origins of circus enter-tainment or eighteenth- and nineteenth-century performance and representa-tion, Dawson's study of the circus recovers its cultural relevance and social contests in this troubling period. She argues that British circus promoters used the circus and the myth of its British genesis to stave off anxieties about global conflict, domestic financial woes and the threat of continental fascism. Far dif-ferent from other mass commercial leisure activities in the technological age, the circus emerged as an unwavering national institution in advertisements when British promoters portrayed it as emblematic of a more stable Victorian era. Circus marketing reflected a nostalgia for British military prowess and the imperial tradition. Its most 'British' characteristic, however, was its democratic and egalitarian atmosphere, leading to its massive growth and commercial expansion after the First World War. The interwar circus was emblematic of British democracy not only because it was accessible to all – though stratified by seating structure and boundaries of privilege – but also because it embodied democratic practices that attracted grassroots activists and lobbyists seeking parliamentary favour and manipulating public opinion. Debates about animal cruelty, regulation, and the influx of foreign circus workers reveal that the circus was renovated through democratic processes and cultural contestation. Recasting the circus as both British and democratic allowed circus promoters such as Bertram Mills to assert that British circuses were not only capable of providing mass entertainment for their citizens but would do so by restoring selected 'British' qualities to this form of leisure.

The emergence of television made leaving the house for entertainment an often more difficult and more expensive alternative than it had been before the Second World War. Drawing on recent historical investigations into the effects of 'Americanisation', Kelly Boyd analyses the impact the American western had on British television. By airing cowboy films and western specials regularly, the British Broadcasting Corporation and other independent media outlets effectively mediated the greater presence of American culture on the screen. As a convenient and cheap way to fill broadcast schedules, westerns became a mainstay of BBC programming. British viewers, however, drew different messages from their American counterparts, who relied on westerns to project aspects of American national character. Television watchers absorbed the dominant messages differently on each side of the Atlantic. For Britons, westerns recreated imperial frontiers and presented highly ethical instruction and clear morals. The format of the western became well worn by the mid-century, articulated not only in television, but earlier in silent films, boys' story papers, and Wild West shows. Boyd argues that even as American westerns expanded in influence and popularity, they did not negate British cultural authority, as British production companies and viewers appropriated the western in their own way. The cowboy pictures on British television came to represent typified national ideals of justice and chivalry, even though they did not challenge the format or framework of the genre. In the end, the article illuminates the manifestations of a single cultural debate – concerns about Americanisation and the western – among several different audiences and groups of British television viewers.

Despite the increase in television viewers throughout the 1950s and 1960s, many still looked to traditional forms of leisure outside the home and often attempted to remake those experiences for their own generation. My own article explores the changing environment of football supporters and the anxieties it brought to this particular leisure industry from the mid-1960s forward. Much of the study of football violence has followed popular interest and gradually devolved into investigations of different club 'firms' and anecdotal pop sociology. Yet the football industry and the practical changes it wrought on the experience of football spectatorship cannot be overstated. Football violence catalysed the evolution of football spectatorship from popular family leisure to territorial, closely monitored and segregated supporters' communities. As I demonstrate in this article, rowdy football spectating occasioned the gradual and partial takeover of British football by state authorities during the 1970s.

Using the Safety at Sports Grounds Act of 1975 as a touchstone – the Act that ushered in tighter government control of football environments and drastic changes to the architecture of stadiums – I explore the political discourses surrounding sports reform in the wake of politically embarrassing football violence. Politicians coupled football spectatorship with sports participation in general, perceiving that watching football encouraged young and old alike to partake of local sports initiatives. Therefore, the emergence of football violence troubled politicians for several reasons.

First, Labour representatives worried about the party's association with sport regulation and sport funding because they perceived working-class sports advocates as their rank-and-file voters. Failing to protect football spectating or reducing funding for sports development both nationally and locally threatened to spoil Labour's courting of these working-class voters.

Second, both Tories and Labour members worried about the costs of regulating football violence and forcing football clubs to make changes to stadiums that facilitated better policing without public subsidisation. Not only had football violence decreased football attendances, and therefore football clubs' revenues, but the British treasury had little money for leisure development in the crippling financial depression of the mid-1970s. In order to justify widespread changes to the football industry and persuade voters of the necessity of public sports expenditure, politicians marketed their involvement in sports as necessary to recapture the family atmosphere that both football spectatorship and sports participation supposedly engendered. Because the football environment had come to be dominated by working-class men, politicians romanticised the 'pre-hooligan' era and promised that football reform would reinstitute football as a safe leisure pursuit for women and children. In the end, both Home Office documents and Parliamentary debates reveal the intimate connections among political competition, football supportership, and family values during this period.

Smoking marijuana, coded from the beginning as both rebellious and criminal, might also be classified as a commonsense form of leisure for many Britons. Chad Martin's article examines the growth of cannabis use and the resulting criminalisation of the drug in post-war Britain. First associated with a small number of post-war immigrants from the colonies, cannabis became increasingly linked with various youth subcultures in the 1950s and 1960s. Press and legislative authorities demonised drug use within these communities, leading to an increased number of arrests and sensationalised media attention. Martin begins by noting the impact of an initial Home Office study, chaired by Baroness Wootton, that took testimony from police authorities, medical experts, social workers and organisations devoted to drug law reform. Though the final report recommended major reductions in the penalties associated with cannabis use, which suggested that drug liberalisation policies could be forwarded, public opinion about drug use became very conservative throughout the late 1960s. Martin convincingly shows that, although other contemporary legislation ended theatre censorship, decriminalised homosexuality and legalised medical abortions, drug reform measures proved particularly polarising and failed to advance. In comparing drug use with other reform discussions, he contextualises the debate within a wide range of discourses in the reform era. By the end of the twentieth century, Britain had the highest number of cannabis users in the European Union, but its cannabis laws were far less liberal than those of other major western European countries.

Martin illuminates the source of this contradiction, suggesting that several government authorities used cannabis penalisation to gain political capital, even though sociological studies and several advisory councils suggested delegalisation of 'soft' drugs. Using a wide range of sources including underground press, Parliamentary debates, government reports and drug reform organisation documents, Martin shows that negative public perceptions of drug use polarised legislative debates about delegalisation, making it nearly impossible for reforms to occur. Antagonising debates on drug use also reflected other cultural disputes and social divisions within British society. Politicians and some press outlets exploited drug use as a method of discrediting and belittling immigrant groups, racialising the discourse on cannabis reform. Police authorities employed drug laws to reinforce their power over rebellious youth and immigrant communities. While Conservatives stressed drugs as a key issue in the perceived national decline they promised to reverse, the Labour party abandoned permissive reforms as a matter of political expediency. In sum, cannabis use became a socially acceptable but politically volatile form of post-war leisure, marked by incensed moral entrepreneurs that called on broader discourses of permissiveness, moral degeneracy and national decline.

In the final chapter, sociologist Cécile Doustaly evaluates research on how gender affected experiences of leisure throughout the century, concluding with an analysis of bingo after the 1960s.

First, in effort to see women's hidden participation in leisure where previous historians and social scientists have not attempted to, Doustaly analyses previous studies and qualitative definitions that have precluded the recognition of women's engagement with leisure. As many historians have noted, defining what leisure is proves difficult, for analysts have to differentiate free time and leisure time, organised and unorganised activities, and individual and collective forms. Using a wide variety of studies from history, sociology and gender studies, Doustaly argues that leisure cannot be defined as merely a matter of taste or personality since it depends on a highly stratified and individual context composed of obligations, external influences and social commitments which tend to affect women more than men. Most women's leisure participation intersects with other professional, family and community responsibilities.

Second, Doustaly questions the positive impact of the 'society of leisure' on women throughout the twentieth century. While many of the spaces where leisure occurs – places such as pubs or bingo halls – remain ordered by masculine codes, women's participation in leisure can also contradict oversimplified binaries of work/leisure and family/leisure. Labour and family life directly impact women's participation in leisure and the forms they pursue, often making leisure far from affirming and recreational.

Third, though traditional inequalities between men and women in access to leisure have changed little, historians and sociologists cannot overgeneralise the impact of gender. Within many of the social groups she explores, such as the wealthy or the young, gender differences are less marked. Conversely, inequalities in leisure tend to affect those women who are already excluded by other social divisions, especially minorities and the poor. Nonetheless, Doustaly's review affirms that leisure not only reflects divisions of gender in twentieth-century British society but also validates them by limiting varied expressions of femininity.

By the last decades of the twentieth century providing and protecting leisure had clearly become a political problem. And yet the concerns of politicians, providers and participants often reflected concerns from the first half of the twentieth century and even the Victorian period. Many of the ongoing questions about the propriety of different forms of leisure, and how to regulate and consume them, were now contested by different social groups, but in new terrains. In particular, conflicts of Britishness, and how British leisure contributed to social cohesion and social anxieties, remained poignant and important to many Britons' lives.

Notes

1 David McCrone, 'Unmasking Britannia: The Rise and Fall of British National Identity', *Nations and Nationalism* 3, no. 4 (1997): 579–96.

2 Richard Weight, *Patriots: National Identity in Britain, 1940–2000* (London: Pan Macmillan, 2002), 1–16.

3 Paul Ward, *Britishness Since 1870* (London: Routledge, 2004).

'What shall we do with them when they're not working?': leisure and historians in Britain

JEFFREY HILL

The literary critic and theorist Terry Eagleton, in a newspaper piece written at the time of the 2010 association football World Cup, played to his readers a familiar refrain about the function of leisure in society: basically, it takes people's minds off more serious matters. Of football he says: '[n]o finer way of resolving the problems of capitalism has been dreamed up, bar social-ism.'[1] For Eagleton, then, the explanatory concept of 'social control', once much used by historians and sociologists, appears still to be in rude health. Can we agree with him? Is leisure simply to be understood as a diversion?

Considering the continual anxiety that 'leisure' has aroused in British society, social historians were a long time in arriving at a systematic study of it. Peter Bailey's elegant analysis of the state of leisure historiography at the end of the twentieth century showed only too clearly that the ball began rolling with any real momentum only in the 1970s. There followed a quarter-century when leisure became a force in the academy, with many new areas opened up and a rich variety of methodologies and theories called into play.[2] Before this, as Emma Griffin, a recent contributor to the field, has noted, much of the writing on leisure tended to be commemorative rather than analytical.[3] However, one important understanding of leisure had been cultivated in nineteenth- and early twentieth-century political circles out of which emerged influential ideas about the nature of leisure and its function in relation to the social order. The notions of 'social control' and 'mass culture', with their origins in continental European socialism, were essential to this discourse, though on the whole in Britain their application took a moral rather than a dialectical turn.[4]

The writings of J. B. Priestley illustrate this well. Priestley was a noted journalist, novelist and playwright, born in the Yorkshire town of Bradford in the 1890s when it was a hotbed of radicalism.[5] It was here that the socialist Independent Labour Party (ILP) was formed and established its first stronghold.[6] Priestley's thinking formed an arch between a Victorian insistence on leisure as 'recreation' and the critique of a new mass culture that became common among intellectuals in the interwar years. In *English Journey*, a state-of-the-nation survey conducted in the early 1930s, he had offered some caustic comments on the newer forms of entertainment encountered on his travels; nowhere more so than in the midlands town of Nottingham where, under the impact of modernity, its medieval Goose Fair had been transformed, he felt, into a site of easy mechanised pleasures.[7] A few years later, in the early stages of the Second World War, Priestley articulated a more rounded stance in the famous 'reconstruction' issue of the progressive photo-journalism magazine *Picture Post*. Priestley echoed some of the views expressed in *English Journey* while at the same time looking forward to a post-war world when life (it was expected) would be better, both materially and spiritually. An anticipated reduction in the hours of labour would be of benefit to all, but what would fill the new 'leisure' time thus achieved?

> Not, I hope, an orgy of silliness and passive mechanical enjoyment. We do not want greyhound racing and dirt track performances to be given at all hours of the day and night, pin table establishments doing a roaring trade from dawn to midnight, and idiotic films being shown down every street. We do not want a terrifying extension of that 'Why Move From Your Armchair?' spirit, which persuades the average citizen that he is really an invalid in one of the final stages of heart disease. If we are all to be freed from hours of work simply in order to lie back and be mildly tickled, then I cannot see that much will have been gained. [8]

Priestley was not himself particularly elitist in his attitudes to culture, but he did believe that people should fashion their own spare-time activities, and there was a warning in this passage against the idea of leisure as a distraction. He had earlier recalled the robust men of his youth who met in pubs to sing. '[T]hey were not being humbugged by any elaborate publicity scheme on the part of either music publishers or brewers … they were singing glees over their beer because they liked to sing glees over their beer.'[9] In putting his faith in an essentially *voluntarist* principle – leisure was something created out of the day-to-day activities of people themselves – Priestley was part of that discourse formed in the previous century and which had certainly not exhausted itself by the mid-twentieth. It continued to show much vitality as politicians, critics and social observers struggled with the problem of leisure in the ages of 'affluence' and 'post-industrialism'.

Priestley's politics were progressive in nature, possibly 'left wing' (his commitment to the Labour Party was evident in the general elections of 1945 and 1950). He did not, however, go as far as those on the left of the labour movement for whom 'culture' was regarded as an instrument to be wielded in the class struggle. Early socialists, especially those who lived in Britain's 'Little Moscows' – the industrial towns and villages where dynamic groups of the ILP or Communist Party attempted to create a distinctive cultural life – complemented their challenge to industrial capitalism in the economic and political spheres with an attempt to oppose capitalist leisure forms.[10] Like Priestley, though in a more explicitly political way, these people felt that leisure in its commercial forms had a capacity to detract from people's 'true' nature. One cardinal feature of leisure was not forgotten; no matter how much importance was placed on 'spare time' – and for many people it was *very* important – it did not exist in isolation. Leisure was intimately connected to work. 'Work/leisure' was an inseparable relationship, though not necessarily an equal one. Leisure – 'non work' – was something earned by working and in many cases made possible by other people's work. But, in an industrial context especially, leisure might carry a qualitatively superior meaning. Whereas paid work is carried out in time bought by the employer, often involving dull machine-related, repetitive tasks, leisure represents 'free' time, time to be oneself, when something of a person's 'true' nature is revealed. Many of these themes ran through Priestley's writings, expressed particularly in his concern that leisure should say something authentic about an individual and not be time given over simply to a passive absorption of 'silliness'.

Theories and histories

Some of the leading practitioners of the first academic phase of leisure history showed traces of this intellectual legacy in their approach. The most significant was Richard Hoggart, who came to the question of leisure from a literary background and produced his seminal study *The Uses of Literacy* almost two decades before the 1970s' take off.[11] Hoggart renewed Priestley's attention to mass culture, portraying a northern working-class community in the first half of the twentieth century whose traditional resilience, humour and collective spirit was under threat from new mass media, largely American in inspiration if not directly in origin. Like Priestley, Hoggart's 'theory' was muted; a sense of social class was certainly there, though in an intuitive sense (you know the working class from how its members speak, dress and where they live). Any Marxist undercurrents were elided into a binary divide of 'them and us' – a division between those who make decisions and those who have to live, as best they might, with their consequences. It was a divide deeply embedded in popular mentalities and language, though this provenance excited little response from other writers, for whom a Marxist analysis seemed more fitting. Robert Malcolmson, for example, was among the first to produce an empirically based historical analysis that linked leisure to economic, social and political conditions. He was very clearly part of the historical movement influenced by E. P. Thompson's thesis on the formation of working-class consciousness in the late-eighteenth and early-nineteenth centuries under the impact of the new economic methods and thinking of industrialisation.[12] Malcolmson focused upon this same problem. In some sense he appeared to share with Priestley a regret about the loss of popular pastimes, though in his case the changes were less to do with the rise of new commercial leisure forms than with new disciplines introduced by factory bosses, moral reformers and legislators. Together they amounted to a social engineering of new habits and relations that profoundly affected leisure, almost redefining it. Some of the vitality that had characterised long-established communitarian pastimes was drained away. Leisure, Malcolmson argued, became a more *controlled* set of activities.[13] a point developed by Eileen and Stephen Yeo in their 1981 collection of essays on popular culture.[14] Malcolmson's was (and remains) an influential book that showed, as befitted the work of a student of Thompson, the dialectical context of leisure – something that could not be detached from 'base-superstructure' models of social analysis, no matter whether 'base' was the determining element or whether relative autonomy was to be found in superstructural forms.[15] The same Marxist (or in some cases quasi-Marxist) methodology was present in many leisure studies of this period. Hugh Cunningham's study of the same processes over a similar time provides a possibly more nuanced and optimistic interpretation of the changes, placing greater emphasis on resistance without necessarily dispensing with the notion of class conflict in leisure.[16] But the Marxist stamp, though common, was not universally accepted. The 'revisionist' work of historians Golby and Purdue showed that leisure and popular culture could be understood without the explanatory tool of class conflict.[17] Some studies perceived changes in leisure as part of a process of modernisation, a concept strongly promoted by non-Marxist sociologists.[18] The predominant focus, as in Malcolmson's work, was the transition from what might be (and sometimes was) termed 'traditional culture' to a modern, commercially influenced world of entertainments: from leisure made, on the whole, by people themselves, to one where it was sold and bought in a market-based relationship.

But the change was not necessarily seen as involving loss. Modernisation, in leisure as in material life generally, could be seen to bring improvements; when they could, people often voted with their feet for the new ways, leaving the countryside for the bright lights of the town. An outstanding study conducted in this vein related to France rather than England. It was Eugen Weber's magisterial *Peasants Into Frenchmen*, [19] which among many other things cast doubt on older interpretations of the impact of the French Revolution. Modernisation theory, however, raised problems of chronology. The idea of a pre-industrial leisure world untainted by business and commerce never really rang true, and in the empirical work of J. H. Plumb there was an early warning shot against too neat a periodisation of leisure. Plumb unearthed plenty of commercialism in eighteenth-century English leisure, a feature re-affirmed in later work by historians of sport, especially David Underdown's study of cricket in southern England.[20] Even it its first flush, then, there were doubts about some of the theory that accompanied leisure history.

The first critical examination of this phase of leisure history was provided by Gareth Stedman Jones in a perceptive essay of 1975 that raised issues still relevant to us several decades later.[21] Considering the inchoate nature of the subject as it had developed at that point, Stedman Jones felt able to propose only 'interim judgements', but he saw two major problems. One, unavoidable at this early stage, was an uneven development that presumably would in part be remedied over time. Its main feature, to Stedman Jones's eye, was the neglect of gender relations in leisure: how, in the historical problem that had chiefly attracted attention at that time – the transition to industrial capitalism – a preoccupation with the experiences of male workers had held back any serious analyses of the sexual division of leisure. The second, and greater, problem was a conceptual or methodological one. In their readiness to borrow from disciplines such as sociology and anthropology (in principle, we may suppose, a good thing) historians had been far too uncritical in their use of the concepts chosen. The chief villain in the piece was 'social control'. Even when applied in a Gramscian sense of 'hegemony', Stedman Jones insisted, the concept was often a crude functionalist device that failed to do justice to the complexities of the historical situations being scrutinised. It made false assumptions, asked the wrong questions and produced unconvincing answers. To resolve such problems he advocated (in addition to a more subtle use of concepts) a situating of leisure within a broader social history. In fact, Stedman Jones seemed sceptical of making leisure a distinct branch of social history at all, for in relation to work, wherein the real problems of class struggle resided, it appeared to him to have a secondary status in historical enquiry.[22]

As Bailey has shown, however, far from vacating the specialist place it was assuming in the mid-1970s, leisure history has grown by leaps and bounds in its separate sphere. It is now difficult, especially in a single chapter, to encompass the whole field, even if we can decide where its boundaries lie. If in its infancy leisure history was the child of the 1960s Thompson-inspired school that revolutionised social history, taking it out of the junior role it had occupied in 'economic and social' history departments and equipping it with an essentially class-based explanatory lexicon, the paradigm represented by that moment is now far less dominant. Class is one among many organising concepts, and theory now draws from a multiplicity of sources. A recent work, Rudy Koshar's edited collection of essays, might be taken (both for its empirical innovation and its conceptual sophistication) as an exemplar of present practice.[23] Koshar's collection broadens out the context of British leisure into a spatial setting that includes Britain, France, Germany, Austria-Hungary and Italy, a much-needed European perspective for a subject that has previously tended to be studied from the perspective of individual national experiences. Moreover, it adds substantially to a currently fashionable interest in cultures of consumption and shows just how much the experience of 'leisure' depended upon the possession of material objects: from relatively expensive ones such as motor cars, bicycles and holidays – and their indispensable supporting text, the travel guide – to cheap popular pleasures like cigarettes and cinema seats. It is important too because, for all its emphasis on consumption, it nevertheless contains a strong element of cultural history and is attentive to matters of *meaning* and *identity*. Two chapters in particular – those of Erik Jensen on boxing spectatorism in Weimar Germany, and Patrick Young on tourism in France between 1890 and 1918[24] – offer a nuanced analysis of how the issue of identity may be teased out of consumerist practices. Jensen's remarkably comprehensive yet succinct analysis of boxing reveals a wide range of enthusiasm for the sport, including that of women, and lays down important markers for the study of a topic seriously neglected in all countries. Young, interrogating the literature of the Touring Club de France, shows how middle-class attention was directed to *la France profonde*, as the regions and localities were represented as repositories of essential 'Frenchness'. The process thus combined the commodification of the provinces as tourist destinations with the creation of an imagined unified France. The chapter connects with many of the themes present in Eugen Weber's great work on the French countryside, which saw modernisation as almost a colonial enterprise.[25] Finally, though not the least important of its attributes, the collection engages with the difficult issue of interpretation. Can the development of 'leisure' be pigeon-holed into an interpretive category, in the way that the once-influential theorists of the Frankfurt School sought to do? Koshar gives a pretty unequivocal 'no' to this question, realising that the field contains too many 'histories' and too many 'varied temporalities and narratives' (p. 15). Where sociologists might still find patterns in leisure development to satisfy their thirst for models, the historian is now confronted with a multiplicity of tendencies that defy straitjacketing. The field, it seems, has grown so rich and varied that it defies any plausible master narrative.

This is not to suggest that it has fragmented into anarchy. Theory itself has become a focus of debate. The old functional problematic contained in social control has given way to issues raised in cultural history, a development that itself reflects the postmodern interest in discourse and language: the 'linguistic (or cultural) turn'. It has brought to the fore what have been called 'signifying practices': that is, historical behaviour represented in texts and lived culture that, as Francis Mulhearn once put it, 'produce sense'.[26] The reception within the academy of methodologies informed by such ideas has not always been a warm one. Many have been repelled by theory, feeling that it predetermines the outcome of enquiry; such sceptics prefer to operate according to a time-honoured empiricist method that lets the facts speak for themselves, the historian being bound (in the well-worn phrase) by 'the rules of evidence'. An early critique of new methods in social history was formulated by the late Tony Judt, by no means a 'traditionalist' in historiographical terms.[27] It failed to deter the experimentalists. By the 1990s there were few areas unaffected by postmodern thinking.[28] The 'challenge' of the new thinking remains. Douglas Booth's *The Field*, an examination of the ways in which the history of sport – a burgeoning addition to the leisure field – has been practised in Britain, Australia and the USA, provides a clear recent example of the rumpus new ideas can cause among a community of historians. Booth's 'deconstructionist' views, cogently argued if perhaps over-stridently expressed, were too much for many.[29] This, to be sure, was an extreme case, and there are, I suspect, few now working in the area of leisure who, while they might demur at Booth's version of fully fledged 'postmodernism', would retreat into a traditional empiricism.

Many acknowledge that 'theory' can be of value. Beyond this, though, there are other questions to be posed. Is the study of signifying practices and representations a worthwhile one? A good deal of recent leisure history has been preoccupied with questions of meaning and identity. Peter Bailey's work, for example, takes ideas from the study of language to examine the development of what he calls 'the new populist ideology of consumerism' in the late-nineteenth century, with a strong emphasis on performative aspects.[30] In sport history there has been a keen interest in on- and off-field activities that has given us important studies of the formation of Welsh, Scottish and Irish and sometimes English identities.[31] In the hands of a historian like Robert Darnton, famous for his deconstruction of the cat massacres in eighteenth-century Paris, such influences and methods are a rewarding way of opening up new insights into popular mentalities.[32] There are, to be sure, doubters. A formidable one is Eric Hobsbawm, who, writing in 2009, had cause to doubt some of the newly laid paths that led to 'feelings'. 'There is a major difference between the traditional scholar's questions about the past – "What happened in history, when and why?" – and the question that has, in the last 40 years or so, come to inspire a growing body of historical research: namely, "How do or did people feel about it?"'[33] The problems for historians in this, says, Hobsbawm, are 'considerable'; they include questions such as how representative feelings are, and how far they can be taken as a measure of popular opinion. It is a matter that should concern historians of leisure, where much of the research deals with people's responses (not always easily verified) on questions of consumption, class, gender, politics, reading, films and so forth. Emma Griffin has been especially dubious about the flight into meaning inspired by anthropologists such as Clifford Geertz. She sees it as tending to 'de-politicise' popular culture, and seeks herself to bring the political back into sports and pastimes. Griffin's work, with its awareness of contested cultural space (village greens, market squares) and the political control exercised over it, harks back in some ways to the ideas of the 1970s cohort, notably Stuart Hall's insistence that the popular must, in the final analysis, be seen in a context of struggle and contestation.[34] On the other hand, though, with its notion of the 'heterogeneity of historical experience' (p. 18), its insistence on the locality, and an unwillingness to see overarching patterns of development, Griffin's work is a very model of the modern idiom in leisure history.

Writing the history of sport

In hoping for a 'more imaginative, more broadly cast, theoretical approach' to the subject, Peter Bailey, himself among the most innovatory of leisure historians, observed at the end of the last century a loss of the imagination among his fellow practitioners: an apparent hesitancy to advance out of fixed positions, which he described (in a metaphor suggesting decline through age – whether in the subject itself or those who practise it is not certain) as a 'hardening of the categories'.[35] Ten years on, it is a charge that might with some justice be brought to the area of leisure that has been among the most energetic in the recent past: sport history.[36] In the 1970s there was very little of it. Few had followed the early initiatives of Percy Young in association football.[37] The breakthrough came with Tony Mason's 1980 study of the same game.[38] Mason's was a book that showed how archival material expertly used could construct a serious and detailed social history of sport. It had a seminal influence. It was followed in 1989 by Richard Holt's very different *Sport and the British*, a scholarly and comprehensive discussion of the place of sport in the formation of a national community.[39] Less archive-based than Mason, it was nonetheless equally influential, and is still read with relish two decades after its publication.[40] These two books established the pattern for much that followed. In many senses they are the Ur-texts of sport history. Neither was especially theoretical in conception; in fact both historians might reasonably be described as following a traditional 'empiricist' path from sources to 'truthful' interpretation. And thus sport history, whether in its British manifestation through the activities of the British Society of Sport History, or in its various other national guises (USA, Australia, Europe), has galloped along, sometimes putting haste ahead of direction. Its content, originally a Masonian interest in how sport was organised and made available (through clubs, press, spectator groups) has broadened out into rather more ideological aspects of the meaning of sport and its links with 'identities' such as region, nation and gender. There are, almost inevitably, gaps in the picture: still very little on sport before about the seventeenth century; a strong emphasis on commercial and elite sport at the expense of recreational amateur sport organised by voluntary bodies; a predilection for the developed world; and a neglect of newer 'extreme' sports – those not circumscribed by the regulations of governing bodies and which often involve breaking the law and exposing the body to physical dangers – that represent therefore the subversive notions of leisure that Peter Borsay has described as 'other'.[41] An important and somewhat surprising omission in a topic for which performance is vital concerns play itself; it is almost as if the big matches are not serious enough material for the academic.[42] For some time, too, woman might have been included in the realm of the neglected, but the work of several (usually female) historians in the 1980s and 1990s has begun to set the problem aright.[43] Whilst British sport history might still be a predominantly male business, it is encouraging that the North American Society for Sport History has a very noticeable female presence. In many cases this has resulted in history that is attuned to real issues of gender and not merely 'her-story'. What is still awaited in Britain, however, is a single book – comparable in vision to Holt's – that squares up to the question of gender in sport.

While content has flourished, conception has shown less vigour. It is here where a 'hardening of the categories' is most evident. Cultural history might be the area to visit to see some of the experimental forms of the discipline, but sport history, as Douglas Booth's book suggests, does not share such a questioning spirit. Inter-disciplinarity, theory, source material, comparative history (let alone a fully transnational compass) are aspects that demand greater attention than they have so far received. The exceptions – highly-imaginative historians such as Murray Phillips,[44] Synthia Sydnor,[45] and Booth himself – point up the orthodoxy. Sport history, a project that represents the convergence of many streams from different parts of the academy as well as amateur history, has succeeded in establishing itself as a distinct sub-branch of the discipline. Compared with the 1970s, it is far less likely now to cause eyebrows to be raised in respectable academic circles. This is partly a reflection of the changes that have occurred in society generally, where popular pastimes now rate as subjects of serious study and the dominance of the old-established elites is less marked in both life and the history we write. Sport history's growth also mirrors the global popularity of sport as both a participant and spectator pastime, its increasing significance as a business, and the multi-disciplinary appeal of sport studies. Sport history, however, remains one of the few aspects of sport studies without a vocational use. When most other disciplines are used in an 'applied' capacity (selling sport, preventing injuries, improving times and techniques, avoiding or pursuing litigation, managing sport businesses) and claim an obvious relevance to the so-called real world, historians have to work harder to justify their academic efforts. They have, nonetheless, succeeded in joining the history 'mainstream', making a mark with their work in research assessment exercises. But at the forefront of conceptual and methodological advances in the discipline they are not. While studies in the various issues raised by the question of identity are fine, more attention should be paid to the broadly political aspects of sport, nationally and internationally. Sport as a 'civil culture' (the term is Ross McKibbin's[46]) is an important area, demanding exploration of the recreational levels of sporting organisation rather than elite activity, and determining the place of sport clubs in the bigger process of constructing a civil society. Recalling Stedman Jones's strictures, working with historians in the 'mainstream' is one prerequisite of this objective.

Consumption and privatised leisure

In other areas, however, there are more encouraging signs of rejuvenation. The work of Koshar and his co-authors gives us a lead into much of the 'new' leisure history; that is to say, approaches to leisure that have broken free of the early class conflict model and taken, to an extent at least, a cue from postmodern ideas about linguistic and textual effects in shaping meaning in historical relationships. The subject of consumption offers fertile territory. Early markers were set out by Stephen Jones.[47] His extensive work on the culture of the British labour movement was done mainly in the 1980s before his tragically early death. Coming from a background in economic history, Jones tended to see leisure as a 'good' made available to people through various channels. There were three main sectors of provision: voluntary association, the market and the state. It is a valuable model if, in its basic form, a little over-schematic. More subtly, we would expect each sector to exhibit tensions and conflicts between its 'actors', to find considerable overlap between the sectors, and to question the applicability of this particular trinity: should not the churches, or employer patronage, also be included if the model is to describe certain kinds of environment (the Catholic Church, for example, in particular areas of Britain and large areas of continental Europe)? Nonetheless Jones's approach has the virtue of organising into an analytical framework an immensely complex and extensive field. One of the implications emerging from it was the redefining of individuals. Social historians used to thinking in terms of class were forced to adjust to new identities shaped around the individual as 'consumer' or 'taxpayer'. This chimed with political attempts, especially in the Thatcher years, at individualising people. In this mindset there was, to be sure, 'the nation' (still an emotive term, used often in contradistinction to 'Europe') but, as Margaret Thatcher once famously claimed, no such thing as 'society', 'only individuals and families'. Few in academic circles took this assertion to quite such a facile length, but it might have served somewhat to hasten a shift already taking place away from class to other social categories based on gender, race, ethnicity, age and religion, and to see them less as rigid collectivities.

The overlap between the main 'sectors' of leisure provision becomes evident when we move away from commercial leisure and begin to look at voluntary activity. This area has received less attention from historians than have those giant leaps in the commercialisation of leisure that occurred from the middle of the nineteenth century, especially in that 'climacteric' of change which pro-duced a 'mass culture' in the thirty or so years before the First World War. But there is good reason for thinking that a great deal of leisure, if not sport, is best understood by considering the changing nature of the home and family. It might be tempting to imagine that commercial leisure displaced a prior family-based focus, and that this was one of the reasons why its presence incurred so much concern on the part of reformers. In fact, however, changes in both commercial and domestic leisure were taking place at much the same time, resulting in new leisure forms in each sector. Home-based leisure was as historically specific as market-based leisure. The changes are expertly charted in three studies of nineteenth-century leisure that have become classics of the historian's craft – Hugh Cunningham's analysis of a broad shift in leisure relations in the mid-century, Peter Bailey's influential *Leisure and Class in Victorian England* and Gareth Stedman Jones's interpretation of work and leisure changes in later nineteenth-century London.[48]

Leisure became implicated in the process of class consciousness at the point when middle-class people began to seek control of formerly public spaces in order to 'privatise' them for approved activity. In a process that had to do with wider middle-class fears of the mass, much of the old cheek-by-jowl public culture of the eighteenth century was re-shaped and became demarcated by social distinction and exclusion. It was a process that frequently invoked state power to achieve its objectives; by-laws removed allotments, for example, to make way for housing or railway development; drinking hours were curtailed; popular sports were driven off the streets in the interests of public order and the protection of property. In one direction, the process produced a new, domesticated middle-class culture, its distinctive symbols of respectability enshrined in the piano, essential for the cultivation of refined tastes (especially among the family's female members), in the improving press such as the *Saturday Review*, in dinner parties, in gardening and, if the household's resources ran to it, in private tennis courts and billiards tables. Working-class households could sustain few of these accoutrements of cultivated domesticity. Working-class leisure developed its quintessential features in a more public and collective form. The neighbourhood public house and the music hall were important focal points, though hardly 'respectable'. One response was 'rational recreation', a largely middle-class inspired initiative through which, it was believed, the minds and habits of the working class would be elevated by inculcating a belief in 'time-budgeting and money management' and introducing them to 'the satisfaction of mental recreation, thus immunising them against the contagion of pub and the publican, and the animal regression of "sensuality"'.[49] Bailey saw this partly as a response to the guilt felt among the bourgeoisie that the culture of the masses had been driven away and neglected. On the whole it failed. But Stedman Jones observed a more suburbanised, privatised working-class culture, with leanings towards the music hall, racecourse, football match and seaside excursion, conservative in its philosophy but nonetheless resistant to attempts by outsiders either to understand or to change it.[50] It was a culture, says Jones, summed up in the characters performed by two of the best-known music hall entertainers, Dan Leno and Charlie Chaplin, the latter's comic creation of the put-upon 'little man' soon to be synonymous with the early cinema.

Until housing changes provided better material foundations for a home-based leisure for all, the ideal of respectable domestic leisure was always going to be out of the reach of many. Radio (wireless) became a major leisure form in Britain by the 1930s, and, as the work of Sian Nicholas has revealed, a very important part of wartime life and morale. [51] Television did not exist on any kind of mass basis until the early 1950s. The first truly mass audiences were for the coronation of Elizabeth II and the Stanley Matthews' Cup Final in 1953. The extensive analysis of television since this time by Jack Williams has brought out the immense social impact of the medium.[52] By any measurement – *Social Trends* is a useful one[53] – television is still the foremost leisure activity in Britain, possibly monopolising time that could be taken up in other pursuits. As Williams points out, we simply cannot ignore television. Its effects are many and various though, to be sure, difficult to assess. Williams raises the question of whether television has altered people's conception of their identity, and advances the proposition that a consciousness of class has been diluted as a consequence of television programmes directing viewers' attention to other forms of identity. In essence the medium is a home-based, private activity – now joined by other electronic forms such as DVDs and various computer-related entertainments – and quite different from older leisure activities such as cinema and the pub in the kinds of social interactions it generates. (Interestingly, however, football coverage on BSkyB, a medium accessed by only a limited number of households in Britain, has caused the public houses that offer live transmissions of games to become rejuvenated centres of male public sociability.) Getting to grips with these questions is not easy, especially since the trend in television studies, where the running has been made by sociology and media studies academics, has been to assume an institutional or programme focus.[54] The view, so to speak, from the viewer has been less often taken, particularly by historians. Williams's work is therefore something of an exception in this respect and should provide a pathway for others to follow.

Changes in the British economy in the later-twentieth century, notably the relative decline of manufacturing industry and the growth of the service sector – trends discernible since the end of the war – greatly strengthened the link between domesticity and leisure. Following the policies of the Thatcher administrations of the 1980s the financial sector came to hold the commanding height of the economy. One effect was to make personal credit available among the mass of the population to a degree not previously seen. Much of this was directed at personal consumption: housing, motor cars, holidays, home entertainments, clothing – in fact, a whole range of material goods and services designed to offer a hedonistic lifestyle. This new leisure form – for such it was – quite properly attracted the attention of the social historian. In the 1980s John Benson brought out the importance of shopping as a leisure activity, and particular shopping venues have since been the subject of study, notably Bill Lancaster's history of the department store.[55] Manchester University Press, in a substantial series on leisure and popular culture edited by Jeffrey Richards, has further advanced the enquiry into the relationship between consumption and leisure, opening up new topics in valuable studies of motor car culture (O'Connell), smoking (Hilton), the seaside (Walton) and tourism (Barton).[56] In some cases the series has extended leisure activity into the broader questions of gender relations (Langhamer) and regionalism (Russell), the latter a fine example of the ways in which the many representations of the north of England have mediated ideas of the region and contributed to a sense of identity.[57] Many of the new areas of leisure investigated in studies such as these still retain an element of public togetherness – holidays, for example, or clubbing – but as befits the period in which much of the activity and its historiography was galvanised, a large proportion are in essence markedly privatised.

History and heritage

One vast area of this new development sits right under historians' noses, but as yet has only sporadically been scrutinised in a scholarly way. This is the study of history itself – or, to be more precise, the study of the past as a leisure pursuit. Professional historians might baulk at describing their job as leisure, but for many millions the subject of history is a fascinating and rewarding source of pleasure. Considering that so many people have traditionally complained of being 'put off' history at school (by all those dates) it is surprising but nonetheless encouraging that they return to it in adult life. Perhaps it is not so surprising. History in various forms is all around, and the subject is blessed with an easy accessibility. The ability to read is the basic requirement of 'doing history', and while some methodological skills are useful, the subject could not be better placed to serve as a popular recreation.

Thus we have a growth area in the economy, animated by a great deal of media interest and activity, that is variously referred to as commercialised history, public history, and heritage.

Important academic interventions in this process were made in the 1980s, a time in Britain when the idea of 'heritage' was in vogue, with various heritage sites emerging.[58] One of the most critical studies of this trend came in Robert Hewison's *The Heritage Industry*.[59] As his subtitle suggested, Hewison was concerned about the political impact of a heritage that he saw as undesirable nostalgia, taking people's minds away from contemporary problems and presenting to them an imagined past that seemed preferable to the present, a parallel universe almost. Hewison also posed an important question about the nature of heritage. It dealt with the past, but to what extent was it history (p. 10)? Similar concerns exercised David Lowenthal. The bringing of the past into the present, so that it was no longer a 'foreign country', is, Lowenthal avers, a compelling, even necessary, requirement. We cannot do without the past, but recalling and restoring it involves a complex interaction with the present. In both writers there is a sense of wariness about the ideological and commercial effects of heritage on history, a concern less evident in the work of Raphael Samuel, writing only a little later but more willing to embrace non-academic forms of historical reconstruction, especially in television.[60]

In an excellent book Jerome de Groot examines the vast growth of popular forms of history in recent years, referring to the process as the *consumption* of history.[61] His thesis suggests a business relationship – popular history as something bought and sold in the market place. A good deal of what he analyses does indeed concern history provided through various commercial cultural forms, but he also recognises that public history encompasses many varieties of what he calls 'amateur histories' – the everyday interests followed up by people, usually as hobby rather than formal study, and which has been especially evident in local history or the tracing of family trees. Only quite recently has the academic history taught to undergraduates in British universities begun to turn its attention to a critical analysis of the histories created and transmitted in this public domain. But the field of public history is vast, and we are reaching a point (perhaps we have already passed it) where what most people's understanding of what history is derives far more from popular representations of it than from academic analysis. Television is quantitatively one of the biggest forms of this public history, and recent research by Angela Piccini underlines the scale of its historical reach.[62]

Cultural production of this kind is a delight for millions, but what kind of history is being purveyed? Much of it seems to work in an *implicit* fashion. How many of Piccini's viewers, one might wonder, would be consciously aware that what they are watching as entertainment was indeed a form of history, a *using* of the past to merge with present interests and concerns: in the case, for example, of the BBC television programme *Flog It!*[63] the past is a collection of relics to be traded in for money. In the different case of David Starkey's Tudor television histories, it is a dramatic power struggle between the rich and famous in the quest for an elusive political stability.[64] The danger of trivialising and narrativising history in these ways has been alluded to by the historian Tristram Hunt in a critique of one particular television programme – the BBC's *Who Do You Think You Are?* It originated as a worthy educational tool for amateur historians seeking to use archive sources to reconstruct their family history; in the course of time, however, the programme was transformed, becoming a showcase for celebrities. In its current form it takes the serious business of family history and deploys it in situations where the potential for human drama and emotion can be maximised. The tedium that attends the 'doing' of history is largely removed – documents magically appear, with experts on hand to interpret them. The celebrity subjects of the programme, whose family history is being traced, are well-known media personalities who possess the requisite screen presence that boosts the programme's human-interest appeal. Notwithstanding the producer's attempt to refute Hunt's argument there are, it seems, times when such programming veers more towards an electronic version of tabloid journalism than serious history.[65]

Many of the problems about popular constructions of history have been evident, perhaps more clearly than in any other leisure form, in the cinema.[66] The 1980s saw a surge of what de Groot calls British 'heritage' films, many of which communicated a conservative vision of the past through stately homes and the aristocracy. *Brideshead Revisited* was a case in point.[67] They are again illustrated in a recent film *The King's Speech*, the awards for which ensured big audiences, in the English-speaking world at least.[68] The film is set in England in the period between 1925 and 1939 with its central story being the struggle of the Duke of York (later King George VI) to overcome, with the help of a speech therapist, a stammer that seriously affected his public appearances and, in a more general sense, the standing of the monarchy. The personal drama, climaxing in an efficiently stage-managed radio broadcast made by the king from a recording studio on the outbreak of war, is framed by two major political episodes – the Abdication Crisis of 1936 and the coming of war in 1939. While the film strives for historical accuracy in representing the built and material environment, and attempts to cast actors who bear some resemblance to the historical figures portrayed, its treatment of the political process is far freer. The story is told with a large serving of hindsight, the script being inscribed with a sense of foreboding about the coming war. However, it makes no mention of the British government's attempts to avert conflict through the policy of appeasement. The leading politicians of the later 1930s (Baldwin and Chamberlain) are marginalised in the narrative, while the figure of Winston Churchill is foregrounded. He appears in situations where his political standing at the time would simply not have warranted his presence.[69] It seems clear that the film-makers' intention was to employ the Churchill character because the name and persona, which the actor playing the part developed almost to caricature proportions, would be readily identifiable to audiences.[70] In doing so they were also able to draw upon a layer of historical knowledge embedded in popular memory. The 'idea' of Churchill has survived, when that of other politicians has been largely forgotten, because it has long been incorporated into a familiar strand of national heritage, with Churchill as public hero and the embodiment of all that is British. It denotes a time of national heroism, with the country united behind its king and prime minister. Thus by building its story upon heritage myths rather than analytical history, *The King's Speech*, which had the potential to be a critical and subtly subversive slant on the British monarchy's problems of communicating with its subjects, became instead yet another comforting version of 'our island story'. Does any of this matter? Not for the film's producers, presumably, whose interest was in box-office takings. For many members of the audience also the film would seem 'true': it looks right, and has known political events and real figures as reference points to complement its largely fictionalised interpretation of the daily life of the monarchy.

Popular history of this kind is very democratic – nobody owns it. Professional historians might once have thought they were the custodians of the past, but they can scarcely harbour such thoughts nowadays when history has become the business of film-makers, television producers, novelists, playwrights and journalists. All work over the past. The results can sometimes be very innovative – the novels of Sarah Waters, to take just one example, have provoked pointed thoughts about both the content and the construction of historical narratives.[71] But in the course of this expansion of history, something has emerged that should concern the professional historian. One of the most pertinent concerns what is selected for the heritage treatment. The transforming of the past into a story about the past (in other words, into 'history') takes place in a context of power, between those who think they are important and those who don't – or to put it more precisely, those who have been encouraged by that very process of producing history to regard themselves as *un*important. Thus a critical perspective on the past, to *question* and *contest* the legacies of dominant historical narratives, to *reclaim* and *re-interpret* the past, is a necessary part of historical discourse; to ask, as the writer Ian Sinclair did in a recent critique of the Olympic Development Agency's claim to be protecting the heritage of east London, 'whose heritage'?[72] Without this critical approach, involving an awareness that the process of historical reconstruction is, to a degree, a *political* one, there is a powerful impetus pulling us into a consensual and conservative wisdom about *our* 'national heritage'. It has been reinforced in public history initiatives such as the BBC's television series 'Restoration'.[73] It can communicate a view of the past that is largely Anglocentric and rural, symbolised in the image and idea of the country house.[74] Gareth Stedman Jones once scorned a particular form of labour history, evident in books like Francis Williams's *Magnificent Journey*, as 'a sort of plebeian variant of the whig theory of history'.[75] In other words, they took a traditional 'great man' approach to the past and brought it down from the level of the old elites to that of ordinary men and women. And for all its apparent 'democratic' content, public history purveyed through media outlets is in danger of a similar fate, with the past served up to us as a commercialised form of the great person theory of history, implicitly freighted with an ideology of 'progress', and with all the uncertainty, debate and sheer hard graft that attends the practice of creating history left largely unconsidered. Recalling Stedman Jones's observations of the 1970s on the history of leisure as a separate category, the very same point might be made today about the need for a convergence of public history with 'mainstream' (i.e. academic) history.

The heritage of sport illustrates some of these issues. The proliferation of sport museums has been welcomed, though it has to be recognised that they often emphasise the glory side of sport rather than what Wray Vamplew has called the 'downside'.[76] Eilean Hooper-Greenhill's work is important here on the complexities of the 'text-reader' relationship as it unfolds in museums between the exhibits and visitors'.[77] Not all sport museums take their historical responsibilities as keenly as the National Football Museum, where the placing of sporting events within their broader context of economic, social and political life is a fundamental means of explaining the history of football to its public.[78] However, attracting visitors is the sine qua non of the sport museums – even the 'serious' ones.[79] The Wimbledon tennis museum is certainly among the leaders in the field of serious sport museums, but even there the star players and the famous events take precedence over those aspects of Wimbledon's history that historians might consider worthy of at least a mention: the problems of sporting injuries and performance-enhancing drugs; the work of the backroom office workers; and the catering staff who actually prepare the strawberry teas that are such an important part of the annual June ritual.

Leisure and gender

Under the influence of cultural history, with its concern for issues of language, discourse and representations, the question of identity has been well to the fore, with some especially interesting work on gender. Stedman Jones's concern over the neglect of the sexual division of leisure has been spectacularly overcome, with a number of outstanding studies of gender relations in leisure. They have shown that traditional definitions of leisure, based on a distinction between work and leisure, are implicitly male-centred and should therefore no longer serve as a starting-point for analysis. Ellen Ross's work on the flexible, often spontaneous, leisure habits of poor women in working-class neighbourhoods of London brings this point out with devastating effect.[80] Angela McRobbie's contributions to the gender aspects of leisure are foundational texts, particularly her celebrated close reading of magazines aimed at teenage girls, who were subjected in the 1970s to many traditional versions of the woman's role in fostering domesticity.[81] Andrew Davies's subsequent study of working-class life in Salford and Manchester, based extensively on oral evidence, presents a full and rather pessimistic picture of women's leisure. For married women especially leisure was a highly circumscribed experience – not altogether absent from their lives (Davies instances the cinema and pubs) but limited compared to the possibilities open to men, even men in poverty. Leisure was often an extension of household duties (sewing, mending, knitting), which were women's primary function. Whatever they did, 'respectability' was the social imperative that reined women in.[82] Another oral history, Langhamer's study of women's leisure in the north of England for a slightly later period, tends to complement Davies's account. Langhamer encompasses a variety of activities, many of them newer forms such as ballroom dancing, cinema-going and the interwar craze for rambling, setting these within a broad social context of family, friendship groups, and boyfriends. By emphasising the longitudinal changes in women's leisure experience between youth and middle age Langhamer confirms that the kinds of leisure we are accustomed to thinking of when studying men were largely confined to younger, single women, though commercial leisure provision was premised upon the expectation of heterosexual liaisons. Marriage effectively brought these relative freedoms to an end.[83]

Quite different in its orientation is Jean Williams's study of women in association football, the quintessential preserve of male leisure.[84] Williams's work has a paramount quality that much leisure history lacks: it is comparative history of the boldest kind, with detailed case studies of football in Australia, Britain, the People's Republic of China and the USA. In each of these countries the game among women has become important in recent years, embellished in the USA through the assistance of federal equal-opportunities legislation (Title IX) that has helped in the achievement of impressive levels of participation in soccer by schoolchildren and young women. Although Williams's typifies what might in some senses be described as a 'classic' historian's method – collecting the evidence, analysing it and writing up the findings in an interpretation – *A Beautiful Game* develops a story begun in earlier work about the place of women in football and their struggle to establish their game in the face of strong male opposition. The theme of the gender war in sport is prominent in Williams's approach to history. It is a project that, among other things, illustrates the truth of Sheila Rowbotham's famous dictum – that women have been 'hidden from history'.[85] Using archival sources from various football governing bodies, including much from the FIFA itself, Williams pieces together the difficult and often discontinuous history of women's football. Britain offers a caution to those who like their history to be of an 'onward and upward' kind; women's football there 'peaked' during and just after the First World War, when the Preston team based on the Dick, Kerr & Co. engineering works achieved much success domestically and, after a tour of the United States in the early 1920s, internationally. Development did not proceed in a uniform fashion, however, and not until the final quarter of the twentieth century were the achievements of the earlier years rekindled. Williams's international conspectus offers interesting discursive forays into questions of sources and of how to fill those awkward gaps faced by historians working in this field; gaps which extend to under-represented areas of Africa and South America. Thus the book amounts to far more than simply a redressing of the balance between men and women in the historical narrative of football. It is a challenge to the cultural and historical construction of football as a 'man's game'. Football must been seen as simply 'football', a game played by men and women and beset, as are all social activities, by tensions arising from gender, class, ethnic, age and other divisions.

Finally, one of the most comprehensive studies of leisure in Britain from this perspective is Catriona Parratt's analysis of working-class women over the period from 1750 to 1914.[86] It registers in a number of ways the advances that have been made in this field. Whilst essentially a project in *women's* history it nevertheless has much to say about gender relations, as well as taking a clear line on questions of continuity and change, and on the place of leisure as both a restricting and liberating force in women's lives. Parratt echoes many of the ideas about the impact of industrialisation originally found in Malcolmson's work, but is keen throughout to characterise the field of leisure as one of contestation: between men and women, and between both and employers, reformers, parliament and opinion formers. She makes clear that differences between women, principally stemming from income, age and marital status, make the concept of 'women's experience' problematical. As Andrew Davies has emphasised, women, far more so than men, had to kick against dominant gendered assumptions about leisure, but they often succeeded in moderating the sterner expectation of their 'betters'. Leisure that was not freely chosen was not leisure worth having. Bound in many ways to the home and domestic care – and if working also in waged labour – leisure offered the space in which women recreated themselves as they would wish to be, free from the ideological labels of 'good wife' or 'dutiful daughter' that society pressed upon them. The music hall, as Bailey has shown, was one of the places where such thoughts were expressed, and contested. Although by the early twentieth century the halls had mostly lost their previous reputation as haunts of low life and become instead respectable theatres of family entertainment, they could still deal in ambiguity and subversion, much to the audience's delight. As the refrain of Marie Lloyd's popular song had it: 'I always hold with having it if yer fancy it … 'cos a little of what yer fancy does yer good.'

Conclusion

We began with a question about social control. Having once carried a certain plausibility, the concept has gradually fallen below the horizon. In the 1970s it was sustained by a dominant theoretical approach that owed much to Marxism, and which therefore gave emphasis to questions of social class and domination as a principal explanatory tool. Since then, as new generations of academics have assumed positions of influence, the subject of leisure has cascaded into a range of topics, themes, methodologies and conceptual leanings. In the process master narratives have been edged out. There is no discernibly 'dominant' theoretical paradigm. A measure of this is the fate of 'social control'. The implication of Terry Eagleton's 'what shall we do with them when they're not working?' – the idea of football as the opium of the masses – does not now tend to spark much debate.

In moving away from overly rigid concepts and interpretations, leisure historians have created a richer terrain; but one in which, as Bailey was intimating in his assertion that leisure has lost 'focus and momentum as a distinct speciality',[87] we are perhaps failing to see the wood for the trees. Instead of a single project we now have leisure 'histories'. As is ever the case with history, though, there are gaps. Among the chief areas that would repay close attention are:

- the history of leisure in an imperial and colonial context examining the two-way effect of this relationship. How did British rule influence leisure in the colonies, and in what senses was this reflected back into metropolitan life?[88] This should fuse with the recent interest in studying 'globalisation'. [89]
- medieval and early-modern leisure. The former in particular, if not neglected, is generally under-represented.
- the post-1945 period in Britain, in contrast with the interwar years which are richly served. Although it is now opened up in studies of an essentially political nature,[90] it as yet lacks specific work aimed at the particular leisure features of this time.
- at a more methodological level (and considering the 'practical' services likely to be expected from academic subjects in the light of the United Kingdom government's Browne Review),[91] the relationship of historical research to the work of those who administer leisure provision, especially at times of budget restraint. What role can historians play here? Sport is a clear case where funding from both public and private sources to analyse contemporary problems (for example, the staging of mega events, or the provision of sport for the disabled) might present opportunities for historians. In an ideological climate where the notion of 'small state/big society' might well prevail the practice of voluntarism in leisure (as in, for example, the establishing of clubs and societies) affords immense scope to the historian's expertise. Nowhere (I might suggest) has the club principle been stronger over a long period of time than in Britain. There is much that leisure administrators ('leisure scientists' as they might be termed in the USA)[92] can learn from this tradition.

Gaps or no gaps, the extensive field of leisure studies does need texts that provide overview, and Peter Borsay's highly-ambitious sweep of the past half-millennium is one of the very few to do this, presenting a challenging thematic re-consideration, especially of the problems of periodising and conceptualising leisure development.[93] In Borsay's 'longue durée' the old convention of a 'great divide' coincidental with the industrial revolution is replaced with a more subtle six-phase periodisation, a final phase of which takes account of recent international linkages in leisure made possible through electronic communications of various kinds. Without by any means neglecting change – after all, it is a fundamental concept for the historian – Borsay sees powerful strands of continuity through the three analytical categories he uses to organise his long perspective: play (the contrast of leisure pursuits with the 'real' world), symbol (the sports stadium, for example, as a symbol of the nation) and the 'other' (something other than the 'normal', such as a holiday or travel experience). Each is seen as a constant in the lives of people over a considerable period of time. Moreover, they together make up something that is very important for those people. Trivial or irrelevant though leisure might be in some ways, it nonetheless remains essential; life without 'play' would be impossible.[94] And that remains a primary justification for our studying it. Therefore, in a new political environment where humanities subjects will probably have to work their passage by producing 'relevant' research and graduates for the needs of business and government, we will need to remind our political masters of the great importance of the irrelevant in our society.

Notes

1 Terry Eagleton, 'Football: A Dear Friend to Capitalism', *Guardian*, 15 June 2010. In his autobiographical memoir a few years earlier Eagleton had claimed: '[m]y own personal proposal for furthering the cause of socialism would be to abolish sport.'

2 Peter Bailey, 'The Politics and Poetics of Modern British Leisure', *Rethinking History* 3, no. 2 (1999): 131–75.

3 Emma Griffin, *England's Revelry: A History of Popular Sports and Pastimes, 1660–1830* (Oxford: Oxford University Press/British Academy, 2005), 9–11.

4 The habit developed among the socialist parties of continental European countries of counterposing socialist practices to 'bourgeois' culture, for example in sport. The German Social Democratic Party is the clearest and best-documented case. See W. L. Guttsman, *The German Social Democratic Party, 1875–1933: From Ghetto to Government* (London: George Allen and Unwin, 1981); A. Kruger and J. Riordan (eds), *The Story of Worker Sport* (Leeds: Human Kinetics, 1996).

5 On Priestley in general, see John Baxendale, *Priestley's England: J. B. Priestley and English Culture* (Manchester: Manchester University Press, 2007).

6 See K. Laybourn, D. James and A. Jowitt, *The Centennial History of the Independent Labour Party* (Halifax: Ryburn Press, 1993).

7 J. B. Priestley, *English Journey* (repr. Harmondsworth: Penguin Books, 1997), 131–43.

8 Priestley, 'When Work Is Over', *Picture Post*, 4 January 1941, 39.

9 Priestley, *English Journey*, 377.

10 See Chris Waters, *British Socialists and the Politics of Popular Culture* (Manchester: Manchester University Press, 1990); Stuart Macintyre, *Little Moscows: Communism and Working-Class Militance in Inter-War Britain* (London: Croom Helm, 1980); Stephen G. Jones, *Workers At Play: A Social and Economic History of Leisure 1918–1939* (London: Routledge & Kegan Paul, 1986). For a local study, see Jeffrey Hill, *Nelson: Politics, Economy, Community* (Edinburgh: Keele University Press, 1997). In general the study of leisure within these political contexts has declined over the past ten years; see, for example, Jeffrey Hill, 'When Work Is Over: Labour, Leisure and Culture in Wartime Britain', in N. Hayes and J. Hill (eds), *'Millions Like Us?' British Culture in the Second World War* (Liverpool: Liverpool University Press, 1999), 236–60; 'Introduction: Sport and Politics', *Journal of Contemporary History* 38, no. 3 (2003): 355–61. The ILP's position is well explained in Arthur Bourchier, *Art and Culture in Relation to Socialism* (London: ILP Publication Department, n.d. [1926]).

11 Richard Hoggart, *The Uses of Literacy: Aspects of Working-Class Life, With Special Reference to Publications and Entertainments* (London: Chatto and Windus, 1957).

12 E.P. Thompson, *The Making of the English Working Class* (London: Gollancz, 1963).

13 It reminds us that the word 'leisure' relates to the Latin 'licere' – to be allowed for/ to be lawful.

14 E. and S. Yeo (eds), *Popular Culture and Class Conflict 1590–1914: Explorations in the History of Labour and Leisure* (Brighton: Harvester, 1981).

15 See Catriona M. Parratt, 'Robert W Malcolmson's *Popular Recreations in English Society, 1700–1850*: An Appreciation', *Journal of Sport History* 29, no. 2 (2002): 313–23.

16 Hugh Cunningham, *Leisure in the Industrial Revolution c.1780–c.1880* (London: Croom Helm, 1980).

17 J. Golby and A. W.Purdue, *The Civilisation of the Crowd: Popular Culture in England 1750–1900* (London: Batsford, 1984).

18 Allen Guttmann's *From Ritual to Record: The Nature of Modern Sports* (1978; repr. New York: Columbia University Press, 2004) is a good example.

19 Eugen Weber, *Peasants into Frenchmen: The Modernization of Rural France, 1870–1914* (London: Chatto and Windus, 1977). In a similar vein is the equally outstanding study of modernization in French sport and leisure during the same period by the British historian Richard Holt, *Sport and Society in Modern France* (London: Macmillan, 1981).

20 J. H. Plumb, *The Commercialisation of Leisure in Eighteenth-Century England* (Reading: University of Reading, 1973); David Underdown, *Start of Play: Cricket and Culture in Eighteenth-Century England* (London: Allen Lane, 2000).

21 Gareth Stedman Jones, 'Class Expression Versus Social Control? A Critique of Recent Trends in the Social History of "Leisure"', in *Languages of Class: Studies in English Working Class History 1832–1982* (Cambridge: Cambridge University Press, 1983). The article originated as a paper presented at the Society for the Study of

Labour History conference on 'The Working Class and Leisure' at the University of Sussex, autumn 1975.

22 The sentiment was echoed a little while later by Stuart Hall in a paper given at the History Workshop conference, Ruskin College, Oxford, 1979. See Stuart Hall, 'Notes on Deconstructing "The Popular"', in R. Samuel (ed.), *People's History and Socialist Theory* (London: Routledge,1981). Hall called for the study of popular culture to be situated in the political and economic struggle 'for and against a culture of the powerful', 239.

23 Rudy Koshar (ed.), *Histories of Leisure* (Oxford: Berg, 2002).

24 Erik Jensen, 'Crowd Control: Boxing Spectatorship and Social Order in Weimar Germany', and Patrick Young, '*La Vieille France* as Object of Bourgeois Desire: The Touring Club de France and the French Regions, 1890–1918', in Koshar (ed.), *Histories of Leisure*.

25 Weber, *Peasants into Frenchmen*.

26 Francis Mulhearn, 'Notes on Culture and Cultural Struggle', *Screen Education* 34 (1980): 31–5.

27 Tony Judt, 'A Clown in Regal Purple: Social History and the Historians', *History Workshop Journal* (1979): 66–94.

28 But see, for example, Jeremy Black: 'Far from being Postmodernists or pomophobes, most historians get on with research, which they generally approach in an accretional fashion, and treat debates about pomo as self-referential, if not self-regarding, and of little relevance to the practitioner.' In 'Past Lives of the Pomos, Proto-Pomos and Pomophobics', *Times Higher Educational Supplement,* 27 August 2004, 24.

29 Douglas Booth, *The Field: Truth and Fiction in Sport History* (London: Routledge, 2005). Some of the rumpus is evident from Allen Guttmann's long critical review, 'Straw Men in Imaginary Boxes', *Journal of Sport History* 32, no. 3 (fall 2005): 395–400.

30 Peter Bailey, *Popular Culture and Performance in the Victorian City* (Cambridge: Cambridge University Press, 1998), i.

31 Among a large output on this topic are: Grant Jarvie, *Sport in the Making of Celtic Cultures* (Leicester: Leicester University Press, 1999); G. Jarvie and J. Burnett (eds), *Sport, Scotland and the Scots* (Phantassie: Tuckwell Press, 2000); G. Jarvie and G. Walker, *Scottish Sport in the Making of the Nation: Ninety Minute Patriots?* (Leicester: Leicester University Press, 1994); H. F. Moorhouse, 'Blue Bonnets Over the Border: Scotland and the Migration of Footballers', in J. Bale and J. Maguire (eds), *The Global Sports Arena: Athletic Talent Migration in an Interdependent World* (London: Frank Cass, 1994), 78–96; D. Smith and G. Williams, *Fields of Praise*, esp. Chs. 5–7; Gareth Williams, *1905 And All That: Essays on Rugby Football, Sport and Welsh Society* (Llandysul: Gomer Press, 1991); 'From Grand Slam to Great Slump: Economy, Society and Rugby Football in Wales During the Depression', *Welsh History Review* 11 (1993): 339–57. See also Martin Johnes, *A History of Sport in Wales* (Cardiff: University of Wales Press, 2005); 'A Prince, a King, and a Referendum: Rugby, Politics, and Nationhood in Wales, 1969–1979', *Journal of British Studies* 47, no. 1 (2008): 129–48; D. Smith, 'Focal Heroes: A Welsh Fighting Class', in Richard Holt (ed.), *Sport and*

the Working Class in Modern Britain (Manchester: Manchester University Press, 1990), 199; Gareth Williams, 'The Road to Wigan Pier Revisited: The Migration of Welsh Rugby Talent Since 1918', in Bale and Maguire (eds), *The Global Sports Arena*, 25–38; Michael Cronin, 'Defenders of the Nation? The Gaelic Athletic Association and Irish National Identity', *Irish Political Studies* 11 (1996): 1–19; 'Sport and a Sense of Irishness', *Irish Studies Review* 9 (1994): 13–18; 'Which Nation, Which Flag?: Boxing and National Identities in Ireland', *International Review for the Sociology of Sport* 32, no. 2 (1997): 131–46; Richard Holt, *Sport and the British*, 239–42. See also M. Cronin and D. Mayall, *Sporting Nationalisms: Identity, Ethnicity, Immigration and Assimilation* (London: Frank Cass, 1998); Michael Cronin, 'Enshrined in Blood: The Naming of Gaelic Athletic Association Grounds and Clubs', *Sports Historian* 18, no. 1 (1998): 90–104; Jack Williams, *Cricket and England: A Cultural and Social History of the Inter-War Years* (London: Frank Cass, 1999), esp. Chs. 1 and 6; J. Hill and J. Williams, *Sport and Identity in the North of England* (Keele: Keele University Press, 1996); Martin Polley, 'Sport and National Identity in Contemporary England', in A. Smith and D. Porter (eds), *Sport and National Identity in the Post-War World* (London: Routledge, 2004), 10–30; Mike Huggins, 'Sport and the Social Construction of Identity in North-East England', in N. Kirk (ed.) *Northern Identities: Historical Interpretations of the North and Northerness* (Aldershot: Ashgate, 2000), 132–62.

32 See Robert Darnton, *The Great Cat Massacre and Other Episodes in French Cultural History* (New York: Basic Books, 1984).

33 Eric Hobsbawm, 'C (for Crisis)', *London Review of Books*, 6 August 2009, 12.

34 Hall, 'Notes on Deconstructing "The Popular"', in Samuel (ed.), *People's History and Socialist Theory*, 227–40.

35 Bailey, 'Politics and Poetics', 155 and 160.

36 For the most recent overview of British sport historiography, see Martin Johnes, 'Britain', in J. Nauright and S. Pope (eds), *Routledge Companion to Sports History* (London: Routledge, 2009).

37 For example, see Percy M. Young, *Football: Facts and Fancies or the Art of Spectatorship* (London: Dobson, 1950); *Bolton Wanderers* (London: Stanley Paul, 1961); *Football in Sheffield* (London: Stanley Paul, 1962). Another notable 'pre-Mason' exception is James Walvin, *The People's Game: A Social History of British Football* (London: Allen Lane, 1975).

38 Tony Mason, *Association Football and English Society, 1863–1915* (Brighton: Harvester Press, 1980).

39 Richard Holt, *Sport and the British: A Modern History* (Oxford: Oxford University Press, 1989).

40 As was illustrated in the annual symposium 'Historians on Sport' (held at De Montfort University, Leicester), which in October 2010 was devoted to a wide-ranging discussion of Holt's book.

41 Peter Borsay, *A History of Leisure: The British Experience Since 1500* (Basingstoke: Palgrave Macmillan, 2006), 6. On an extreme sport – 'base jumping' (i.e. leaping off high buildings or cliffs) – see Barney Ronay, 'You Only Get One Chance', *Guardian* (G2), 6 August 2010, 6–9.

42 It was encouraging to hear, at a recent gathering of sport historians, the view that the performative elements of sport were worthy of greater attention than they had previously been given (10th anniversary symposium of Historians on Sport, De Montfort University, Leicester UK, 30 October 2010).

43 For example, Patricia Vertinsky, *The Eternally Wounded Woman: Women, Doctors and Exercise in the Late Nineteenth Century* (Urbana, IL: University of Illinois Press, 1994); Jennifer Hargreaves, *Sporting Females: Critical Issues in the History and Sociology of Women's Sports* (London: Routledge, 1994); Kathleen E. McCrone, *Sport and the Physical Emancipation of English Women 1879–1914* (London: Croom Helm, 1988).

44 See Murray Phillips 'A Critical Appraisal of Narrative in Sport History: Reading the Surf Lifesaving Debate', *Journal of Sport History* 29, no. 1 (2002): 25–40.

45 See Synthia Sydnor, 'A History of Synchronised Swimming', *Journal of Sport History* 25, no. 2 (1998), 252–67.

46 Ross McKibbin, *Classes and Cultures: England 1918–1951* (Oxford: Oxford University Press, 1998), 332.

47 Among many publications are: Stephen G. Jones, *Workers At Play: A Social and Economic History of Leisure 1918–1939* (London: Routledge and Kegan Paul, 1986) and *Sport, Politics and the Working Class: Organised Labour and Sport in Interwar Britain* (Manchester: Manchester University Press, 1988).

48 Hugh Cunningham, *Leisure in the Industrial Revolution c.1780–c.1880* (London: Croom Helm, 1980) esp. Ch. 3; Peter Bailey, *Leisure and Class in Victorian England* (London: Routledge and Kegan Paul, 1978), 59–61 and 170. Gareth Stedman Jones, *Languages of Class: Studies in English Working Class History 1832–1982* (Cambridge: Cambridge University Press, 1983), Ch. 4.

49 Bailey, *Leisure and Class*, 59–61.

50 Stedman Jones, *Languages of Class*, Ch. 4.

51 Sian Nicholas, *The Echo of War: Home Front Propaganda and the Wartime BBC, 1939–45* (Manchester: Manchester University Press, 1996).

52 Jack Williams, *Entertaining the Nation: A Social History of British Television* (Stroud: Sutton Publishing, 2004).

53 Office of National Statistics, *Social Trends* (London: Stationery Office) published annually.

54 See, however, the audience research of David Morley, *The 'Nationwide' Audience: Structure and Decoding* (London: British Film Institute, 1980); Tim O'Sullivan, 'Television Memories and Cultures of Viewing 1950–65', in J. Corner (ed.), *Popular Television in Britain: Studies in Cultural History* (London: British Film Institute, 1991).

55 John Benson, *The Rise of Consumer Society in Britain* (London: Longman, 1994); Bill Lancaster, *The Department Store: A Social History* (London: Leicester University Press, 1995).

56 Matthew Hilton, *Smoking in British Popular Culture 1800–2000: Perfect Pleasures* (2000); Sean O'Connell, *The Car and British Society: Class, Gender and Motoring 1896–1939* (1998); John K. Walton, *The British Seaside: Holidays and Resorts in the*

Twentieth Century (2000); Susan Barton, *Working Class Organisations and Popular Tourism 1840–1970* (2005); and *Healthy Living in the Alps: The Origins of Winter Tourism in Switzerland 1860–1914* (2008), all published by Manchester University Press.

57 Dave Russell, *Looking North: Northern England and the National Imagination* (Manchester: Manchester University Press, 2004); Claire Langhamer, *Women's Leisure in England 1920–60* (Manchester: Manchester University Press, 2000).

58 They included: the Jarvik Centre (York); the Tales of Robin Hood (Nottingham); The Way We Were (Wigan Pier Heritage Centre).

59 Robert Hewison, *The Heritage Industry: Britain in a Climate of Decline* (London: Methuen, 1987).

60 Raphael Samuel, *Theatres of Memory, Volume 1, Past and Present in Contemporary Culture* (London: Verso, 1994); *Volume 2, Island Stories: Unravelling Britain,* ed. Alison Light (London: Verso, 1998).

61 Jerome de Groot, *Consuming History: Historians and Heritage in Contemporary Popular Culture* (London: Routledge, 2009).

62 Angela Piccini, *A Survey of Heritage Television Viewing Figures* (Council for British Archaeology, York, 2007).

63 Broadcast by BBC2 television from 2007 (www.bbc.co.uk/programmes)

64 Starkey has been associated with a number of television programmes including *Monarchy*, broadcast by Channel 4 (2004–06), which is a good example of his approach.

65 Alex Graham, 'Who Do You Think You Are, Tristram Hunt?' *Guardian Media*, 17 September 2008, 7; Tristram Hunt, 'The Time Bandits', *Guardian Media*, 10 September 2008.

66 The work of Jeffrey Richards has been particularly important. See *Visions of Yesterday* (London: Routledge and Kegan Paul, 1973); *The Age of the Dream Palace* (London: Routledge and Kegan Paul, 1984); *Films and British National Identity: From Dickens to Dad's Army* (Manchester: Manchester University Press, 1997); *Cinema and Radio in Britain and America, 1920–60* (Manchester: Manchester University Press, 2010); with D. Sheridan (ed.), *Mass Observation at the Movies* (London: Routledge Kegan Paul, 1987). See also Christine Geraghty, *British Cinema in the Fifties: Gender, Genre and the 'New Look'* (London: Routledge, 2000). See also Jeffrey Hill, *Sport, Leisure and Culture in Twentieth-Century Britain* (Basingstoke: Palgrave Macmillan, 2002), Ch. 4.

67 See de Groot, *Consuming History,* 211–14.

68 *The King's Speech*, directed by Tom Hooper (2010).

69 Churchill was out of government for ten years until recalled in Chamberlain's war cabinet (September 1939); he himself described the period as his 'wilderness years'. In the film we see the Churchill character counselling the Duke of York during the Abdication Crisis when in reality Churchill supported Edward VIII.

70 This point was acknowledged by the film's 'royal adviser' in the *Guardian* (www. guardian.co.uk, 9 January 2011)[accessed 20 January 2011].

71 See, for example, *The Night Watch* (London: Virago Press, 2006), which deals with the Second World War and its aftermath, though not in that order.

72 Iain Sinclair, 'The Scam of Scams', *London Review of Books* 30, no. 12 (19 June 2008), 17–23.

73 Broadcast 2003–6 (www.bbc.co.uk/history/programmes/restoration/)

74 Simon Schama, a professional historian based in the USA and much in evidence as a television don in recent years, has joined a current debate about the place of history in the British school curriculum, where its importance has gradually been reduced. Schama argues forcibly for history as a major subject, and outlines an interesting, though largely 'Anglo-centric' syllabus. See Simon Schama, 'Kids Need to Know They Belong', *Guardian (G2),* 9 November 2010, 6–11.

75 Gareth Stedman Jones, 'History: the Poverty of Empiricism', in R. Blackburn (ed.), *Ideology in Social Science: Readings in Critical Social Theory* (London: Fontana, 1972), 107. Francis Williams's book was published in 1945.

76 Wray Vamplew, 'Taking a Gamble or a Racing Certainty: Sports Museums and Public Sports History', *Journal of Sport History* 31, no. 2 (2004): 177–91.

77 Martin Johnes and Rhiannon Mason, 'Soccer Public History and the National Football Museum', *Sport in History* 23 (2003): 115–31; Eilean Hooper-Greenhill, *Museums and the Shaping of Knowledge* (London: Routledge, 1992); *Museum, Media, Message* (London: Routledge, 1995).

78 The museum has now moved to Manchester from its original location in Preston, a site closely associated with the origins of football but not the most advantageous from a commercial point of view.

79 See, for example, the several problems faced by a museum in an urban context. See Kevin Moore, 'Sports Heritage and the Re-imagined City: The National Football Museum, Preston', *International Journal of Cultural Policy* 14, no. 4 (November 2008): 445–61.

80 Ellen Ross, 'Survival Networks: Women's Neighbourhood Sharing in London Before World War I', *History Workshop* 15 (1983), 4–27.

81 Angela McRobbie, *Feminism and Youth Culture: From 'Jackie' to 'Just Seventeen'* (Basingstoke: Macmillan, 1991).

82 Andrew Davies, *Leisure, Gender and Poverty: Working-Class Culture in Salford and Manchester, 1900–1939* (Buckingham: Open University Press, 1992), esp. 61–3, 73, 172.

83 Langhamer, *Women's Leisure in England.*

84 Jean Williams, *A Beautiful Game: International Perspectives on Women's Football* (Oxford: Berg, 2007).

85 Sheila Rowbotham, *Hidden From History: 300 Years of Women's Oppression and the Fight Against It* (London: Pluto Press, 1973).

86 Catriona M. Parratt, *'More Than Mere Amusement': Working-Class Women's Leisure in England, 1750–1914* (Boston: Northeastern University Press, 2001).

87 Bailey, 'Politics and Poetics', 131.

88 Important pointers are provided by: John M. MacKenzie (ed.), *Imperialism and Popular Culture* (Manchester: Manchester University Press, 1986); *European Empires and the People* (Manchester: Manchester University Press, 2011); *Museums and Empire* (Manchester: Manchester University Press, 2009); Stuart Ward (ed.), *British*

Culture and the End of Empire (Manchester: Manchester University Press, 2001).

89 See John Tomlinson, *Cultural Imperialism: A Critical Introduction* (London: Continuum, 1991).

90 The work, for example, of Peter Hennessy, *Having It So Good* (London: Allen Lane, 2006); Dominic Sandbrook, *Never Had It So Good* (London: Little Brown, 2005); and especially David Kynaston, *Austerity Britain 1945–51* (London: Bloomsbury, 2007), *A World to Build* (London: Bloomsbury, 2008), and *Family Britain* (London: Bloomsbury, 2009).

91 *Securing a Sustainable Future for Higher Education: An Independent Review of Higher Education Funding and Student Finance* (October 2010) www.independent.gov.uk/ browne.report [accessed 15 January 2011].

92 See Chris Rojek, *The Labour of Leisure: The Culture of Free Time* (London: Sage Publications, 2010), 110–13, for the distinction between 'leisure studies' and 'leisure science'.

93 Peter Borsay, *History of Leisure*.

94 See Johann Huizinga, *Homo Ludens: A Study of the Play-Element in Culture,* trans. R. F. C. Hull (London: Routledge and Kegan Paul, 1944).

2

Dancing in the English style: professionalisation, public preference and the evolution of popular dancing in Britain in the 1920s

ALLISON ABRA

In the months after the end of the First World War, many Britons observed that the nation had entered a veritable dancing craze. As the *Daily Express* proclaimed in October 1919, 'Dancing mad! London is stricken with the craze, and so also are the great towns throughout the country. The adult population … at the present time can be roughly divided into three classes – those who are dancing, those who are learning, and those who want to do both.'[1] Other press reports described how businessmen were leaving their offices in the middle of the day, or how women were stopping by a public ballroom in the midst of their shopping, to take a turn about the floor.[2] Another article reported that special dancing classes were being held in Marylebone, London, to instruct disabled war veterans how to dance with artificial limbs,[3] while one Londoner expressed annoyance in a letter to the editor that authorities appeared to be prioritising the building of dance halls over regular household waste disposal services.[4] In an article announcing weekly dances at the Masonic Hall in Leyton, a northeastern suburb of London, the *Eastern Mercury* summed up the general situation: 'We venture to think that never in history has dancing been indulged in to the extent it is this season, doubtless the re-action after the dreary days of the past five years, has something to do with this.'[5]

Much of the contemporary coverage of the dancing boom similarly attributed its occurrence to euphoria over the end of the war, but a reaction to those 'dreary days' was in fact only one element of a much larger transformation and restructuring of British popular dance culture. Indeed, a renewed fervour for dancing had been building even before the war, with the arrival in Britain of a number of 'modern' dances from beyond the British Isles. In the midst of the dance craze some fundamental questions thus began to emerge about this plethora of new dances, and how Britons should be dancing them. At the fore-front of this debate was a group of dancing teachers, performers and writers who sought to take hold of the reins of the new dancing juggernaut and influence its continued evolution. Between 1920 and 1929, these dancing aficionados held a series of meetings and purpose-driven dances in which they deliberated over what was being danced in Britain, and how these dances were being taught and performed. The result of this process was twofold, leading to the further profes-sionalisation of ballroom dancing and to the development and standardisation of what became known as the 'English style' of ballroom dancing.[6]

As its very name suggests, the new dancing style was self-consciously national, with professionals habitually suggesting that the English style was more refined and graceful than American and European dancing, and better suited to the British character and temperament. The national dancing style was also meant to be national in scope and accessibility, comprising dances that were acceptable to and easily mastered by the vast majority of Britons. Further cementing the linkages between dancing and the nation's people and culture, the dance profession consistently proclaimed that decisions related to the content and appearance of the national style should remain in the hands of the British dancing public, rather than in the control of teachers and other pro-fessionals. However, as this discussion will show, dance professionals wielded considerable authority in shaping the English style, and had significant finan-cial motives for continuing to intervene in the evolution of British ballroom dancing. Through a close examination of the emergence and progression of the foxtrot, the tango, the blues, the Charleston and other dances, this chapter will show that the preferences and agendas of the dance profession often diverged from those of the dancing public. The result was that determinations over which dances the national dancing style should contain were forged through ongoing negotiations between the profession and the public, which played out in dancing schools, at dance competitions, in print culture and on the floors of the nation's ballrooms.

The professionalisation and standardisation of modern ballroom dancing

British popular dancing had been in a state of considerable flux since approximately 1910, and the ensuing period witnessed the proliferation of many new dances of divergent styles and origins. The first major innovation was the transformation of the waltz, which had remained the 'unchallenged queen of ballroom' for nearly a century after its initial introduction to Regency-era dancers.[7] A variation on the dance known as the Boston arrived in Britain from America and enjoyed a short-lived heyday in British ballrooms. The Boston especially appealed to younger Britons because it represented a significant departure from its Victorian predecessor, with the only real similarity being that it was performed to waltz music. Arguably its greatest legacy, however, was that it introduced the relaxed and natural movements that would become the hallmark of the English style of ballroom dancing. Meanwhile, other new dances were also helping to 'modernise' British dancing styles.[8] Following on the heels of the Boston, the tango came from Argentina by way of Paris, which caused a sensation in the winter of 1912–13 and saw a ubiquitous number of 'tango teas' take hold across British Isles. Around the same time, the introduction of American ragtime music to Britain, usually associated with the arrival of Irving Berlin's song 'Alexander's Ragtime Band' in 1912, also led to the importation of multiple dances designed to accompany the new musical form's syncopated melodies. These included the so-called 'animal dances', such as the Bunny Hug, Turkey Trot, and Grizzly Bear, as well as the one-step and by the first year of the war, a rudimentary version of the foxtrot.

There are two elements important to note about these developments: the rapid and chaotic manner with which new dances were being introduced to British ballrooms, and the fact that none of these dances were home-grown. Rather, all of the new dances enjoying success in Britain came from the European continent, from Latin America or, increasingly, from the United States. The interruption caused by the devastating war, however, meant that these were not issues that would be addressed in any meaningful way until the Armistice, at which time Britons quickly became absorbed in a confused *mélange* of music and dances collectively understood as 'jazz'. This umbrella term included both the new musical form that had travelled to Britain with American troops bound for the Western Front in the final year of the war and a dance step known as the 'jazz roll'.[9] The one-step and particularly the foxtrot also still dominated British ballrooms, but with very little cohesion as to how these dances were being performed.

With the peace, the already disorderly dancing terrain was soon made even more ungovernable by the dance craze, as well as several other developments which concurrently helped to foster the revolution in popular dance. First of all, dance culture was strongly affected by the many wider social and cultural changes that emerged from the war years, particularly the changing status of women. The new freedom and independence enjoyed by female war workers, nurses and auxiliary military servicewomen found further expression in the dancing craze, as these young women, soon to be dubbed 'flappers' or in some cases merely the 'dancing girl', became dancing's chief enthusiasts.[10] At the same time, the widespread expansion and commercialisation of leisure that would continue throughout the interwar years also influenced the growth and dissemination of dance culture, as dancing shows and dance music dominated wireless programmes and gramophone record sales. Finally, with the opening in October 1919 of the Hammersmith Palais, London's first purpose-built dancing space, a new entertainment industry – the dance-hall industry – was inaugurated. Dance halls and new public ballrooms began to crop up throughout the country, with one estimate suggesting there were as many as 11,000 by 1926.[11]

Throughout this period, leaders within the dancing community looked upon the untamed and mutable British dancing scene with no small degree of trepidation. Foremost among those seeking to intervene was Philip Richardson, editor of the *Dancing Times*, and one of the most prominent figures in ballroom dancing during the interwar years. Richardson's greatest cause for concern was the undisciplined and untutored manner in which Britons performed the new dances. As he later recalled, the quick tempo of jazz, combined with the near-constant emergence of wild new steps and figures, placed 'the smooth foxtrot which had been slowly developing in grave peril. There was much freak dancing to be seen and freak variations'.[12] Richardson did not place the blame for 'freak' steps solely on the dancers, however; he was also concerned about how Britons were being *taught* to dance. Post-war enthusiasm for the activity had seen dancing schools crop up by the hundreds, as eager Britons sought tutelage in the modern styles. Indeed, with respect to the number of schools in the city of Leeds, the *Dancing Times* noted, '[dancing] classes are springing up in nearly every street, and municipal authorities will seriously have to consider the advisability of opening up new streets to enable teachers to have one each'.[13] But while dancing schools existed in abundance, there was little to no regulation of who was teaching the classes – essentially, anyone could set up as an instructor – or consistency as to how the dances were being taught. Richardson and a number of others sought to regulate this state of affairs by creating a proper system of accreditation for teachers and, even more importantly, by standardising the steps of the dances that they were teaching.

In addition to restoring order to chaotic ballrooms, Richardson articulated another rationale for the necessity of standardising ballroom dancing steps:

in order to deflect public criticism away from the modern styles. Throughout 1919 and 1920 he and other dance professionals followed with perturbation the attempts by Catholic Church authorities in France to stamp out dances like the foxtrot and the tango. Cardinal Amette, Archbishop of Paris, and Bordeaux's Cardinal Andrieux, condemned the dances for their perceived indecency, frivolity and 'unseemly gyrations'.[14] At the behest of the Church, the Marquise de Monstier also produced a report that decreed modern ballroom dances 'ugly and indecent',[15] and there were attempts in Paris to establish a dance censorship board, which would evaluate new dances in much the same way that films underwent review.[16] There was no similar campaign in Britain, but from the pages of the *Dancing Times* Richardson expressed considerable concern about the possibility that one could emerge, writing in May 1920, 'Now, you and I know that these dances are perfectly clean, but unless we make a little counter-attack the very large number of people who do not dance will begin to pay attention to the other side.'[17] A few months later, he similarly cautioned, 'They have not seriously attacked dancing in England yet … Believe me, it is a very serious danger if allowed to develop.'[18]

While Richardson was no doubt sincere, it must be noted that he and other dance professionals had another, less overt reason for seeking to standardise the instruction and steps of modern ballroom dancing. Richardson decried what he called 'freak' variations as a threat to the aesthetics, integrity and reputation of ballroom dancing, yet these movements also represented improvisation and originality on the part of dancers. The lack of standardisation, or of a 'correct' way to dance, undoubtedly posed a considerable threat to those who earned their income as dance instructors. As dance scholar Juliet McMains has noted, 'if dancing became a free-form frenzy with no standards or techniques, dance teachers would soon be out of jobs'.[19] Indeed, though the criticisms of modern ballroom dancing were never as vociferous in Britain as they were in France and elsewhere, some teachers were not above fomenting the notion that dancing was under public scrutiny and attack in order to fill their classes. For example, one advertisement for the Méthode Sielle School of Dancing featured a heading that screamed 'Vulgarity in the Ballroom!' before going on to assert that this claim was being buoyed by:

> people of unimpeachable character who would be most insulted if told of their responsibility. Their well-meaning but untutored movements are nine-tenths of the cause of the present absurd outcry in the Daily Press, in which one sees dancing described as negroid, indecent and vulgar. It is because many dancers do not know how to hold themselves that their dancing calls forth this strong condemnation.[20]

The idea that dancing, particularly improperly performed dancing, was a source of controversy and condemnation thus provided dancing teachers with a justification for their profession's continued existence. The teachers' professed concerns about the reputation and aesthetic value of their art existed alongside their status as entrepreneurs running commercial enterprises and their need to maintain a reason for Britons to continue attending dancing classes. As will be shown, this need also existed in tension with the burgeoning profession's continually avowed desire that the dancers, and not the teachers, should be the ones to direct the future of British dancing.

Thus, in early 1920, with a variety of motives both declared and undeclared, Richardson and other teachers began to discuss the need for a meeting that would assess the state of ballroom dancing in Britain, and the first 'Informal Conference of Teachers of Ballroom Dancing' was accordingly convened at the Grafton Galleries in London on 12 May of that year. Organised under the auspices of the *Dancing Times*, and chaired by Richardson, the conference brought together about two hundred teachers and members of the press. Over the course of the afternoon, the teachers debated what should be the standard steps of the foxtrot, one-step, and modern waltz, and an exhibition of the three dances was performed by famed dancing teacher Monsieur Maurice and his partner Leonora Hughes.

After the fact, Richardson summed up the goals of the event, writing that 'the business of the recent conference may be put under two headings. Firstly to eliminate what is bad. Secondly, to put what is good on a firm basis.'[21] In pursuit of the first goal, all of the teachers at the meeting avowed to 'do their very best to stamp out freak steps'.[22] These specifically included excessive lifts and dips, which were viewed to be poorly performed by ordinary dancers and only attractive or appropriate in professional exhibitions. Freak steps were further defined by professionals as those movements which produced havoc in crowded ballrooms (a common reality in the midst of the nation's dance craze), such as an over-pronounced pause in the waltz, or side and backward steps in the foxtrot. It must also be acknowledged that those steps and movements deemed unacceptable or 'freak' were often those associated with the perceived African-American origins of most of the new dances. As one dancing professional mused about 'negro dances' several years after the standardisation process had begun, 'Of course, [these dances] had to be refined and adapted to civilised life before [they] could be countenanced in European ballrooms. The sawing movements of the arms, shaking shoulders, and close embraces, the incessant tom-tom beating and clatter had to be modified.'[23] The standardisation of ballroom dancing therefore had a distinct racist undertone, and professionals were quite invested in developing a national dancing style that was fundamentally 'anglicised' and in keeping with the national character. The implications of this goal, and the part played by the dancing public in helping the profession to articulate the cultural meanings about race and nation associated with popular dancing, are complex and beyond the scope of this discussion.[24] However, it should be briefly noted that the profession viewed the new British versions of the dances under review at the initial and subsequent conferences of teachers to be entirely made-over and distinct from their foreign precursors, celebrating them for their fluidity, grace and refinement. As Richardson noted in 1923, 'the ingredients of the foxtrot came from America, but the foxtrot as danced to-day in London is essentially an English dance, with considerable difference from its prototype in New York'.[25]

While the first conference of teachers was clearly quite sure as to what constituted bad dancing, there was less consensus about what was acceptable or good. Therefore, the decision was taken to form a smaller committee responsible for establishing the recognised steps of the major modern ballroom dances, which would report back to the larger group later that year. The process of creating a specifically British style of ballroom dancing had officially commenced, and over the course of the next few years, the fledgling dance profession continued to work towards standardising ballroom dancing steps in a number of different ways. The small committee formed at the first meeting of dancing teachers issued a preliminary report, and further conferences were convened at the Grafton Galleries and other dancing spaces. Richardson and the *Dancing Times* also began organising less formal events, most notably special dances at which teachers could practise and confer about the steps of specific ballroom dances. The 'Tango Ball' was held in May 1922, and the 'Blues Ball' in the autumn of 1923. In this way the steps of the foxtrot, one-step, tango, and modern waltz were gradually standardised, and these dances (known as 'standard four') formed what became recognised as the English style of ballroom dancing.

Throughout the period during which it held conferences and special dances, the dance profession also continued to expand into other areas, which further affected the evolution of the English style. Starting with the *Daily Sketch*'s sponsorship of a national foxtrot and waltz competition in 1921, the 1920s saw the emergence of serious competitive dancing. Many nationwide competitions were inaugurated, with complex definitions of professional, amateur and novice eventually emerging. Local heats would be held throughout the country, followed by well-publicised grand finals, typically at venues in London such as the Queen's Hall or Royal Albert Hall. There were also frequent and less elaborate dance competitions, local or one-night-only events at a public ballroom. However, competition dancing's premier event was undoubtedly the annual Blackpool Dance Festival. Debuting around 1920, Blackpool eventually became the location for the British Professional and British Amateur Dance Championships, and has often been seen as ballroom dancing's version of the Wimbledon tennis tournament.

Beyond taking part in dance competitions, many professional dancers were also employed in exhibition dancing, which in its simplest definition was any dancing performed before an audience. In the 1920s, ballroom dancing became an increasingly popular performance art in public ballrooms, music halls, theatres and even department stores, as professional dancers performed the dances of the English style with the goal of both entertaining and instructing their audience. The interwar years also saw the expansion of dance print culture. While the *Dancing Times* continued to predominate, a number of other dance-themed periodicals and popular newspaper columns began to emerge. Hundreds of dancing teachers also took to print-based instruction, and a voluminous number of dance instruction manuals were printed and reprinted. Victor Silvester's *Modern Ballroom Dancing*, for example, was first published in 1927 and went into dozens of editions, remaining in print for decades afterwards.

Competitions, exhibition dancing and print allowed dance professionals around the country to forge further connections and collaborate on steps and figures. All of these elements contributed to the continued professionalisation of ballroom dancing. Even more significantly, however, these dance-related events and print outpourings provided a connection between the dance profession and the rest of British society. The instructional benefits of dance manuals were likely self-evident, but many professionals felt that the general public could also learn a great deal from witnessing an exhibition dance or dance competition, or by following the extensive coverage that the major events received in both the dance and popular press. Accordingly, professionals sought to use these forums to educate the public as to correct steps and figures, to introduce a new dance or to alert dancers to the latest trends.[26]

Of course there was some debate, even at the time, as to how effective these measures were in guiding how the average Briton danced. The ever-expanding market for dance manuals, the impressive salaries commanded by the most accomplished exhibition dancers[27] and the large crowds and extensive press coverage that many dance competitions generated all point to considerable public interest in the dictates of the dance profession. As one dancing enthusiast wrote in a letter to the editor of *Modern Dance*, 'As a keen amateur dancer, whenever I can get the opportunity I never miss seeing our leading professionals, and have attended the finals in Blackpool for the last four years, and seen most of them dancing at the Astoria, Hammersmith, and other London dance places.'[28] Many Britons therefore did look to the example and tutelage of the dance profession in ways above and beyond enrolling in dancing classes.

Yet at the same time, there is evidence that professional activities were not all geared towards tutoring the public in correct dancing, and that the public frequently ignored or remained oblivious to the suggestions and innovations of the profession. For example, there were those professionals who felt that exhibition dancing or even competitions should really be focused on providing entertainment rather than instruction. Instead of performing the standardised, simplified versions of the standard four dances of the English style, many professionals chose to exhibit more complex figures or different dances. As exhibition dancers Marjorie and Georges Fontana told the *Dancing Times*, 'the audience at most modern dances can do the ballroom dances now in vogue quite well themselves, and … they would prefer to see an exhibition couple do something that they cannot do …We make a point therefore of giving dances of a far more elaborate nature.'[29]

It is also clear that many Britons participated in dancing without ever having taken a lesson, attended a competition or read a dance manual. As *Oxford Magazine* noted in 1929, 'Ballroom dancing appeals to thousands upon thousands … its followers form two great camps, those who learn to dance, and that quite appreciable number who dance without learning.'[30] Dance halls and other public ballrooms were important spaces for socialisation and romance, food and drink, or simply listening to the music, and many patrons, assuming they danced at all, did so merely by emulating others on the floor. In addition, even those Britons who did take dancing seriously continued to control their own experience to a great extent, despite the best efforts of the profession to shape the national style. By choosing to dance a foxtrot when a tango was being played by the band, or improvising their own steps while performing one of the standard four, or simply walking off the floor when a dance they disliked was being performed, Britons individualised their dancing experience and helped to shape the nation's dance culture. As Julie Malnig has noted with respect to the standardisation of modern ballroom dancing in the United States, 'one could not always account for what bodies were doing *in the moment* of dance'.[31]

Indeed, the complexities of the relationship between the dance profession and dancing public were highlighted at what was known as the Great Conference, held at the Prince's Galleries on 14 April 1929. Nearly a decade of discussion and debate on the content and specific steps of the English style culminated in this event, at which the dance profession agreed on two primary points. First, the Great Conference saw the establishment of the Official Board of Ballroom Dancing, the committee which would consider all major issues of concern to professionals, and the general state of ballroom dancing in Britain, for years to come. With this move the profession affirmed its continued relevance, and its ongoing intervention in the instruction and development of British ballroom dancing for the foreseeable future. Yet at the same time, the profession also used the Great Conference to formally mandate that in standardising modern ballroom dancing their focus should be on the public rather than on professionals such as themselves. They further declared that the basic steps of the four standard dances must therefore be kept as simple as possible in order to remain accessible to the majority of British dancers.[32]

This had been the professional mantra throughout the 1920s: that the development of dancing should be controlled by the aptitudes and preferences of the public, rather than by the directives of the profession. Yet there can be little question that through its series of conferences and other events, dance competitions and exhibitions, and voluminous production of dance manuals and periodicals, the profession had sought and achieved a critical influence over the evolution of the English style and popular dance culture in general. It is also apparent that the profession consistently had motivations above and beyond the public interest, seeking out new ways to fill dancing classes and maintain its *raison d'être*. The preferences and agendas of the profession and public were not always aligned. Accordingly, the national dancing style was forged reciprocally by the profession and the public, with each taking a role in determining what dances would be included, how they would be performed, and what cultural meanings were attached to them. This becomes acutely apparent through a closer examination of some of the most successful dances of the 1920s, which is the focus of the next section.

Negotiating a national dancing style

In 1921, famed dancing teacher Monsieur Pierre wrote an article for the *Dancing Times* which offered the following query in its title: 'Who makes new dances?'[33] In the course of the discussion that followed, Pierre categorically asserted that it was 'not the teachers' who controlled which dances would take hold in Britain's ballrooms. Describing how, in the midst of the present dancing boom, new dances were appearing on the nation's dance floors almost daily, Pierre decreed that this was a phenomenon being directed entirely by the dancing public. For his part, Monsieur Pierre appeared to lament the fact that 'teachers, powerless to exercise any control, have had no alternative but to follow the lead of the very people they had once hoped to govern'.[34] However, his concerns were not universal among teachers of dancing. Rather, the oft-expressed belief among many within the dance profession, and the one that purportedly governed the actions of those involved in developing and standardising the English style, was that the progression of British dancing should be in the hands of the public, not the professionals.

In particular, Philip Richardson was a strong proponent of this position. Richardson often suggested that the greatest charm of the modern dances that characterised the English style was that they were simple and easily mastered. This accessibility, Richardson posited, placed dancing back in the control of dancers rather than the dancing master, a figure who in his Victorian or pre-war incarnation was illustrated as positively tyrannical. In 1920, Richardson even hyperbolically compared the public's casting off of the shackles of the dictatorial dancing master to the events of the recent war: 'The modern ballroom dancer has revolted against the despotism of the Victorian dancing master in the same way that … in the great world of which the dancing world is but a microcosm, the free nations have revolted against the military autocracy of the Teutonic peoples.'[35] And yet, what would have been the fate of the fledgling modern ballroom dance profession had the public chosen to abandon its guidance too?

Significantly, the dance profession's stated desire that the public should control the development of dancing in Britain had to constantly be negotiated in terms of its own need to remain relevant and to maintain its bottom line. As will be shown, in the case of a number of dances public preference did not always ally with professional will, and the profession consistently and power- fully intervened in the continued development of dance culture in Britain. Specifically, the profession actively promoted certain dances such as the tango and the blues, and resisted other dances, notably the Charleston, which the public embraced and chose to perform in a manner beyond the control of the profession. Indeed, this negotiation between public and profession as to the content and development of a national dancing style became strongly evident even in the case of a dance that the profession and the public both admired: the foxtrot.

Throughout the 1920s, as the steps of the standard four were formalised by the dance profession and new dances were consistently introduced each season, the foxtrot clearly remained the favoured dance of the public. As the manager of the Hammersmith Palais told a writer for *Popular Music and Dancing Weekly* in 1924, 'We find that the fox trot is the most popular dance, then the waltz and the one-step, and finally the Blues and the tango.'[36] There are a number of reasons for this predominance, which were to some extent cyclical and self-per-petuating. Public enthusiasm for the dance meant that music composers and publishers produced far more foxtrot songs than any other, which then became the most commonly played songs by the dance bands in public ballrooms. The effect of this abundance of foxtrots was that the public continued to perform the dance the most frequently and remained more comfortable with it than with any other dance. Many Britons also seemed to favour the foxtrot simply owing to its attractive appearance and relative lack of complexity. As one pro-fessional dancer observed in 1925, the enduring appeal of the foxtrot was easily accounted for because, 'It is an easy, healthy and natural dance, combining a pleasing rhythm with an ease of accomplishment which is greater than that found in any other dance.'[37]

As this comment suggests, the dance profession also valued the foxtrot, and recognised it as the staple dance of the English style. However, the state of foxtrot – and the question of whether or not any dance could seriously chal-lenge its supremacy – was also an issue of incessant discussion among pro-fessionals. In fact, despite its acknowledgment of the foxtrot's attributes, the profession increasingly lamented the dance's pre-eminence. Pointing to the influence of dance bands in maintaining the foxtrot's ubiquity, teacher Santos Casani complained, 'Because nine out of ten dances that are played are fox trots … consequently dancers have every opportunity of becoming proficient. If only dance-hall bands would play different dances in turn, and so give dancers an opportunity of practising other steps, the fox trot would soon topple from its pedestal and fall into line with the other dances.'[38] From the pages of the dance press, many other professionals similarly expressed boredom with the dance, and began to suggest that this boredom was shared by the public. As early as 1922, the *Dancing Times* reported: '[the foxtrot] has almost become stereotyped, and dancers feel that they want something a little different in this present winter from the foxtrot of a year ago.'[39] By 1926 the periodical decreed that the dance had been in a 'rut' for some time.[40]

Given the profession's control over much of the dance press, it is difficult to discern from these sources whether or not the dancing public actually shared the profession's tedium with the foxtrot or not. What is certain is that just as it had been to the professionals' advantage to suggest that dancing was being attacked by social purists, it was also to their advantage to suggest that interest in the foxtrot was waning and that Britain needed a new dance. The foxtrot's continued supremacy meant that once dancing enthusiasts had perfected the dance they might cease taking lessons, which represented a significant threat to a profession dominated by teachers of dancing. The *Dancing Times* actually acknowledged this reality in 1921, suggesting that with no new dance on the horizon for the upcoming season, 'a number of teachers w[ould] complain that this absence' was 'very bad for business'.[41] The result was that despite its avowal that the dancers and not the teachers should shape the development of the national dance culture, the profession regularly intervened in that development. In particular, the profession was constantly on the lookout for new dances that it could use to draw Britons into dancing classes.

Indeed, one of the dance profession's major efforts in this respect involved not a new dance, but an old one: the tango. While the dance remained enormously popular in Paris after the war, it never replicated the success it had enjoyed in Britain during the 1912–13 season. In a 1920 letter to the editor of the *Dancing Times*, exhibition dancer Robert Sielle bemoaned this fact, writing, 'Although we now have a tango remarkable for its beauty, simplicity, and general suitability to the requirements of ballroom dancing, we are still faced with the difficulty of overcoming the public timidity which invariably heralds the opening bars of tango music. No one seems to care to be the first to get up and dance.'[42]

Other professionals clearly shared Sielle's concerns, for there were persistent attempts by the dance profession to transform and publicise the dance in ways that would make it more palatable to the public. New variations of the tango were frequently introduced, and it formed a major component of the debates and events associated with the standardisation of the English style. The tango was also frequently displayed before the public through competitions and exhibitions, and at the start of each new dancing season professionals declared in the dance press that the tango would almost certainly be back in vogue in the coming year. For example, in the autumn of 1924, *Popular Music and Dancing Weekly* averred, 'There is much talk of a revival of that exotic Southern dance.'[43] Two years later, the same periodical similarly asserted, 'I hear that the Tango is going to be a definite feature of the new season's dances. This is as it should be.'[44]

Yet simply stating that the tango would rally could not make it do so, and the public generally remained wary of the dance. At the root of the public's reticence appears to have been the belief that the tango was more difficult than the other standard dances of the English style. In 1926, a writer for *Popular Music and Dancing Weekly* recounted that she had undertaken a small study of the tango problem at a London dance hall. 'June' reported to have overheard one dancer proclaiming, 'Tango music is sweet and I like listening to it, but the dance looks as if only an expert should attempt it.'[45] The result, June further noted, was that 'when a tango tune was played a few couples with a conscious air of bravery left the crowded floor-side to attempt the tango – lonely souls in a vast Sahara!'[46] Dance professionals worked hard to overcome these qualms and to encourage Britons to experiment with the tango. One writer commented: 'during the last week or so, I noticed that nearly all the dance halls include a tango in their programmes, but – I also noticed – that at such times there was more than a plentiful supply of space on the dance floor. I wonder if any of you have ever tried the tango, or if you realise how very fascinating a dance it really is?'[47]

Ironically, the same periodical speculated that the perception that the tango was difficult, and the public's reluctance to attempt it, were in large part owing to the profession's preoccupation with the dance: 'The tango died almost before it was born, the result, I am convinced, of so many teachers trying to improve it by introducing their own steps.'[48] In an attempt to perfect, and perhaps renew public interest in the dance, the profession may well have scared casual dancers away from the tango. Throughout the 1920s, therefore, the tango remained a topic of considerable interest to professional dancers, and a staple of competitions and exhibitions, but not a prominent element of popular dancing. The dance reveals the extent to which the profession and public were not always united in determining which dances should form the content of the national style.

This fact was showcased repeatedly throughout the 1920s as the dance profession introduced (or reintroduced) a series of dances to the dancing public. There was a determined quest to locate 'standard five', a fifth dance that could enter into the English style canon. Professional motivation was undoubtedly composed of both a sincere desire to elevate the art and the need to maintain enrolments at dancing academies. But whatever their basis, these efforts by the profession generally failed. For example, in 1923 the dance profession grew extremely enthusiastic about the 'blues', another new dance imported from America. Philip Richardson proclaimed in the *Dancing Times* in August of that year, 'A new dance at last. We shall all be dancing "Blues" this autumn.'[49] Like the foxtrot, the blues was performed in 4/4 time, but at a slower tempo. It was introduced at a time when foxtrot tempos began to speed up in public ballrooms, culminating in the development of the quickstep, so it was perhaps not surprising that the blues never achieved great success with the dancing public. The dance profession continued to engage with the blues for a number of years, both in print and at conferences and special dances, but the public did not embrace the dance. As Richardson himself later admitted, 'The dance intrigued professionals, but never really took off with the public.'[50] So like the tango, the blues was a dance that the profession saw great potential in, but to which the public remained indifferent; professional zeal was simply not enough to ensure a dance's success. Yet significantly, another dance was about to demonstrate that professional ambivalence was also not enough to ensure a dance's failure.

In 1925, a new American dance called the Charleston was introduced to Britain through the musical revue *Midnight Follies*. It was not until later that year, however, when dance professionals Robert Sielle and Annette Mills witnessed an exhibition of the ballroom version of the Charleston in New York, that the dance found a route to Britain's dance floors. In July, in conjunction with the *Dancing Times*, Sielle and Mills staged a 'Charleston tea' at a Soho dancing club in order to experiment with the dance and introduce it to other professionals. As one teacher present at the event later recalled, 'Questions, comment, argument, discussion went on for hours. Oh yes, the Charleston had hit London with a resounding thud.'[51] Teachers across the country immediately began offering lessons in the dance, and the demand was great. Famed ballroom dancer and dance bandleader Victor Silvester recalled in his autobiography that he and his wife taught thirteen hours a day at a profit of a hundred pounds per week, a number that, given a larger dance studio, he believed they could have doubled.[52]

However, despite the boon to the dancing schools brought about by the Charleston, when the new dancing season commenced that autumn, still more Britons chose to attempt the wild new dance without instruction. Two professional dancers described the situation in the *Dancing Times*: 'Hundreds of wild youths endeavoured to copy [the exhibition dancers'] kicking and stamping steps and to adapt them to the ballroom, with disastrous results. It was positively unsafe to go within two yards of any couple performing these ridiculous antics.'[53] The result was that some dance professionals turned on the Charleston. They decried it for reintroducing wildness and 'freak' steps to the ballroom, and condemned it as a threat to serious dancing. In an article in *Popular Music and Dancing Weekly*, one writer dismissed the dance altogether in an account of the season's dancing: 'So far I have intentionally omitted the Charleston because no one seems to have taken it seriously.'[54] Other professionals acknowledged the dance's popularity, but also its perceived deficiencies and liabilities. In June 1926 the *Dancing Times* observed, 'First, a very large section of the dancing public wish to dance the Charleston. Secondly, the majority of those who do Charleston are not only a nuisance but even a source of danger to other dancers.'[55]

It should be noted that not only the dance profession but also the general public were strongly divided on the Charleston. Dance-hall proprietors were greatly concerned about the effect of the dance's wild steps on their wooden dance floors, and the general disruption it caused in the ballroom. Some dancing spaces banned the dance outright, while others displayed signs with the letters 'P.C.Q.' for 'Please Charleston Quietly.' Meanwhile, for a time the Charleston was denounced daily in the pages of the popular press. The dance was deemed vulgar and coarse, and even dangerous, as certain newspapers suggested it could cause permanent damage to the ankles or paralysis-inducing shocks to the body.[56] Much of the criticism of the dance was also strongly racialised, given the dance's African-American origins. A *Daily Mail* correspondent declared the dance to be 'a series of contortions without a vestige of charm or grace, reminiscent only of the Negro orgies from which it derive[d] its creation'.[57] The *Mail* also quoted a Lady Walpole, who declared that watching a couple perform the dance was like watching 'two Christy Minstrels on the beach'.[58]

Condemnations of the Charleston from the dance profession and elsewhere did little to diminish its widespread popularity, however. As Victor Silvester later recalled:

> Wherever you went people seemed to be practising the Charleston – in bus queues, in Tube stations waiting for a train, at street corners, in shops; even policemen on point duty were seen doing the steps – because in practically every ballroom in London every second dance was the Charleston, although ministers fulminated against it from their pulpits, schools banned it, and various cultural societies staged protest marches.[59]

Moreover, the popular press, one of the primary sites of Charleston condemnation and criticism, also reported on and helped to perpetuate the dance's success. National dailies like the *Daily Mail* would fulminate against the Charleston on one page, but on another would discuss its influence on fashion, or report that the Prince of Wales was a keen enthusiast of the dance.[60]

Confronted with intense public ardour for the dance, the ballroom dance profession knew that action had to be taken. In October 1926, Richardson acknowledged that the Charleston juggernaut could not be stopped:

> The rhythm and beat of [Charleston] music has obtained too firm a hold upon the popular imagination for any official 'bannings' or attacks by disgruntled correspondents in the daily Press to stop it. It has got to come and those halls which attempt to 'bar' the Charleston would be doing good dancing a far greater service if, instead of telling their patrons they must not do it, they would help them to dance it in a quiet and simple manner.[61]

In the months that followed, Richardson and other professionals sought to formalize the second part of this assessment of the Charleston situation by developing a 'quiet and simple' form of the dance. Known as the 'flat progressive Charleston', the milder form of the dance was a smoother, more refined version of the original that eliminated the violent side-kicks. Much in the same way that the dance profession had taken up the foxtrot, tango, waltz and one-step and developed them into the English style, it now transformed the Charleston in a manner deemed more appropriate for British ballrooms.

The Charleston craze reached its zenith in December 1926 with the star-studded 'Charleston Ball' at the Royal Albert Hall, which featured a cabaret, competition and general dancing, and was attended by many of the leading dance professionals and celebrities of the day. The event arguably marked the Charleston's achievement of general social acceptance, but soon afterwards the craze for the dance began to dissipate. It was around this moment that a quick-tempo version of the foxtrot began to take hold, and rather than entering into the English style canon in its own right, the Charleston's long-term significance was the influence it had on the development of this new dance, called the quickstep. Indeed, it was the latter, and not any of the dances that the dance profession had sought to promote or obstruct in the 1920s, that would finally supplant the foxtrot as the nation's favoured dance by the next decade.

Conclusions

While the fervour for the Charleston was rather short-lived in the final analysis, it is illustrative about the processes of cultural negotiation that occurred between the dance profession and dancing public when it came to the introduction and evolution of a new dance, and of the national style in general. In its continued quest to locate 'standard five', and to maintain the ongoing evolution of the English style – both for its own sake, and to keep people attending dancing classes – the profession latched on to the Charleston as a new dance to introduce to the public. However, some professionals soon came to regret this move, since the dance proved to inspire the very experimentation and improvisation that represented such a threat to 'correct' dancing and to their own expertise and *raison d'être*. Others also despised the dance for its wild appearance and the rough element it introduced to the ballroom, which stood in direct contrast to the graceful elegance professionals had tried to inculcate into the English style.

Yet despite these concerns, the dance profession could not, and would not, reject the Charleston out of hand. In fact, the *Dancing Times* espoused the opposite, labelling calls in the popular press for the abolition of the dance as 'ridiculous' and 'harmful'.[62] Even those professionals who were wary of the Charleston recognised that it had to be embraced for two primary reasons. First, public enthusiasm for the dance brought many new students to dance classes, which was clearly to the dancing teachers' economic advantage. Second, the profession's persistent belief, and the one eventually codified at the Great Conference in 1929, was that the public should largely determine the direction that popular dancing in Britain would take. In embracing the Charleston, or in rejecting other dances like the tango or the blues, the public played an important role in shaping the national dancing style simply by determining which dances would be well-received and successful. In order to remain relevant, the dance profession was required, and indeed expressed their desire, to respond accordingly. As dance professional Josephine Bradley later recalled:

> [The Charleston] illustrated a viewpoint that I have always had that in reality the public lead the teachers in dancing taste and fashions. You cannot foist a new dance arbitrarily upon the general public. Looking back over my twelve years as a West End dancer and teacher, this has been proved over and over again. New dances have been put forth as the latest fashion – and what has happened to them? They have quietly faded away in a few weeks.[63]

But while the dance profession sought to acknowledge and even promote the agency of the dancing public, this power of the people to shape the nation's dance culture should not be over-stated. First of all, the channels through which the dancing public was exposed to new dances – dancing classes, exhibitions, competitions and print – were strongly mediated by the profession; even the Charleston had, after all, been introduced to Britain by two professional dancers. The dance profession also continued to exert a strong influence on how a dance would evolve once the public had embraced it, as was made evident in the creation and dissemination of the flat progressive Charleston. In this case, the profession once again took up a dance that it found objectionable and contrary to how the British were 'supposed' to dance and transformed it into something more aligned with the graceful elegance of the English style. So while the dancing public helped to influence which dances would find success in Britain, it was the profession that continued to determine which dances the public would be exposed to, and how they would develop once they had been publicly embraced. Of course, even this form of professional control had its limits, since all of the personal instruction, dance manuals, competitions and exhibitions in the world could not dictate what would happen once Britons actually ventured onto the dance floor. In the fleeting moment of physically performing a dance, dancers always had the ability to defy professional expectations and to embody their own vision of what the national style should be.

Notes

1 'London's Orgy of Dancing', *Daily Express*, 30 October 1919, 7.
2 'Tea-dancing', *Daily Mail*, 27 January 1919, 4.
3 'One-legged Dancers', *Daily Express*, 22 December 1919, 6.
4 S.A.M., Letter to the Editor, *Daily Express*, 31 January 1920, 4.
5 'Select Dances', *Eastern Mercury*, 21 October 1919, 4.
6 It must be acknowledged that naming the national dancing style the 'English style' represented an exclusion of Scottish and Welsh dancers on the part of the contemporary dance profession. However, there is little doubt that in their efforts to create a standardised national style of ballroom dancing, professionals did mean for it to extend throughout the whole of the British Isles. Indeed, some contemporaries frequently stated that given its breadth and ubiquity, both in dancing schools and public ballrooms, the English style really should be called the 'British style', and it was so-named in some of the primary material upon which this chapter is based. The goal of the standardisation of the English style was that there would theoretically be no difference in how Britons danced from London to Edinburgh to Cardiff, and I am therefore discussing it as the 'national' style, despite its problematic nomenclature.
7 Philip J. S. Richardson, *A History of English Ballroom Dancing* (London: Herbert Jenkins, 1946), 18. The waltz was not the sole dance to appear on public dance programmes prior to 1910. Also in favour were the two-step, the lancers, the quadrille, the galop, or sequence dances such as the valeta or military two-step, but none of these threatened the waltz's supremacy.
8 The dances in vogue after 1910 were collectively referred to as 'modern' ballroom dances, and there was much discussion in both the popular and the dance press about the perceived modernity of the new dancing styles. In referring to them in this way then, I am referencing how they were understood by contemporaries, in alignment with much recent work on modernity. See Martin Daunton and Bernhard

Reiger (eds), *Meanings of Modernity: Britain From the Late-Victorians Era to World War II* (Oxford: Berg, 2001).

9 The so-called 'jazz roll' was a dance figure that comprised three smooth steps performed to four beats of music, and while it would eventually fade out as a separate dance, it had an important influence on the continued development of the foxtrot in the early 1920s.

10 It should be noted that prevalent social anxieties about women's increased emancipation and their perceived pleasure-seeking excesses inevitably produced some controversy around dancing, their favoured pastime, as well. However, whether dancing women were being praised or castigated, I argue elsewhere that this discussion only served to raise dancing's profile and influence within wider society. See Allison Abra, 'On with the Dance: Nation, Culture, and Popular Dancing in Britain, 1918–1945' (PhD diss., University of Michigan, 2009). See also Billie Melman, *Women and the Popular Imagination in the Twenties: Flappers and Nymphs* (Basingstoke: Macmillan, 1988); Claire Langhamer, *Women's Leisure in Britain, 1920–1960* (Manchester: Manchester University Press, 2000); Selina Todd, *Young Women, Work, and Family in England, 1918–1950* (Oxford: Oxford University Press, 2005).

11 See J. McMillan, *The Way it Was, 1914–1934* (Kimber, 1979), 76, as cited in James Nott, *Music for the People: Popular Music and Dance in Interwar Britain* (Oxford: Oxford University Press, 2002), 151.

12 Richardson, *A History of English Ballroom Dancing*, 39.

13 Provincial Notes, *Dancing Times*, November 1919, 135.

14 Daily Express Correspondent, 'Seven Sinful Dances', *Daily Express*, 18 December 1919, 1.

15 Daily Express Correspondent, 'Dances to Prelates. Marquise in a Campaign Against the Fox-Trot', *Daily Express*, 8 March 1920, 1.

16 'Tango Without the Tang', *Daily Express*, 26 January 1920, 5.

17 The Sitter Out, *Dancing Times*, May 1920, 606.

18 The Sitter Out, *Dancing Times*, November 1920, 84.

19 Juliet McMains, *Glamour Addiction: Inside the American Ballroom Dance Industry* (Middletown, CT: Wesleyan University Press, 2006), 80.

20 'Vulgarity in the Ballroom!' *Dancing Times*, January 1921.

21 The Sitter Out, *Dancing Times*, June 1920, 687.

22 Richardson, *A History of English Ballroom Dancing*, 44.

23 F.A. Hadland, 'Negro Influence in Dancing', *Dancing Times*, April 1927, 73.

24 The goal of 'whitening' black dances for more widespread social consumption was not unique to Britain during this period. For more on similar efforts in the United States, see McMains, *Glamour Addiction*; Danielle Robinson, 'Race in Motion: Reconstructing the Practice, Profession, and Politics of Social Dancing, New York City, 1900–1930' (PhD diss., University of California, Riverside, 2004). For more on the relationship between popular dancing and British national identity, see Allison Abra, 'Doing the Lambeth Walk: Novelty Dances and the British Nation', *Twentieth Century British History* 20, no. 3 (2009): 346–69.

25 Ballroom News, *Dancing Times*, October 1923, 17–19.

26 Authorities such as Richardson argued that the *Daily Sketch*'s decision to include the waltz in the programme of their 1921 dance competition was a significant factor in bringing the dance back to public favour. The inclusion of a dance in a competition or exhibition could therefore prove strongly influential in determining trends.

27 By way of example, during a week-long engagement at the Glasgow Norwood Ballroom, famed dance team Santos Casani and Jose Lennard were purportedly paid a hundred pounds per day to perform exhibition dances. See Elizabeth Casciani, *Oh, How we Danced! The History of Ballroom Dancing in Scotland* (Edinburgh: Mercat Press, 1994), 49.

28 Richard S. Gray, Letter to the Editor, *Modern Dance*, October 1936, 14.

29 Marjorie and Georges Fontana, 'Ballroom and Exhibition Dancing', *Dancing Times*, December 1920, 176.

30 S.G.R., 'Rhythmic Dancing', *Oxford Magazine*, 28 February 1929, 453, as quoted in Nott, *Music For the People,* 162.

31 Julie Malnig, 'Women, Dance, and New York Nightlife', in Julie Malnig (ed.), *Ballroom Boogie, Shimmy Sham, Shake: A Social and Popular Dance Reader* (Urbana, IL.: University of Illinois Press, 2009), 82.

32 Richardson, *A History of English Ballroom Dancing*, 75–6.

33 Monsieur Pierre, 'Who Makes New Dances?' *Dancing Times*, December 1921, 299.

34 *Ibid.*

35 The Sitter Out, *Dancing Times*, May 1920, 606. See also Richardson, *A History of English Ballroom Dancing*, 32.

36 Draycot Dell, 'Dance Halls of To-Day', *Popular Music and Dancing Weekly*, 29 March 1924, 194.

37 Isobel Elsom, 'After the Fox Trot – the Fox Trot', *Popular Music and Dancing Weekly*, 18 July 1925, 246.

38 Santos Casani, 'The Dances of To-morrow', *Popular Music and Dancing Weekly*, 31 May 1924, 112.

39 The Sitter Out, 'In the Ballroom', *Dancing Times*, October 1922, 23.

40 'Are Ballroom Dancers too Conservative?' *Dancing Times*, September 1926, 530.

41 The Sitter Out, *Dancing Times*, January 1921, 306.

42 Robert Sielle, Letter to the Editor, *Dancing Times*, November 1920, 95.

43 Around the Dance Halls, *Popular Music and Dancing Weekly*, 13 September 1924, 157.

44 Around the Dance Halls, *Popular Music and Dancing Weekly*, 23 October 1926, iii.

45 June, 'Dancing in 1926', *Popular Music and Dancing Weekly*, 9 January 1926, 232.

46 *Ibid.*

47 Around the Dance Halls, *Popular Music and Dancing Weekly*, 8 November 1924, 53.

48 Around the Dance Halls, *Popular Music and Dancing Weekly*, 15 March 1924, 148.

49 Philip Richardson, 'A New Dance At Last', *Dancing Times*, August 1923, 1061.

50 Richardson, *A History of English Ballroom Dancing*, 57.

51 Josephine Bradley, 'My "Cavalcade" of Dancing', *Popular Music and Dancing Weekly*, 27 October 1934, 3.

52 Victor Silvester, *Dancing is My Life* (London: William Heinemann, 1958), 88–9.

53 Phyllis Haylor and Alec H. Miller, 'Taming the Charleston', *Dancing Times*, October 1926, 9.

54 June, 'Dancing in 1926', *Popular Music and Dancing Weekly*, 9 January 1926, 232.

55 The Sitter Out, 'Some Thoughts on the Present Situation', *Dancing Times*, June 1926, 255.

56 John Collier and Iain Lang, *Just the Other Day: An Informal History of Great Britain Since the War* (Hamilton, 1932), 171–3, as cited in Frances Rust, *Dance in Society* (Routledge and Keegan Paul, 1969), 90.

57 'The Charleston Dance – A Protest', *Daily Mail*, 26 April 1926, 7.

58 'A Vulgar Dance', *Daily Mail*, 27 April 1926, 7.

59 Silvester, *Dancing is My Life*, 88.

60 See *Daily Mail*, November/December 1926.

61 The Sitter Out, 'Ballroom Notes', *Dancing Times*, October 1926, 35.

62 The Sitter Out, 'Some Thoughts on the Present Situation', *Dancing Times*, June 1926, 255.

63 Josephine Bradley, 'My 'Cavalcade' of Dancing', *Popular Music and Dancing Weekly*, 27 October 1934, 3.

3

Going to the cinema: mass commercial leisure and working-class cultures in 1930s Britain

BRAD BEAVEN

Mass commercial leisure came of age between the wars. A visit to at least one mass commercial leisure venue, be it a football match, music hall or cinema, had become an important weekend ritual for many working people by 1939.[1] Since professional sport and the music hall had their foundations in Victorian society, contemporary observers tended to divert their critical gaze towards the new technological developments that could disperse 'popular' leisure to an unprecedented number of people. The explosion of commercial literature and cinema and the inception of public broadcasting were all significant new cultural developments that permeated the daily lives of working-class people during the interwar period. Technical innovation, and with it the growth of more sophisticated propaganda techniques, marked the interwar period as the era of mass communication. For the British establishment, this brought unprecedented access to working people through print, film and wireless.[2] The historiography of mass leisure during the interwar period has focused on whether new forms of leisure, such as cinema, transformed authentic and robust working-class leisure traditions into safer and more compliant forms of culture. Historians have largely turned their attention to the cinema and adopted one of two lines of enquiry. The first centred on whether the cinema helped nurture a 'national culture' in which working people came to identify themselves with 'British values' that reinforced the status quo.[3] The second

The author thanks Drs John Griffiths and Brett Bebber for reading and commenting on earlier drafts of this study.

strand of historiography investigated the depiction of empire in popular films and assessed whether cinema was a potent force in disseminating the imperial message.[4] This chapter will focus on the impact of cinema on society, assessing the establishment's concerns with this new medium and the constraints and influences on working people and, importantly, the audiences' behaviour in the 'picture houses'.

The most significant mass commercial institution during the inter-war period was undoubtedly the cinema. Although it had its origins in the period before the First World War, Philip Corrigan has described 1914 as 'the moment of cinema'. The number of cinemas had grown rapidly in all major cities in Britain, and overall audience figures were estimated to be some 350 million per year in a population of 40 million.[5] In 1917, an independent inquiry undertaken by the National Council of Public Morals (NCPM) attempted to take stock of the rapid acceleration of the industry. It concluded that cinema-going had become for many working people a popular and dearly held leisure routine, and it estimated that approximately 100,000 people were employed in the trade.[6] At first glance, the rise from 4,000 cinemas in 1921 to about 4,300 in 1934 does not seem to match the phenomenal increases of earlier years. However, these figures hide a significant transformation. By the 1930s, the small hall cinemas had generally been phased out and replaced by large and ostentatious 'Picture Palaces' owned by 'The Big Three': The Odeon, Gaumont-British and Associated British Cinemas. Unlike earlier forms of cinema, the 'Picture Palace' was a truly mass form of entertainment: not only were the interiors of cinemas considerably enlarged to seat over 4,000 people in some cases, but the domineering influence of 'The Big Three' also ensured that audiences were watching the same films with the same stars throughout the country.[7] By the mid-1930s, then, 'the pictures' was the most popular form of leisure activity, with annual admissions to the cinema totalling 963 million and box-office receipts of approximately £41 million.[8]

With this great numerical impact, it is tempting to suggest that the act of cinema-going, and the influence of the films themselves, fundamentally re-shaped working-class leisure patterns. For some historians, the cinema was another agency spawned in the late nineteenth and early twentieth centuries that further fragmented a robust working-class culture down the fault lines of geographical region, generation and gender. Davies has argued that access to commercial leisure was 'structured by class, income, gender and age', which could dictate whether men or women were able to participate in these new forms of mass leisure.[9] The cinema's influence on working-class culture has been taken a stage further by a number of leading historians who have argued that popular British films intentionally and successfully promoted social consensus. Richards and Aldgate have shown that 'stars' such as Gracie Fields and George Formby became national symbols who advocated support for existing institutions, rather than working-class heroes who might have exposed the social tensions of the 1930s.[10] Furthermore, Richards has concluded that 'the public seem on the whole to have been happy with the films they were given during the 1930s, and those films for the most part played their role in maintaining consensus and the *status quo*.'[11] For Stevenson and Cook the cinema helped forge a 'British culture' that differing social classes could identify with and thus prevented the social tensions and revolutionary fervour of continental Europe during the interwar period.[12] This theme has been taken up more recently by Sedgwick, who has argued that, combined with a passive working-class culture, the cinema helped forge social stability during the 1930s:

> A reading of the provincial daily newspapers of the period, with their combination of national, international and local news and local advertisements, leaves little doubt that at a local level Britain was a socially and politically cohesive and coherent nation. Even in the face of mass unemployment and poverty, local institutions such as the town council, the courts and police acted with legitimate authority and maintained order. It is quite clear that a complaisant working-class culture pervaded in Britain … Within this environment, cinema performed the important role of diffusing widely an aesthetic experience which served the dual function of increasing the general level of well-being while reinforcing the status quo.[13]

While some historians have argued that the cinema relieved socio-political tensions, other historians have shown how films provided a window on to the empire. For the working class, the cinema was their only relationship with imperialism since, according to some historians, the empire did not impinge on everyday working-class lives.[14] For Ward, the cinema was a 'prime vehicle for the diffusion of an imperial outlook', while Richards has cautiously argued that the success of imperial films at the box office is powerful evidence of the diffusion and ultimate acceptance of the imperial message.[15] More recently, Thompson has argued that while the quality of imperial films was uneven, 'it would be difficult to deny the British public's enthusiasm for this genre of film.'[16] Prior to investigating these claims, this study will begin by examining contemporary concerns that the cinema was a corrupting and uncivilising influence. We shall then turn to investigate the impact of the cinema on its audience by exploring the various constraints and choices made by cinema-goers. This study will argue that sweeping statements on working-class engagement with the cinema are insensitive to the influences of income, generation, gender and class. Finally, it will examine the effectiveness of cinema propaganda by shedding light on the often overlooked subject of audience behaviour.

Popular cinema and contemporary anxieties

As the most popular leisure activity, cinema-going unsurprisingly became the centre of a number of moral panics linked to its supposed negative impact on citizenship and morality in the British working class. These anxieties were embodied in a group calling itself the Birmingham Cinema Enquiry, establishing the organisation after a conference in Birmingham in 1930. The group, which later became known as the National Cinema Enquiry, was led by the Vice-Chancellor of Birmingham University and comprised magistrates, doctors, teachers and clergymen, most of whom had tended to hold a rather hostile position towards the cinema even before investigations began. It was clear from the start that the group perceived a perilous tension between the cinema and the future of British citizenship. Grant Robertson, the Enquiry's leader, outlined their underlying concerns: 'The basis of our British civilization, and I do not put it too strongly, is built upon some very fundamental ideas, and certain fundamental standards, and standards upon which we have built at any rate our British life. If these go, what remains?'[17] This pressure group was joined by like-minded organisations such as the Mothers' Union, the National Council of Women and the Public Morality Council in calling for the government to impose a more rigorous form of censorship. While these organisations received enthusiastic support from the national press and were successful in making representations to Prime Minister Ramsey MacDonald, their demands ultimately failed.[18] Although the Enquiry campaigned for tighter censorship, the government was reluctant to become involved, declaring that the current arrangements with the British Board of Film Censors were working well. Following the repeated failure of the National Cinema Enquiry to provoke government intervention, its influence petered out after 1935.[19]

While the National Cinema Enquiry's research was established with the sole purpose of investigating the cinema, film-going invariably became a significant issue in more general contemporary surveys of working-class leisure patterns. For some contemporary researchers glamorous film and the luxurious conditions of the new picture palaces engendered an apathy within the working class and a dislocation from their immediate socio-economic environment. In one report, *The Coming of Leisure* published in 1936, it was noted:

> Standards of value and emotional reactions of large numbers of people are being moulded unconsciously by the standards implicitly embodied in the fictitious characters for whom the emotional sympathies of the audience are won, while their critical faculties are dulled by the glamour and the general conditions in which films are shown.[20]

In the same year another survey, entitled *The Challenge of Leisure*, reported:

> It is obvious that most films present common problems in a peculiar and non typical form and solve them, too often, in an arbitrary and illogical manner, with the result that many millions of cinema-goers may easily be educated to accept submissively the vicarious satisfaction of instincts and desires which could and should be actually satisfied. The unreal world presented for our entertainment in the great majority of films may make us less capable of living a satisfying and useful life in the real world which awaits us outside.[21]

Finally, the perceived passivity of the cinema audience was the main criticism of film-going in Rowntree's report on life and leisure in 1930s York:

> Undoubtedly the cinema shares with other forms of entertainment the danger that it may become to some merely a way of escape from monotony rather than a means of recreation. True recreation is constructive, and wholesome recreation implies *re-creating* physical, intellectual, or moral vitality. As one among several ways of spending leisure, visits to the cinema may be re-creative. But some cinema 'fans' rely on the cinema too exclusively as a way of passing their leisure hours. It becomes for them a means of *escapism* rather than of *re-creation*, and this arrests their development.[22]

The implications were clear: during the frenzied domestic political and economic turmoil of the 1930s, a considerable number of working-class males were lulled into apathy, too consumed with the world of film fantasy to embrace their democratic duties as British citizens. The film was perceived as a new and potent influence on working people which, according to F. R. Leavis, could damagingly encroach higher and more civilised cultural planes. Thus cinema-going entailed the audience surrendering 'under conditions of hypnotic receptivity, to the cheapest emotional appeals, appeals the more insidious because they are associated with a compellingly vivid illusion of actual life'. Leavis went on to say that mass film-going was helping to shape a standardised popular leisure which could eventually infect and jeopardise elite civilisation.[23]

A solution to this problem, in some quarters, was for more active state intervention to ensure that good citizenship and the film industry worked in harmony. Writing immediately after the Second World War and in the shadow of the 1930s, the sociologist J. P. Mayer made a plea for the state to formulate a cultural policy, asserting that it was 'possible to make the film medium into an active and dynamic instrument of an all-round citizenship'. Although, he rejected the elitist cultural policies adopted by writers such as Leavis, Mayer did advocate active state intervention to realise an improved mass culture that was both uplifting and civically aware.[24]

However, the role and duties of the British citizen were further confused by the impact and popularity of Hollywood films, which were considered to be importing an alien American culture to British shores. *The Times*, never one to underestimate moral decline, reported in 1932 that 'the United States film industry has done more to Americanize the world than ever Julius Caesar and his legions to Romanize it.'[25] For some contemporaries, the new American 'talkies' were not only corrupting English speech but also introducing hot-headedness and sensationalism which were, according to one youth worker in the 1930s, 'foreign to our national temperament'.[26] Indeed, it was young male youths who were considered the most at risk since it was thought that a significant minority were replicating American habits and, at worst, gangster behaviour on British streets. One newspaper commentator articulated the received wisdom of the early 1930s when he declared: 'it is impossible to deny the enormous and pernicious effect that the innumerable crook films from Hollywood have had on the adolescent with lawless tendencies.' He concluded that the imported American films were increasingly perverting young male minds with 'the muck which exalts lawlessness into a virtue and the murderer and racketeer into heroes'.[27] However, despite these fairly widespread anxieties, researchers consistently failed to find links between juvenile crime and the cinema. Cyril Burt, perhaps not the most liberal researcher of his era, found that the imitation of gangster films by adolescent males was 'exceptional and rare' and concluded that in general 'the picture house provide[d] an alternative, not a provocative, to mischievous amusement'.[28] In this view he was supported by a number of Police authorities, who during the 1920s and 1930s, dismissed the gangster film's perceived link with crime, pointing to the reduced intemperance in British cities during this period.[29]

Trends in cinema-going: class, gender and generation

Fortunately for the historian, the anxiety that the cinema provoked among social commentators generated a number of surveys across the country on the impact of film-going on the British public. The Carnegie Trust's study of young unemployed in Glasgow, Liverpool and Cardiff, Rowntree's investigation in York, and the *New Survey of London Life and Labour* all singled out cinema as an important influence and attempted to categorise patterns of attendance. The evidence gleaned from contemporary surveys on popular cinema-going habits illustrates that attendance patterns were not overly shaped by issues of poverty. A lack of income, though cited by historians as a barrier to cinema attendance, does not appear to be an overriding factor. The cinema was extremely cheap: half of the seats during the 1930s cost less than sixpence, a price which gave access to social groups historically unable to attend commercial entertainment on a regular basis.[30] Such was the importance of cinema to working people that even those who occasionally lacked sufficient funds to visit the cinema were supported by their peer group. H. A. Secretan, a youth worker in London, reported that teenage male youths would perceive a visit to the cinema as an important group activity that was worthy enough to subsidise among themselves. He observed that sometimes one youth would find, due to unemployment or bad luck, that he would be out of coppers:

> probably he will feign a headache and say he means to sit at home. No word will be said but when they get to the booking office, one will slip in front and buy two tickets, with the casual 'I've got yours, chum'. The others will pay up their proportion of the cost later for the gang shares and shares alike. Such is true comradeship below the bridges.[31]

The Carnegie Trust's research into the unemployed confirmed these observations when it discovered that about 80 per cent of the unemployed men attended the cinema at least once a week and 25 per cent of these attended more often. Respondents to the survey regarded films as important topics of discussion within their peer group as the report found that 'it appears just as necessary for many of these young people to be able to discuss the latest film as it is for other people to be able to talk about the best seller in literature.'[32] Such was the cultural significance of the cinema; those on low incomes made every effort to attend at least once a week.

Where perhaps differences between those on low incomes and the so-called affluent workers did lie were in the type and location of the cinemas visited. The survey reported that the more affluent workers attended the cinema during the evening at the more lavish venues in the heart of the city, while the unemployed cut their cloth accordingly and visited the suburban cinemas for the cheaper matinee showing.[33] Even working-class communities in regions which had suffered from the worst consequences of the 1930s depression continued to patronise the cinema. For example, William Woodruff, recalling his financially austere childhood in Blackburn, remembered that he was able to gain admittance into the local cinema 'by handing over two empty, clean, two-pound jam jars' to the cashier.[34] Indeed, for children especially, jam jars appear to have been an accepted currency for cinemas across many parts of the country.[35] In addition, one historian of South Wales has noted that even in the poverty-stricken mining towns the cinema was 'cheap and accessible' and 'was generally within reach of the poorest sections of the community'.[36] Moreover, there is not a clear correlation between workers' affluence and increased cinema-going, since those in the north of England were twice as likely to visit the cinema as those in the south. These striking regional variations continued into the post-war era. In 1950–51, it was estimated that the average person in Preston went to the cinema fifty-three times a year compared with the twenty-seven visits of the residents in the comparatively prosperous Coventry.[37]

There is evidence, however, that generation and gender did structure cinema-going. Although younger males and females were fairly entrenched in the cinema-going habit, older married women were more likely to attend than their husbands. A survey in 1946 reported that 68 per cent of the 16-19 year-olds, compared with only 11 per cent of those over sixty, went to the cinema at least once a week.[38] Older married women appear to have adopted the cinema as a break from the daily chores of housework and shopping, visiting the matinee showing before the children came home from school. *The New Survey of London* reported that about 70 per cent of the weekly cinema consisted of women and girls and it was 'not an uncommon sight to see women slipping into the cinema for an hour, after they have finished their shopping'.[39] In addition, women and girls were also more likely than men to attend the cinema by themselves. Older males, on the other hand, 'tend to go only when they have nothing better to do, or when they have a girl friend to take out'. Indeed, Richards concluded that a large proportion of the population that attended the cinema were the young urban working class, who were more likely to be women than men.[40] It is clear, then, that the explosion of the cinema in mass commercial leisure had a greater impact on youth and older women than adult males. Cheap prices and the flexibility of matinee showings allowed women to adopt the cinema at an early stage of its development and ensure that it was one of the few 'respectable' leisure institutions available to them. For adult males, on the other hand, the cinema was one of many commercial institutions competing for their custom. The gendering of the cinema experience should not, however, be overestimated. Robert Roberts remembered that it was one of the first leisure institutions in which men and women would attend together:

'Many women who had lived a kind of purdah since marriage (few respectable wives visited public houses) were to be noted now, escorted by their husbands to the "pictures", a strange sight indeed and one that led to much comment at the shop.'[41] Moreover, for unattached young men and women, it was the ideal place to meet members of the opposite sex.

Although we can identify agencies such as region, generation and gender which helped shape audience patterns, the experience of cinema-going was not shorn of class-distinctive traits. While the cinema attracted all classes, as Richards has pointed out, cinema-going was not a classless form of leisure. In cinemas where there was a socially mixed audience, differing admission prices would ensure that social distinction was often preserved within the auditorium. The stratified seating arrangements in the cinema ensured that seats in one auditorium could cost from as little as threepence to as much as two shillings and sixpence.[42] Indeed, some middle-class patrons urged cinemas to extend the social ordering of film-goers to the streets outside, requesting the forma-tion of orderly and separate queues according to seat prices.[43] The increasing numbers of middle-class film-goers patronised the more purpose-built venues in the suburbs with their elegant decor and tea rooms, a far cry from the tradi-tional 'flea-pit' institutions found in working-class neighbourhoods. Cinemas, then, were often class-specific institutions with working-class audiences exhib-iting rather different behavioural traits from their middle-class counterparts. Whereas, middle-class patrons would 'make the cinema a genteel recreation and choose their films with care, boycotting anything with a dubious title', working-class audiences were altogether more gregarious and less discerning.[44] In addition, traditional concerns about respectability within working-class culture, did, however, come to the surface as W. E. Bakke and Robert Roberts recalled. Bakke noted that 'one interesting feature of the cinema audience is its sense of class distinction'. Two theatres in Greenwich were spoken of by skilled workers as 'not attended by a very good class of people'.[45] Similarly, Roberts reported that during the early years of the cinema:

> would-be patrons of two-penny seats literally fought each night for entrance and tales of crushed ribs and at least two broken limbs shocked the neighbourhood. In the beginning cinema managers, following the social custom of the theatre, made the error of grading seats, with the cheapest at the back of the house. For a short time the rabble lolled in comfort along the rear rows while their betters, paying three times as much, suffered cricked necks and eye strain at the front. Caste and culture forbade mixing. A sudden change-over one evening, without warning, at all the local cinemas caused much bitterness and class recrimination.[46]

The fledgling nature of the cinema during the interwar period, then, allowed both working- and middle-class patrons to shape their own traditions and habits in cinema-going that were largely drawn from long-standing leisure pursuits such as the music hall and theatre respectively.[47]

Popular film in the 1930s and the propagation of empire

Despite the differing cinema-going habits that were influenced by age, gender and class, historians have argued that those who attended the picture house were exposed to propaganda that diminished social divisions. Historians who adopt this perspective see popular British films as performing a pivotal role in transferring the underlying message of social cohesion to the masses. Aldgate's work on the propaganda potential of 1930s films such as *Sing as We Go*, where Gracie Fields triumphantly leads a cheerful and very compliant unemployed workforce back to a re-opened mill, demonstrates that film-makers were consciously attempting to engender an acceptance of existing institutions in a society which was far from stable.[48] Likewise, historians have argued that the depiction of empire helped fuel support for the imperial cause and thereby further distanced working people from political radicalism or subversive groups in society. Imperial films provided swashbuckling excitement that even drew in those hostile to imperialism. For example, Richards cites Bertolt Brecht's reflections on having seen the epic *Gunga Din* (1939) to illustrate the powerful affect of film. Brecht wrote:

> In the film *Gunga Din* … I saw British occupation forces fighting a native population. An Indian tribe … attacked by a body of British troops stationed in India. The Indians were primitive creatures, either comic or wicked: comic when loyal to the British and wicked when hostile. The British soldiers were honest, good humoured chaps and when they used their fists on the mob and 'knocked some sense' into them the audience laughed … I was amused and touched because this utterly distorted account was an artistic success and considerable resources in talent and ingenuity had been applied in making it.[49]

Clearly, Brecht's firm opposition to imperialism would not have been moved by enjoying one film. However, Richards speculates that the picture may have had an 'immense' impact on those cinema-goers who had no previous knowledge or opinion of empire. However, the theory that cinema helped engender a social cohesion or imperial fervour in British society through the messages embedded in popular films tends to underestimate the audience's power of choice. Cinemas and film-makers were, after all, commercial institutions that relied on popular support. Social surveys noted that working-class audiences were drawn towards certain genres of film that were essentially escapist in narrative. Indeed, the desire for an escapist adventure might well be a reason why imperial epics were so popular during the 1930s. Films with an imperial theme regularly featured in the top fifty British films throughout the 1930s, with almost all of them celebrating the imperial cause.[50] As Richards has suggested, you did not need to know a great deal about the workings of imperialism to enjoy a film on empire, since for most people 'the Empire was the mythic landscape of romance and adventure. It was that quarter of the globe that was coloured red and included "Darkest Africa" and the "mysterious East". In short it was "ours".'[51] Furthermore, cinema-goers were not only treated to adventures in the far flung reaches of the British Empire, they were also often transported back to the pomp and glory of the Victorian and Edwardian eras – a far cry from the depression-ravaged Britain of the 1930s. As MacKenzie has rightly argued, although cinema was a new technology, it was disseminating material that had first been popular in the late nineteenth century. For example, although Kipling's reputation underwent a damaging re-evaluation after the First World War, the appetite for Kipling stories in the cinema went unabated in the interwar period and beyond. The film *Elephant Boy* (1937) was followed by *Gunga Din* (1939), *The Jungle Book* (1942) and *Kim* (1951). Other Victorian or Edwardian novels transferred to cinema included Rider Haggard's *King Solomon's Mines* (book 1885; film 1937), A. E. W. Mason's *Four Feathers* (book 1902; film 1939) and Edgar Wallace's *Sanders of the River* (book 1911; film 1935). Many imperial films such as the account of *Rhodes of Africa* (1936), *Lives of a Bengal Lancer* (1936) and *We're Going to Be Rich* (1938) that celebrated a past imperial age were written in the 1930s.[52] Given the success of these films, it would be difficult to argue with MacKenzie's assessment that:

> The public remained set in the late nineteenth-century view of the world, and popular preoccupations – military and naval adventure, oriental fascinations, racial condescension, deference to royal and patriotic symbols – survive from decade to decade, stimulated rather than stifled by warfare. The 1930s represented an extraordinary renaissance of the imperial adventure tradition, made all the more potent by Hollywood's eager participation.[53]

Along with empire, other popular genres were crime, comedies and westerns, leading one cinema manager to complain that:

> The crowd you get here doesn't like anything that makes it think … prefers mostly blood and thunder and sophisticated comedy. Spencer Tracy and Gable

get over well. The Marx Brothers fell flat; they just don't see the point. What I think is the best policy is just to get people into a seat and simply pour entertainment into them.[54]

When asked in social surveys why they preferred certain types of films, 'escapism' was the most featured response by working-class audiences irrespective of age or gender. For example, one survey on working-class youth noted that a film's ability to provide a form of 'escapism' for the audience was the most important variable in the popularity of a film.[55] In another survey, unemployed men explained that the 'pictures help you live in another world for a little while'.[56] Mayer believed that his research had not only uncovered discernable differences in film tastes according to gender and class but also revealed that the adolescent working-class boy was more likely to be attracted to lowbrow pictures. Certainly, boys favoured the action films, as one thirteen-year-old boy wrote that 'the picture I like best is the *Eve of St. Mark*. Why I like it is because it has fighting in it. I like fighting pictures. The picture I dislike is *Rose-Mary*. I dislike it because it is so much singing and Romance.' This and other responses from boys in his study provoked Mayer to conclude by asking 'how can their minds resist the emotional temptations that films offer? How can they become appreciative of life, its obligations, its beauties, its disappointments? They are "movie-made", even before they begin to live.'[57] Even in the heavily trade-unionised communities of South Wales, workers' film groups struggled to compete with adventure and escapist films. It soon became apparent that the hardened politicised trade unionist much preferred the Hollywood films since, as one historian has noted, 'the typical working-class cinema-goer in the depressed south Wales valleys of the 1930s was already fully cognisant with the lives and struggles of the workers without having to see them drearily restaged on the screen.'[58] Indeed, a group of unemployed miners in Blaenavon who filmed, acted and produced their own silent film in 1928, provides a rare insight into male working-class film tastes. The film included a 'highway robbery, high upon the windswept moors of Blaenavon, a duel in a garden, a dramatic escape of a lovely heroine from a picturesque Welsh castle, set amid the romantic mountains of Gwent; a family feud, a wicked Major and a highwayman'.[59] Clearly, this melodrama and escapist action were far removed from the day-to-day realities of Welsh coalmining.

The cinema, then, was *the* most important commercial entertainment in working-class communities, integrating effortlessly into working-people's leisure habits, surpassing the popularity of the music hall and becoming a key cultural institution. Although older males were less enthused than their younger counterparts and female devotees, there can be no doubt that the popularity of the cinema cut across gender and generation and was infused with working-class traits. Audience behaviour, at times, resembled the horse-play of working-class neighbourhoods while, like the music hall, the cinema became a meeting place for men and women alike. The choice of films also shows a continuity in working-class entertainment tastes with the escapist and often crude comic plots of popular films representing a smooth transition from the similar music hall genre. The escapist nature of the cinema also ensured that film-makers' messages of social cohesion were left behind in the cinema auditorium. Contemporaries and subsequent historians have underestimated the ability of working people to consume mass commercial leisure on their own terms and within their own forged environments. The cinema, then, must be seen in a broader cultural context, since it was more than simply a house to view pictures but had become an important cultural institution within the working-class neighbourhood. Indeed, the cinema, rather like its predecessor the music hall, was a crucible in which certain traditional working-class behavioural traits were allowed to flourish. We must now examine audience behaviour in detail, since it directly relates to claims that the cinema's influence helped engender a passivity and acceptance of social structures among working class men and women.

Cinema-going in a cultural context: audience behaviour

The important research on reading the texts and propaganda that underpinned popular films should not, however, cloud important issues such as the motivation for film-going and audience behaviour while in the cinema. Kuhn has recently argued that because film studies have privileged the film text, they downplayed 'not only the reception of films by the social audiences but also the social-historical milieus and industrial and institutional settings in which films and consumed'.[60] There is a great leap from identifying a film's underlying socially inclusive message to asserting that cinema helped nurture a socially cohesive culture during the 1930s. For this to occur we must accept that the audience's role was largely a passive one in which the film's underlying message seeped into the targeted group's consciousness. Harper's research on audiences' responses to 'lowbrow' films in the 1930s suggests that audiences were far from passive consumers of leisure, with working-class men in particular keen to express their film tastes to contemporary researchers.[61]

During the 1930s, audience members were keen to express their views about films in the cinema auditorium, which casts doubt on the assumption that cinema-going was a straightforward process where 'people in their billions went to the cinema primarily to watch films, normally under conditions of quiet and comfort'.[62] Contemporary cinema managers would not have recognised this rather cosy image of the cinema of the 1920s and 1930s. Audience participation, often with rowdy cat-calls, wolf-whistles and guffaws, was commonplace and demonstrated the wildly active mood of the viewers. William Woodruff remembered that cinema-going in the interwar period was:

> a wild affair where a man kept order with a long bamboo pole. If we were caught blowing rice or rock-hard peas at the pianist, or spitting orange pips from the balcony, or whistling too long at the kissing scenes, we ran the risk of getting whacked over the head – a real hard whack.[63]

Indeed, Mayall has shown in his work on Birmingham that cinema management was not for the faint-hearted, as they often struggled to maintain order and discipline among the audience.[64] In addition, it is clear that for working-class people a trip to the cinema was not motivated solely by the desire to see a picture, an experience which cut across generation and gender boundaries. For working-class male adolescents, it was the camaraderie of the group and the gregarious behaviour that went on inside the picture house that was the cinema's chief attraction. A disgruntled adult cinema-goer in Birmingham shed light on young male activity in the cinema when he complained about the 'gangs of young "roughs" whose sole entertainment appears to be to see who can make the "cleverest" remarks and shout them out during a programme … Fortunately, these disturbances are rarely met in better cinemas, but they are a continued source of annoyance in cheaper houses.'[65] Likewise, one early police report on the activities of a cinema in London noted that the young men and women gathered in the cinema's coffee shop with no intention of watching a film. The report notes: 'Many young girls and youths between the age of 16 and 18 have assembled there indulging in horseplay causing annoyance to pedestrians and nine males have been charged with insulting behaviour.'[66] A further report confirms that the cinema's coffee shop 'appears to be a place of meeting for young courting couples, many of whom partake of refreshments and leave without visiting the pictures'.[67] Clearly, for these youths film-watching was not the chief motivation for attending the cinema complex. However, it is an undercover policeman's report on the behaviour of a cinema audience which raises doubts over whether the underlying messages of films were successfully transmitted to a receptive audience:

In the ground floor there were seats filled with couples of opposite sexes, all closely embraced and not in the slightest way interested in the pictures which were being shown on the screen. Many of the couples lay in a reclining position in lounge seats which occupied one corner of the building ... I frequently saw the manager walking about various parts of the house and apparently taking no action whatever regarding the conduct of couples lying in indecent attitudes. The film which was being shown on the screen at the time I was in the 'cinema' was very interesting but many couples were taking no interest whatever in the picture, but were embraced in each other's arms apparently oblivious to what was appearing on the screen.[68]

Despite the policeman's insistence that the film was a very interesting one, the couples in this cinema seemed to have had more pressing romantic matters on their minds.[69] In fact, working-class youths were transferring the audience participation of the music hall and horseplay of the street into the arena of the cinema. The film, in this context, was of secondary importance. Likewise, when a teenage girl in one contemporary social survey could not recall the plot of a film she had seen twice, the researcher suspected that the respondent visited the local cinema with the prime intention of meeting local boys.[70] The regular habit of cinema-going ensured that films did not have a lasting impact on their audience, a situation confirmed by Kuhn, who in a recent study has argued that 'for the typical young cinema-goer of the thirties, then, going to the pictures was a part of everyday life: easy sociable, pleasurable – and still fondly remembered'.[71] Indeed, once in the cinema Fowler discovered that 'cinemas were by no means simply institutions where a passive working-class audience would sit in silence and receive unquestioningly all the images and messages peddled in the films'.[72]

If film propaganda had difficulty in distracting impressionable youths from their more preferable activities, how did older working-class people react? Surviving evidence gleaned from the few contemporary studies of cinema audiences suggest that working-class youths and adults shared similar behavioural traits in the auditorium that distinguished them quite markedly from their middle-class counterparts. During one week in 1934, a reporter for *Film Weekly* observed three very different cinemas audiences in London. He noted that in the large West End cinema the audience was 'a lively, good-humoured and intelligent house' in which couples took interest in the film rather than solely in themselves, and that 'audible comment on the film was conspicuous by its absence'. Moving on to a cinema located in a middle-class suburb, the reporter observed that the afternoon matinee had attracted a small, largely female audience whose members disturbed his concentration of the film with 'the clatter of jugs and requests for more milk and fresh buns from the harassed attendant'. Finally, he moved on to a 'different class of cinema in a less prosperous district'. He reported:

> I encountered a packed house and a perfect roar of sound. Every single person present constituted him or herself a loudly vocal critic of the fare provided. I have never heard so loud a noise accompanied by such violent behaviour. Yet an attendant explained to me that this was a comparatively quiet night. Only the fact I had seen the film before (about a year ago) made me aware that it was indeed a talkie and not the revival of some old silent film. Had I gone in to see the film and not the audience, I should undoubtedly have walked straight out again, for it was a very bad one – and not for a moment did sickly tolerance cloud the audience's recognition of its badness. No lapse was allowed to pass unnoticed. Yet despite their unusual method of showing it, they were utterly absorbed in the film. They missed nothing – their appreciation was all-embracing. It was an abject lesson to other more expensive audiences. When I had entered the spirit of the thing I began to enjoy myself thoroughly – a perfect example of the effect of an audience on the appreciation of a film.

According to the reporter, the audience behaviour reminded him of 'the early years of film-going', adding, however: 'naturally, I do not commend this example of audience behaviour for wider circulation.'[73] Clearly, this form of cinema-going was a new and compelling experience for our intrepid reporter who, after initial doubts, thoroughly enjoyed the occasion. Indeed, working-class cinema-going consisted of more than just simply watching the film: it was 'a night out'. The film was important, though watching a 'bad' film in a vocal and energised atmosphere was, it seems, as entertaining as watching a critically acclaimed picture.

For working-class adults, a visit to the pictures could mean that the film was one of a number of entertainments on offer. The newer, purpose-built picture palaces employed page boys, usherettes, doormen and chocolate girls and offered a luxurious environment, some cinemas containing cafes, restaurants and bars .[74] As we have seen, the new cinema complexes proved more of an attraction to older working-class women than their male counterparts, who still preferred traditional masculine pursuits. However, evidence suggests that the groups of females who visited the cinema perceived film-watching as only one of a number of activities associated with the cinema. Once again, the cinema's coffee shop was the focal point of the afternoon, with many women preferring this leisure activity to the film itself.[75] Likewise, older men would often attend the cinema as part of a weekly routine. One survey noted that 'it was perhaps inevitable, but none the less unfortunate, that many [men] acquired a habit of attending the cinemas regardless of the standard of films'.[76] This particularly infuriated film aficionados who complained that people would '"pop in" at any old time without regard to what films [we]re showing' and on leaving the auditorium were often unable to recall the film's title or plot or any of its actors.[77] In addition, Orwell observed that cinemas, particularly in areas hit by the 1930s' depression, were densely populated by unemployed men whose first concern was to find a warm and dry place away from inclement weather. He reported: 'in Wigan a favourite refuge was the pictures, which are fantastically cheap there. You can always get a seat for fourpence, and at the matinee at some houses you can even get a seat for twopence. Even people on the verge of starvation will readily pay twopence to get out of the ghastly cold of a winter afternoon.'[78] These sentiments were shared by a correspondent to *Film Weekly* who commented that dole and cinema queues were both growing rapidly in 1934:

> The reason is simple. The cinema is an entertainment which is within reach of all. Even the man with only a few coppers in his pocket can have two or more hours enjoyment and forget his worries for a time. It is impossible to get the same value for money elsewhere. In my opinion it is wrong of people to condemn the out of work man for spending time and money at cinemas. The entertainment is a tonic.[79]

Working-class people's use of the cinema, then, was perhaps more complex than some historians have described, a situation that confirms William Farr's observations of cinema audiences during the 1930s. In 1936 Farr was a member of the British Film Institute when he wrote that 'the millions of people who visit cinema each week – and very many go more than once a week – go to be entertained. With some the motive may not even be as explicit as that; they go to the cinema as a way of spending the evening.'[80] Thus, film choice and the influence of propaganda on working-class audiences ought not be over-stated. Audience behaviour and motives for cinema-going suggest a far from passive response from working people regardless of gender and generational divides.

Conclusion

The old nineteenth-century term 'pleasure seekers' was a never more apt description of working-class mass leisure habits of mass commercial leisure between the wars. Contemporary anxieties of degeneracy in a higher culture and citizenry pervaded the two decades, while more recent historians have claimed that the new forms of mass communication, such as the cinema, were powerful forces of social cohesion. This study has argued that there can be little doubt that a significant section of film entertainment was, conscious or not, actively supportive of the status quo and social stability. However, the assumption that this propaganda was successfully transmitted to a wide-eyed public is fraught with difficulties. Generalisations about working-class cinema-going overlook the constraints of poverty and the peer influence of age, gender and class. Furthermore, cinema managers were highly conscious of popular demand since their highly competitive business would only survive with well-attended feature films. As Robert James has argued, the film industry often tailored its product to meet a demand.[81] This popular demand could be detected through full houses or through audience behaviour within the auditorium. Audience behaviour, a much neglected area of study, reveals that working-class people during this period were manipulating their environment for their own ends and finding a commercial sector willing to respond. Within the context of the cinema, working-class audiences were able to impose their own layer of meaning and enjoyment, a trait in their culture which stretched back into the nineteenth century.[82]

Notes

1 S. G. Jones, *Workers at Play: A Social and Economic History of Leisure 1918–1939* (London: Routledge and Kegan Paul, 1986), 38.

2 The British establishment is taken to mean the Government, as well as establishment press such as the *Times* and public broadcasting through the newly established BBC.

3 For example, see J. Stevenson and C. Cook, *Britain in the Depression: Society and Politics 1929–39* (London: Longman, 1994), Ch. 14; J. Sedgwick, *Popular Filmgoing in 1930s Britain: A Choice of Pleasures* (Exeter: University of Exeter, 2000), 47.

4 S. Ward (ed.), *British Culture and the End of Empire* (Manchester: Manchester University Press, 2001), 15; J. Richards, 'Boy's Own Empire: Feature Films and Imperialism in the 1930s', in J. M. MacKenzie (ed.), *Imperialism and Popular Culture* (Manchester: Manchester University Press, 1986), 162.

5 P. Corrigan, 'Film Entertainment as Ideology and Pleasure: A Preliminary Approach to a History of Audiences', in J. Curran and V. Porter (eds), *British Cinema History* (London: Weidenfeld and Nicolson, 1983), 27–8.

6 The National Archives, Public Records Office (hereafter PRO) HO45/10811/312397/1 'Cinema Commission Inquiry', 1917.

7 Corrigan, 'Film Entertainment as Ideology and Pleasure', 27–8.

8 Jones, *Workers at Play*, 37.

9 A Davies, 'Cinema and Broadcasting', in P. Johnson (ed.), *Twentieth Century Britain* (London: Longman, 1994), 265, 270; A. Davies, *Leisure, Gender and Poverty. Working-Class Culture in Salford and Manchester: 1900–1939* (Milton Keynes: Open

University Press,1992), ix.

10 J. Richards and A. Aldgate, *Best of British: Cinema and Society from 1930 to Present* (London: I.B. Tauris, 1999).

11 J. Richards, *The Age of the Dream Palace: Cinema and Society in Britain 1930–1939* (London: Routledge, 1984), 324.

12 Stevenson and Cook, *Britain in the Depression*, Ch. 14.

13 Sedgwick, *Popular Filmgoing in 1930s Britain*, 47.

14 B. Porter, *The Absent Minded Imperialists: Empire, Society, and Culture in Britain* (Oxford: Oxford University Press, 2004), Ch. 9.

15 Ward, *British Culture and the End of Empire*, 15; Richards, 'Boy's Own Empire', 162.

16 A. Thompson, *The Empire Strikes Back?: The Impact of Imperialism on Britain from the Mid-Nineteenth Century* (Harlow: Pearson, 2005), 94.

17 Richards, *The Age of the Dream Palace*, 58–60.

18 S. J. Jones, *The British Labour Movement and Film, 1918–1939* (London: Routledge, 1987), 110.

19 Richards, *The Age of the Dream Palace*, 58–60.

20 E. B. Castle, A. K. C. Ottaway and W. T. R. Rawson, *The Coming of Leisure: The Problem in England* (London: New Education Fellowship, 1935), 68.

21 W. Boyd (ed.), *The Challenge of Leisure* (London: New Education Fellowship, 1936), 132.

22 B. S. Rowntree, *Poverty and Progress: A Second Social Survey of York* (London: Longmans, 1941), 46–7.

23 F. R. Leavis, *Mass Civilisation and Minority Culture* (Cambridge: Minority Press, 1930),10 and 30.

24 J. P. Mayer, *British Cinemas and their Audiences* (London: Dennis Dobson, 1948), 249.

25 *The Times*, 5 March 1932.

26 H.A. Secretan, *London Below Bridges: Its Boys and its Future* (London: Geoffrey Bles, 1931), 86.

27 *Truth*, 6 September 1933.

28 C. Burt, *The Young Delinquent* (London: University of London Press, 1925), 147–150.

29 Richards, *The Age of the Dream Palace*, 62.

30 P. Miles and M. Smith, *Cinema, Literature and Society* (London: Croom Helm, 1987), 164.

31 Secretan, *London Below Bridges*, 84.

32 C.A Cameron *et al.*, *Disinherited Youth: A Report on the 18+ Age Group. Enquiry Prepared for the Trustees of the Carnegie United Kingdom Trust* (Edinburgh: T&A. Constable, 1943), 104.

33 Cameron *et al.*, *Disinherited Youth*, 104.

34 W. Woodruff, *The Road to Nab End: An Extraordinary Northern Childhood* (London: Abacus, 2002), 176.

35 A. Kuhn, *An Everyday Magic: Cinema and Cultural Memory* (London: I. B. Tauris, 2002), 48.

36 S. Ridgwell, 'Pictures and Proletarians: South Wales Miners' Cinemas in the 1930s', *Llafur* 7, no. 1 (1996): 70.

37 R. McKibbin, *Classes and Cultures: England 1918–1951* (Oxford: Oxford University Press, 1998), 422.

38 McKibbin, *Classes and Cultures*, 420; see also M. Chamberlain, *Growing Up in Lambeth* (London: Virago, 1989), 26.

39 H. L Llewellyn Smith, *The New Survey of London Life and Labour: Life and Leisure* vol. IX (London: P.S. King & Son, 1935), 46; Jones, *Workers at Play*, 60.

40 Richards, *Age of the Dream Palace*, 15.

41 R. Roberts, *The Classic Slum: Salford Life in the First Quarter of the Century* (Manchester: Manchester University Press,1971), 175.

42 Kuhn, *An Everyday Magic*, 2.

43 *Film Weekly*, 14 September 1934.

44 Richards, *Age of the Dream Palace*, 17; S. Harper, 'A Middle-Class Taste Community in the 1930s: The Case of the Regent Cinema, Portsmouth', *Historical Journal of Film, Radio and Television* (forthcoming).

45 Richards, *Age of the Dream Palace*, 16.

46 Roberts, *The Classic Slum*, 176.

47 For an analysis of the cultural continuity of working-class male leisure between the nineteenth and twentieth century, see B. Beaven, *Leisure, Citizenship and Working-Class Men in Britain, 1850–1945* (Manchester: Manchester University Press, 2005).

48 Aldgate, 'Comedy, Class and Containment: The British Domestic Cinema of the 1930s', 268–70.

49 Richards, 'Boy's Own Empire', 144.

50 Thompson, *The Empire Strikes Back*, 92.

51 Richards, 'Boy's Own Empire', 143.

52 References from the British Film Institute's online film database, http://www.bfi. org.uk

53 J. M. MacKenzie, *Propaganda and Empire* (Manchester: Manchester University Press, 1986), 91.

54 G. Cross (ed.), *Worktowners at Blackpool: Mass-Observation and Popular Leisure in the 1930s* (London: Routledge, 1990), 135.

55 C. Cameron, *Disinherited Youth*, 104.

56 E.W Bakke, *Unemployed Man: A Social Study* (London: Nesbit & Co, 1933), 182.

57 Mayer, *British Cinemas and their Audiences*, 130–1.

58 Ridgwell, 'Pictures and Proletarians', 78.

59 *Film Weekly*, 7 November 1928.

60 Kuhn, *An Everyday Magic*, 4.

61 Harper, *Picturing the Past*, 61.

62 Sedgwick, *Popular Filmgoing in 1930s Britain*, 6.

63 Woodruff, *The Road to Nab End*, 176.

64 D. Mayall, 'Palaces for Entertainment and Instruction: A Study of Early Cinema in Birmingham, 1908–18', *Midland History* 10, no. 2 (1985), 98.

65 *Film Weekly*, 16 February 1934.

66 PRO, MEPO2/7497/8, 'Report on the Rank Picture Show', (1916).

67 PRO, MEPO2/7497/7, 'Report on Rank Cinema', (1916).

68 PRO, MEPO2/7497/13, 'Report on Rank Cinema', (1916).

69 For more examples of this type of behaviour, see N. Hiley, '"Lets go to the pictures": The British Cinema Audience in the 1920s and 1930s', *Journal of Popular British Cinema*, no. 2 (1999); J. Hill, *Sport, Leisure and Culture in Twentieth Century Britain* (Basingstoke: Palgrave, 2002), 59–63.

70 A. Kuhn, 'Cinema-going in Britain in the 1930s: Report of a questionnaire survey', *Historical Journal of Film, Radio and Television* 19, no. 4 (1999), 540.

71 Kuhn, 'Cinema-going in Britain in the 1930s', 540.

72 For contemporary survey on teenage leisure and Fowler's conclusions on the impact of cinema, see D. Fowler, *The First Teenagers: The Lifestyle of Young Wage-Earners in Interwar Britain* (London: Woburn Press, 1995), 132.

73 *Film Weekly*, 9 November 1934.

74 McKibbin, *Classes and Cultures*, 423.

75 M. Abendstern, 'Expression and Control: A Study of Working-Class Leisure and Gender 1918–39. A Case Study of Rochdale using Oral History Methods' (PhD diss., University of Essex, 1986), 109.

76 C. Cameron, *Disinherited Youth*, 104.

77 *Film Weekly*, 4 January 1935.

78 G. Orwell, *The Road to Wigan Pier* (1937; repr. Harmondsworth: Penguin, 1974), 72.

79 *Film Weekly*, 6 March 1934.

80 W. Boyd *et al.*, *The Challenge of Leisure*, 131.

81 R.T. James, *Popular Culture and Working-Class Taste in Britain, 1930–39: A Round of Cheap Diversions?* (Manchester: Manchester University Press, 2010), 203.

82 For a more detailed overview of leisure between 1850–1945, see Beaven, *Leisure, Citizenship and Working-Class Men in Britain, 1850–1945*.

4

Selling the circus: Englishness, circus fans and democracy in Britain, 1920–45

SANDRA TRUDGEN DAWSON

Writing in 1935, circus fan and amateur historian William Bosworth made some extraordinary claims. He wrote, 'An Englishman, Philip Astley, invented the circus' and 'an Englishman, George Sanger', invented the travelling circus. Bosworth also attributed the revival of the circus in the 1930s to 'another Englishman', namely, Bertram Mills. Indeed, Bosworth exclaimed, 'Circus history is inextricably and inevitably woven into the tapestry of the history of Britain.'[1] For this fan, the modern circus was very much an English invention and an important aspect of the nation's history and character. Bosworth was not the only one to think of the circus in this way. Maurice Willson Disher, drama critic for the *Daily Mail* and ardent circus fan, authored several books in the 1920s and 1930s that romanticised and popularised the circus and the notion of its particularly 'English' origins.[2]

Disher and Bosworth were both founding members of an organisation of circus fans, the Circus Fans Association of Great Britain. Formed in 1934, with the explicit desire to promote the circus in their creative image, this organisation, together with circus proprietors and sympathetic Members of Parliament, appropriated nationalistic discourse to re-imagine and sell the circus as an important part of British heritage. By staging circus art exhibits, publishing circus novels, biographies and histories, and launching opposition to anti-circus legislation, this unlikely collaboration sold the idea of the circus as a national and democratic institution.[3] Enjoyed by all ages and socio-economic groups, the modern circus for fans amply illustrated the democratic traditions of the nation. At a time when democracy was under threat in Europe, these agencies presented the circus as a part of an expressly democratic British historical past, in order to meet the challenges of the present and navigate the ambiguities of an uncertain future.

Indeed, during the interwar years, the number of circuses in Britain grew and more people attended performances. The growth of the circus industry coincided with the general interwar expansion of popular leisure, as well as the introduction of paid holidays.[4] Yet while new sites of pleasure like the cinema and dance halls flourished, other, older types of leisure entertainment, like the music hall, declined.[5] The circus, hugely popular in Victorian Britain and yet nearly extinct before the First World War, might have disappeared but for the interwar efforts to support the circus as an irreplaceable piece of national history. Unlike the music-hall acts that seemed antiquated, circus performances were constantly updated and re-invented. Yet the timelessness of the circus remained embedded in the advertising, offering audiences a nostalgic connection with a more stable national past. This study examines the specific marketing of the circus in the interwar period and explores why the articulation of the circus as an 'English' invention and an essential part of national heritage resonated so strongly with consumers. Through an examination of circus books, programmes, ephemera, press articles and journals, I argue that between 1921 and 1945, fans, politicians and the industry successfully promoted the modern circus as a historically British creation, not only to increase its popular appeal but also to offer a vision of the nation as a democratic and unified entity.

The British circus has received considerable scholarly interest. Recent works have focused largely on the eighteenth and nineteenth centuries and the way the modern circus moved from the margins of society to gain respectability.[6] Other studies survey the history of the British circus from medieval times or stress the cultural significance of the circus as vehicle of metaphor and representation.[7] This article, however, focuses on a particular moment in the twentieth century when the circus was promoted as a symbol of national unity able to negotiate the domestic and international crises that shaped anxieties about the nation and the British Empire.

The First World War seriously weakened Britain's political and cultural Empire. It was in this milieu that Maurice Willson Disher first popularised the circus as part of an expressly 'English' cultural heritage and a visible example of democracy. As a drama critic for a popular and conservative newspaper with a circulation of two million, Disher had a degree of cultural prestige and authority.[8] In *Clowns and Pantomime* (1925), and *The Greatest Show on Earth* (1937), Disher maintained that Philip Astley, a recently de-mobbed cavalry horse-trainer, invented the modern circus in 1776 when he opened his amphi-theatre in London and demonstrated trick riding.[9] Considered by contem-poraries to be the definitive history of the circus, *The Greatest Show on Earth* claimed the modern circus was established first in Britain by Astley.[10] Historian Marius Kwint has recently argued that Astley was by no means the first or the only trick rider at the time, but the myth conveniently established the inven-tion of the circus as doubly British: founded by an Englishman and originating from within the nation's capital.[11] The date, 1776, was significant as the year when Britain lost the colonies in America to the ideals of democracy. When Disher wrote in the aftermath of the First World War, Britain once more stood to lose parts of the empire in the name of American principles of democracy and the self-determination of nations.[12] It was not, however, the recognition of America's new and elevated political position on the world stage, or even the eighteenth-century loss of the colonies that was of significance to Disher. Rather, it was the increased consumption of American entertainment in the twentieth century that Disher resented, as well as the implied notion that America somehow 'invented' both democracy and popular leisure.[13] At a time when American democracy was held up as the world standard, when imported American entertainment flooded Britain, and P. T. Barnum was credited with establishing his circus as 'the greatest show on earth', Disher made alternative claims about the modern circus and its British origins. By maintaining that an Englishman created the circus first in England in 1776, and by arguing that the circus represented a truly democratic form of entertainment, Disher not only appropriated the circus as part of British national heritage but he also denied the implication that America was the original source of both democracy and popular leisure.

Disher's books were certainly popular, yet the degree to which this con-struction of Britishness in the circus resonated with the general public is not easily quantifiable. However, the number of circuses in Britain did quadruple between 1921 and 1945,[14] suggesting that this strategy, along with other forms of marketing, found some degree of currency among circus fans in a period marked by economic insecurity and the mass importation of foreign entertain-ment.[15]

Disher gave literary merit to an idea that was later expanded on and reiter-ated by circus fans like Bosworth and circus proprietors. Bertram Mills, the owner of a new circus that opened in December of 1920, readily adopted the idea that the circus was an eighteenth-century British invention and emblem-atic of the national character. Mills, a de-mobbed army officer, bet a friend in

1919 that he could create an annual horse show in London that would surpass the pre-war shows. The result was more than simply a horse show.[16] It was a hugely popular and successful annual circus at Olympia that 'enraptured' over a quarter of a million children and adults alike, and coincided with the famous Sanger Circus centenary celebrations.[17] Within four years, *The Times* claimed that daily audiences of 10,000 at Mills' annual show 'proved that the attraction of the circus' in Britain, its birthplace, was 'eternal'.[18]

By 1925, Mills consciously used history to market his show at Olympia in London. The annual circus featured a number of prominent international performers. The programme, on the other hand, related the history of the modern circus and the circus founder, Philip Astley, in a way that rooted Mills' own new circus in its historical context and emphasised the connection of the circus to British military and imperial tradition.[19] Astley was not simply an Englishman, the programme explained; he was a former soldier, like Mills and approximately one and a half million men in post-war Britain.[20] Astley's own experience in the service of the nation, along with his horse-riding skills, combined images of military precision with feats of athletic prowess and connected them directly to the idea of 'Englishness'. By emphasising Astley's cavalry acumen, Mills effectively aligned circus tradition with the palpable military experience of a more recent past. As marketed by Mills, the circus not only had securely historical national origins, it was a physical manifestation of British character. In fact, the two notions were inextricably entwined in the programme when Mills described the circus as '"ultra" British, masculine, and virile', the very characteristics embodied in British soldiers and the imperial imagination of the nation.[21] The appeal of the circus then was tied to, and represented in, an essential national character performed as 'virile' masculinity. And, according to Mills, the love of the circus was somehow embedded in the national psyche. Consequently, Mills claimed, the appeal of the circus would never evaporate, because 'there w[ould] always be an England.'[22] Like the author of the earlier article in *The Times*, Mills believed the circus, like the nation, was 'eternal', as the recent victory in war revealed.[23] This romantic genealogical rhetoric tied the circus to the larger idea of an older and irrepressible national identity, one that had survived the ravages of the Great War intact, as demonstrated by enthusiastic audiences. The fact that many of the performers were not British was of no concern. It was the expression of admiration and support for a historically British institution that was the essence of the nation's identity.

The interwar revival of the circus owed much to the efforts of Bertram Mills. The elevation of the circus to the level of the nation in the marketing of Olympia helped reinstate the circus as a respectable and historical form of British entertainment and promoted Mills' new business venture to two important groups: consumers and the Showman's Guild of Great Britain.[24] Mills was an outsider to the industry. He was not born into a circus or a Showman family and he needed the support and recognition from the Guild for success and to attract Showmen to work for him.[25] Mills was extraordinarily successful in this respect. Not only was his circus hugely popular, he was the first non-Showman ever to be admitted to the Guild, and in an unprecedented decision, Mills was made Chairman of the Showman's Guild of Great Britain in 1938 before he died later that year.[26]

One of the ways Mills persuaded the Showmen to accept him and his circus was to stimulate interest in the circus industry through the promotion of the annual show at Olympia. The popularity of the circus in Britain had declined dramatically since the end of the nineteenth century. As a shrewd businessman, Mills used art and publicity to stimulate a serious interest in the circus after the First World War. He invited fashionable artists like Dame Laura Knight, Stephen Spurrier and Clifford Hall, and photographer Baron Nicholas de Rakoczy, to paint and photograph images of the performance and the behind-the-scenes details of his circus.[27] The results were then published or displayed in art exhibitions around the country, making the circus accessible to a wider audience and advertising the Mills circus and its venue at London's largest exhibition hall at Olympia.

Mills' marketing strategies for Olympia also helped stimulate consumer demand for other seasonal circuses in the capital. A number of travelling tenting circuses that usually disbanded in the winter opened for business in permanent structures. For example, Fred Ginnett's circus performed for a month at the Crystal Palace in December 1922 and again in the 1923 winter season.[28] In 1925, Ginnett combined with the Robertson circus to host a huge summer show at Wembley Stadium, which was attended by members of the Royal Family. This added to the argument that the circus was a democratic institution, accessible, affordable and enjoyed by all social classes.[29] By 1928, the popularity of the circus in London encouraged Bostock's circus to purchase a permanent building at Earl's Court for winter performances each year.[30]

The Bostock, Ginnett and Mills circuses featured acrobatic horse-back riding and dozens of finely groomed horses, popular with fans of all social classes. Mills had over eighty horses in his show. In fact, the Olympia circus boasted the largest equine display of superior-quality black 'liberty' horses in Britain. Liberty horses performed as a group in the circus ring without riders.

These displays attracted an upper- and middle-class audience who were often invited to watch the circus animals being trained in their winter quarters at Ascot.[31] Mills also capitalised on the penchant of the British peerage for good 'horseflesh', by offering Members of the House of Lords personalised pre-performance tours of his stables. Mills then used the names of the prominent fans in advertising, reinforcing the notion that the circus was a 'democratic space' attracting all groups, from manual workers to the highest echelons of Britain's post-war social scene.

All circuses advertised the presence of important people at their shows, but Mills courted socially influential people as a way to defuse the negative press received from members of the Royal Society for the Prevention of Cruelty to Animals (RSPCA). In December 1920, just days after the first performances at Mills' new Olympia circus, Captain Edward Fairholme, a leading member of the RSPCA, wrote a letter to the editor of *The Times* to 'educate public opinion' about the cruelties inflicted on circus animals through training and the 'unnatural' housing conditions. Fairholme claimed these conditions caused the animals 'severe nervous tension' that was magnified by forced public performances. This, according to Fairholme, constituted 'cruelty', a distinctly 'un-British' characteristic which was then displayed on English streets and in English towns.[32] By 1925, the RSPCA successfully lobbied Parliament to pass the Performing Animals (Regulation) Act (1925). The legislation required all trainers and exhibitors to register themselves and their animals and allow 'experts' to inspect their charges for signs of cruelty or suffering. When Mills invited the public to look behind the scenes at his circus, it was part of a wider strategy to respond to the accusations of the RSPCA. The presence of socially influential guests, including peers, helped dispel the idea that circus trainers and exhibitors mistreated their animals. It also helped create a stronger fan base for the circus.

Before the start of each winter season, Mills sent luncheon invitations to scores of distinguished people, with individualised directions from their homes to Olympia. With the invitations came personalised gifts such as luxury choco-lates in horseshoe-shaped boxes with horse brasses attached, or commissioned Wedgwood plates, imported Cuban cigars, and handkerchiefs embroidered with the Bertram Mills insignia.[33] Members of Parliament, the Lord Mayor of London, Aldermen, Sheriffs, novelists and artists enjoyed the pre-performance luncheon presided over by Lord Lonsdale, the 'president' of the Mills circus.[34] The sumptuous meal with high-profile guests was a publicity stunt held in the presence of several members of the press, including Disher.[35]

Personal invitations to the pre-season luncheon at Olympia were clearly predicated on social status and influence in the political, social and business worlds. As a result, the gatherings attracted the attention of 'anti-circus' activists. On Christmas Eve in 1932 Captain MacMichael, the secretary of the Performing and Captive Animals' Defense League was arrested for obstruction outside Olympia as he attempted to pass the league's pamphlets to Prince George and other guests.[36] Despite his failure, MacMichael's protest and the publicity surrounding his arrest brought public awareness to the idea that circus animals were treated cruelly. By lobbying the politically and socially influential guests at Mills' circus, protesters like MacMichael were able to gain support in Parliament. Thus both circus supporters and protestors capitalised on the public opinion generated by the presence of celebrities and the social elite at Mills' circus.

In spite of the occasional interruption from activists like Captain MacMichael, the circus remained a relatively cheap and popular form of entertainment. Ticket prices ranged from as little as a penny to as much as a guinea. The prices and the seat arrangements mirrored the economic disparities within the general population. Yet Disher, Bosworth and other fans continued to represent the circus as a democratic institution because it was still affordable entertainment and accessible to all social classes. Fans advanced this argument just as the idea of Britain as a democratic nation entered public discourse and popular belief. The nature of that democracy, however, remained the source of considerable debate. While there was a general belief in the nation as a democratic entity in the interwar years, not all members of that entity necessarily agreed on what democracy meant or should mean.[37] Circus supporters made claims about the nation's democratic credentials at a critical juncture when imperial Britain's future looked uncertain. As politicians debated the establishment of the British Commonwealth as a league of 'free and equal nations' in keeping with Britain's democratic values, circus fans eagerly took up the rhetoric.[38] For fans, the circus demonstrated the nation's democratic ideals because it was the site of egalitarian pleasure. Democracy for circus-goers meant the ability not only to consume the same entertainment as other social groups but also to obtain the same enjoyment. For fans, the circus was an important democratising agent because it provided collective enjoyment and leisure to all ages and all classes. Circus advocates like Disher and Bosworth appropriated the discourse of democracy to sell the circus as egalitarian and thoroughly 'English' entertainment. Thus the multiple anxieties about the meanings of democracy and the future of the empire during the interwar years made the reassertion of the circus as a democratic and a historically British institution meaningful to fans.

However, even notions of democracy could not counteract the effects of competition from other forms of 'classless' entertainment such as radio, dance halls and cinema. In 1923 there were half a million licensed radio listeners in Britain, but by 1932 the number had risen to over five million.[39] In addition, between 1932 and 1937 nine hundred new cinemas were built to showcase American movies that were especially popular with British audiences.[40] Similarly, dancing also became a lucrative interwar business and several 'chains' emerged to cater to millions of dancers. The largest, Mecca, boasted two thousand dance-halls with three hundred bands, successfully competing with other popular leisure entertainment like the circus and music-hall.[41] To remain viable, circuses lowered their seat prices and looked for alternative venues and audiences. Circuses performed on stages and even in department stores, complementing shows in permanent amphitheaters such as the Blackpool Tower and Yarmouth Hippodrome, as well as the seasonal circuses held in exhibition halls.[42]

Some circuses, however, were unable to remain afloat. After 127 years, the Bostock and Wombell travelling circus and menagerie was sold in 1931.[43] The circus's failure came at a time when Britain faced enormous economic problems and mass unemployment as a result of worldwide economic depression. The hardships faced by thousands of families meant that many simply could not afford even the cheapest forms of pleasure.[44] Yet Mills announced the launch of a new enterprise in 1930 – a six-month tour of a one-ring tenting circus to entertain the country. The tent seated five thousand and was the largest in Britain.[45] Mills' decision was an attempt to recoup the losses of the previous Christmas season and survive the depression years. The strategy proved successful. Within two years, Mills and other proprietors discovered that the most profitable shows took place in small towns that had little competition for entertainment.[46] The number of tenting circuses increased as profits grew and the interwar circus in Britain remained competitive. The circus, like the cinema, was relatively cheap and a perfect form of fantasy and distraction from the monotonous realities of daily life.

Travelling circuses, however, were not always welcomed by provincial towns. This was partly due to prejudices against itinerant showmen, but also because circuses relied on forward advertising in the form of handbills and posters often displayed indiscriminately on walls or bridges.[47] Furthermore, the circus habitually left town in the middle of the night, leaving behind the debris of the previous evening's performance. This practice offended the growing movement to preserve the countryside and to maintain a 'natural' and tidy environment.[48] Circus advertising frequently contravened local by-laws and resulted in prosecution and fines.[49] These cases set precedents and empowered town authorities to attempt to prevent itinerant entertainment in their locales.[50]

The reluctance of town councils to allow circus advertising was a relatively small problem, however, compared to increased opposition from those who accused circuses of animal cruelty. Since its formation in 1824, the RSPCA claimed that any use of animals for public performance was cruel. The increased visibility of performing animals at circuses like Olympia in the interwar years fuelled the RSPCA's campaign to abolish all public performances that included animals. The success of the Performing Animals Act (1925) effectively gave the RSPCA more leverage to inspect and critique animal handling techniques in private and in public. Shortly after the passage of the 1925 Act, Miss Ginnett, daughter of the proprietor of the Ginnett Circus, was accused of cruelty to her horse. Observers claimed that they saw 'evidence of pain' in the tail action of Miss Ginnett's horse as she spurred the animal to trot or canter to music on command in the circus ring. Although the judge dismissed the charge, the RSPCA continued to place pressure on proprietors and performers.[51] Other charges of cruelty, however, were not dismissed. A Dutch clown performing with a mule at Pepino's Miniature Circus in Kingston was fined for 'jabbing' the animal to make the mule buck.[52] The RSPCA also brought another successful accusation of cruelty against a trainer and groom employed at Chapman's Circus. Both men were found guilty of forcing a horse to perform when in 'an unfit condition' and fined £2 each, the equivalent of a week's pay.[53]

The circus industry challenged the claims of the RSPCA and argued that their animals were properly treated. Members of the public were invited to visit 'behind the scenes' at the circus and to inspect the animal housing and husbandry. Proprietors like Mills invited members of the press to view his stables and meet the resident veterinary surgeon, to dispel any idea of animal cruelty in his circus.[54] These assurances of kind treatment of animals did not, however, prevent animal activism in Parliament. In April 1933, a Bill introduced by Lord Danesford to limit performing animals to horses, elephants and dogs, narrowly failed the first reading in the House of Lords. The *World's Fair* reported the failure of the proposed legislation with relief, while in the same week two notable (and foreign) leopard trainers faced charges of cruelty brought by the RSPCA.[55] Although the judge ruled in favour of the trainers, the society continued to exert pressure on the industry by bringing charges of cruelty against circus performers and proprietors, with varying degrees of success.[56]

Despite the negative press that accompanied the RSPCA's accusations and the proposed legislation to limit animal performances, fans throughout Britain continued to attend circus shows. Yet the vigour of the opposition alarmed many fans and prompted the formation of the official Circus Fans Association of Britain (CFA), which pledged to protect the circus from unfair legislation.[57] The CFA officially met for the first time during the 1933–34 Christmas circus season, the same year the Performing Animals Act narrowly failed to pass into law. In an opening speech, Edward Graves, the association's secretary, pledged that the CFA would fight legislation against the circus and opened membership in the organisation to 'all true lovers and ardent admirers of the circus' prepared to take up this challenge.[58] While some proprietors regarded the new organisation with suspicion, Mills realised that an organisation like the CFA could help combat prejudice and ignorance about the circus, and so he invited the members to hold their first annual meeting in the ring at Olympia.[59] Mills provided a sumptuous inaugural lunch, a special performance and an 'official' circus proprietor's blessing on the new organisation. This effectively sealed an alliance between the CFA and Olympia and encouraged Bosworth to declare that 'Bertram Mills brought about the present revival in the circus' in his 1935 circus book.[60]

Indeed, many of the founding members of the CFA were people whom Mills had courted and sent personalised invitations to past pre-performance luncheons. Albeit true circus lovers, many CFA members held a degree of social influence as novelists, artists, cultural critics, reporters, civil servants or ex-military personnel.[61] The first chairperson was Lady Eleanor Furneaux-Smith, a well-known socialite who wrote books and novels about circus life in the interwar years.[62] Other members, like Bosworth and Disher, were also well-respected authors who contributed to the official fan publication, *Sawdust Ring*. This monthly publication featured biographies of great circus performers and histories of the British circus. The editors encouraged members to attend as many circuses as possible with friends in order to make more fans.[63] One founding member and civil servant, Raymond Toole-Stott even ventured to start his own small circus in 1936.[64] The CFA also made use of the *World's Fair*, the Showman weekly, to publish current 'CFA Notes' and stimulate conversations about the circus between fans, performers and proprietors. Fans used CFA Notes to write letters of encouragement or criticism to proprietors. Proprietors, in turn, used the CFA column to respond to criticism or advertise new performances. The column also served as a space where fans could depict their efforts to refute opposition to the circus. Most CFA members, like Bosworth and Disher, ardently believed the circus to be an important part of Britain's history. Fans used their talents to promote the 'Englishness' of the modern circus and to defend a part of British heritage from opposition like the RSPCA. The CFA was not simply a consumer group concerned to preserve access to a commodity; the organisation actively engaged in marketing the circus as a national emblem continuous with a laudable, stable past. As part of a grassroots movement, members continued to lobby Parliament and to publish circus literature and novels designed to promote the circus as a part of British heritage under threat of extinction. In many ways it was the multiple anxieties of the interwar period – economic depression, unemployment, commercial competition – that made the assertion of the circus as co-equal with the nation meaningful to fans who desired to convince the broader public to view the institution in the same way.

While the ongoing conflicts over animal cruelty and entertainment legislation caused problems for circus proprietors who already faced mounting economic difficulties, they also reveal several aspects of the democratic process in interwar Britain. The debates themselves embodied democratic principles that included the exchange of ideas at a grassroots level. Not only did these debates result in legislative reforms, they also reflected other aspects of democracy such as grassroots activism, lobbies and interest groups vying to control the content of legislation, as well as the use of a free press to publish articles, letters and books aimed at shaping public opinion. Both those that supported the circus and those that opposed it mobilised the tools of democracy to air their opinions. Both sides used the idea of nation to support their arguments. The RSPCA claimed the use of performing animals to be cruel and 'un-British', while fans argued that the circus was continuous with a historical tradition of British leisure which exhibited British national values.

Ironically, even as fans and proprietors marketed the circus as a British institution, some of the most sensational and admired performers came from all over the globe. So did some of the most popular circuses. At the height of the economic depression in 1932, Gleich's International Circus planned to tour Britain. Fans were thrilled, but British circus performers feared for their livelihoods and registered an 'emphatic protest' against the Government's decision to grant visas to the German-owned circus.[65] The protest resonated with the Minister of Labour, who gave permission to Gleich's International Circus on the condition that at least fifty per cent of performers and staff engaged were British.[66] The Minister hoped the compromise would satisfy circus fans who desired to see one of the best circuses in the world as well as create opportunities for unemployed British circus personnel. Thus the protectionism served as a method to preserve the idea of the circus, even a foreign-owned circus, as a 'British' institution.

The following year, as the economic depression continued and unemployment deepened, circus proprietors faced condemnation from jobless British performers for including artists from all over the world. The international nature of Bertram Mills' show at Olympia garnered severe criticism in the press. The 1933–34 winter programme included artists from America, Austria, the Caucuses, China, Japan, Morocco, Poland, Spain and Switzerland.[67] Mills answered the criticism. He supported the decision to employ foreign performers at Olympia because, he argued, British audiences 'deserved to see the best performances in the world'.[68] Yet the controversy in the press, coupled with the poor economy, led to low profits for the Mills circus in the winter season of 1933–34.[69] Perhaps as a reflection of the deepened economic crisis and the success of the Government-sponsored 'Buy British' campaign, the underlying issue for the press appeared to be the contest between the idea of the circus as a British institution versus the circus as British entertainment.[70] While Mills saw his role as a facilitator bringing the best circus acts to audiences in Britain, the press believed Mills should use his position as a British employer to use only British acts and employ British workers. Public opinion, then, insisted the circus was an exclusive British institution that should showcase the nation's talent to appreciative audiences.

The newly formed CFA spoke out in defence of the circus industry as a whole and Olympia in particular. The President of the organisation, Lady Eleanor Furneaux-Smith, emphasised the fact that a circus consisted of more than just performances. 'Every important tenting circus not only carries a permanent staff of English workmen', Lady Eleanor claimed, but 'furthermore, seeks additional labour among the unemployed in every town it visits'. Giving the journalist firm numbers to make her point and deflect the criticism, Lady Eleanor explained that the Mills circus employed eighteen hundred permanent 'behind the scenes' staff as well as hundreds of other labourers around the country. Not only did Mills and other proprietors help keep 'men off the dole', Lady Eleanor claimed, they also provided a securely British infrastructure to the circus.[71]

Despite the intervention of the CFA, criticism levelled at circus proprietors who continued to employ foreign performers increased as tensions rose in Europe. The censure came largely from within the industry itself, especially as performers from Nazi Germany sought refuge and work in Britain when the

German circus was reorganised to 'conform to Nazi principles'.[72] Later that year, as fascist Italy faced international sanctions for the invasion of Ethiopia, British artists were denied visas to perform in Italian circuses.[73] As British circus acts faced shrinking opportunities in Europe, performers placed pressure on proprietors to give employment to domestic circus workers. A letter to the editor of the *World's Fair* criticised the circus in Britain and argued that proprietors should not 'seek foreign artists' but rather should give British performers the chance to work in their own country.[74] As European powers made their own circuses exclusive, British performers became increasingly nationalistic and critical of an industry that did not seem to support them, especially when they were displaced by circus workers from nations like Italy and Germany, hostile to the ideals of democracy.

Bertram Mills appeared to heed the criticism. In an account of the sixteenth annual Christmas circus at Olympia in 1935, the correspondent for *The Times* claimed the 'great and gorgeous annual show at Olympia grows each year a more genuinely British affair'. A new lion act by a 'lady tamer' of just twenty-two years thrilled the audience, especially when they learned that she was 'English too'. The article went on to describe the individuals and the acts that made up the Christmas circus as essentially 'English' not, as the correspondent pointed out, because of any 'narrow nationalism'. Rather, the author maintained, 'it is simply that we like to see the country which was, after all, the original home of the circus continuing to take its full share in the development of the art.'[75]

Indeed, the leading editorial in *The Times* on the same day claimed that the large number of winter circuses in London was 'striking proof of the vitality of an institution ... cradled in England ... and so peculiarly congenial to the English character'. The national attraction of the circus, claimed the editor, was because of a 'sense of kinship with the higher animal creation that slightly bewilders foreigners'. This sense of kinship was peculiar to the national character, and ensured that the vigilant English public would take 'every precaution ... to prevent the ill-treatment of the animals'. To this critic, England was a nation of animal lovers whose very nature delighted in the circus and prevented cruelty to animals because of an intense feeling of affinity to the animal world. It was the revival of the circus, brought about by men like Bertram Mills, that revealed this unique national trait.[76] Thus *The Times* promoted the circus and animal husbandry as essential parts of the English 'character', and Olympia as a space where this 'national' quality was made known.

Incidents in foreign circuses served to underscore the idea that 'foreigners' did not share that same sense of kinship with animals that ensured good husbandry, on which the English often prided themselves. In early 1937 in Vienna, 'Jumbo', an elephant with the Circus Busch, consumed 1,400 dough-nuts when left unattended for 'some time'. Although Jumbo appeared no worse for his mass consumption of pastries, the fact that he was left unsupervised by the German circus staff caused a concern among British fans for the elephants' welfare.[77] A few months later, Eva, another elephant belonging to a Detroit circus, was not so lucky. The keeper removed his boots and fell asleep while supposedly taking care of the elephant. Eva, unsupervised, consumed the boots and died within a week.[78] The lack of 'genuine' concern for animal welfare could have serious consequences. Just weeks after the death of Eva, three lions escaped from a German circus. One lion jumped on a circus horse, breaking its neck, and another consumed a performing donkey. All three lions were even-tually captured, but for the overseas correspondents reporting the incidents above, animals were clearly safer in British circuses where their well-being was assured.[79] As the interwar circus and its fans sought to reassure the public that British circuses maintained the highest standards of animal husbandry, the foreign 'other' served as both a caution and as an example of inferior national character. Britain, the birthplace of the modern circus, deplored cruelty to and neglect of animals. Indeed, the British character, according to circus fans, was such that animals received only superior care born of a special bond between Britons and their animals.[80]

Within months, however, the well-being of all performing animals and the circus industry in general was under threat. Immediately following the declara-tion of war with the Axis powers on 3 September 1939, all cinemas, theatres and other places of entertainment were closed. The Ministry of Information argued that falling bombs would kill or injure many people at any crowded place of entertainment. This essentially stopped all circus shows. In addition, the conscription of able-bodied young men seriously depleted performances on the stage as well as the sawdust ring. However, the government soon recog-nised the importance of entertainment to the maintenance of civilian morale and the circus received a boost from supporters in Parliament.[81] In a speech to the Showman's Guild of Great Britain, Lord Strabogli, MP, underscored the circus as a vehicle of national unity when he spoke to circus proprietors and explained, 'You will be doing a great deal if you can only keep going and keep up the spirit of the people … especially the children … they are the citizens of the future. Help brighten their lives and you will be helping the future of the nation.'[82] To him, the circus was a symbol of national unity and future regen-eration, and a British tradition worth fighting for.

During the war, the circus renewed its image as 'a national institution in fact, not just in name', and promoters marketed the circus as a vehicle that rendered a public service at a time of national need.[83] To propagate that image, proprietors allied themselves with prominent politicians and members of the Royal Family. Winston Churchill was photographed alongside the proprietors of the Pinder Circus,[84] while the Lord Provost of Scotland visited the Royal George Circus in Edinburgh and declared the circus a 'wonderful [British] tradition'.[85] The Duke and Duchess of Kent, along with their children, visited a performance of the Sanger Circus at Windsor Great Park to emphasise the 'classless' nature of popular British leisure and the role of the circus in maintaining a unity that cut across class lines.[86] In return, the circus changed names to invoke confidence in the war effort. Reco Brothers became the 'Empire Circus', and a new 'Royal Allied Circus' opened in June 1941. Harry Benet renamed his company 'The Royal Britannic Circus', and still another, the 'Great Dominion Circus', opened in 1942.[87] Circus fans were euphoric when the 1943 season broke all circus records.[88] CFA member B. Harris claimed 1943 'the best circus season ever' despite the hardships, and he predicted the next season to be even better.[89]

The reasons for the success of the circus in the war years stemmed from leisure policies adopted by the wartime coalition government. Law-makers recognised the value of recreation to the war effort and swore not to repeal the Holidays with Pay Act (1938). The Minister of Labour, the National Joint Advisory Council and the trade unions agreed to stagger workers' holidays between June and September and encourage workers to vacation away from home.[90] In addition, the traditional May to October amusements, fairgrounds and tenting circuses continued to amuse the masses. For some holiday resorts, such as Blackpool on the northwest coast of England, the 1940 summer season proved a tremendous success without parallel in history.[91] The circus, like Blackpool, retained its popularity and its image as an affordable and accessible space that transgressed all socio-economic barriers.

Unlike for some other circuses, however, 1940 was not a successful year for the Mills circus. In mid-June, police seized two Italian clowns from the Mills circus tent while they performed in Swansea, south Wales. Under the newly expanded Treachery Act (1940), the Manetti brothers faced internment with several other Italian civilians arrested in Britain since Italy's declaration of war on 10 June. Despite having more than fifteen years of continuous residence and employment in Britain as prominent circus performers, the 'un-naturalized' Manetti brothers were considered 'enemy aliens'.[92] Less than a month after this incident, the Mills circus closed for the duration of the war.[93] Bertram Mills had died in 1938 and his sons joined the armed forces, planning to reopen the circus when hostilities ceased. By 1941, Sanger's Circus, one of Britain's oldest, sold its animals and capital, but the family bought both the goodwill and the name. Like the Mills brothers, they planned to open again after the war.[94]

Most other circuses benefited from wartime policies. By 1942, in response to a severe petrol shortage, the national government promoted the provision of recreation for workers in their own towns. The Holidays-at-Home scheme solved the problem of 'unnecessary' civilian travel, created new opportunities for travelling entertainment, and brought much needed revenue to local authorities.[95] Holidays-at-home policies ensured work and pleasure for millions of Britons and increased opportunities for the circus. In Birmingham alone, the council proposed forty-eight sites for continuous fairs and circuses during the summer of 1942.[96] In Croydon and Edinburgh authorities paid to have circuses as part of their home entertainment,[97] and North Shields even asked the Reco Brothers Circus to provide unprecedented Sunday performances.[98] Thus government leisure policies like Holidays-at-Home, combined with affordability and accessibility, increased the popular appeal of the circus. As wartime propaganda focused on the lack of personal freedoms in totalitarian states, the scheme to provide affordable entertainment for all Britons supported fans' arguments about the democratic nature of the circus and indeed, the nation.

Not all local authorities allowed the circus to perform as part of their planned holidays-at-home. Liverpool, home to an active branch of the RSPCA, chose to ban circuses. CFA members wrote to urge the Liverpool council not to exclude this popular entertainment from their city.[99] Circus fans responded to the 'attack' on the circus with familiar and nationalistic discourse. Emulating Churchillian rhetoric used during the 'Battle of Britain', Mr Malcolm, a pro-circus member of the Liverpool Holidays-at-Home committee claimed, 'To stop circuses is killjoyism at its very worst. Never was there a time when so few would appear to be trying to prevent the enjoyment of so many.'[100] Another fan described the RSPCA as 'un-English', and 'Hitler's Seventh column', helping to bring down the morale of the nation.[101] One more stressed the 'democratic' nature of circus entertainment as important for audiences 'from royalty to commoners'.[102] Yet another fan pointed out that 'more than any other form of amusement the circus contributes to democracy', and commented, 'It is strange that those who prate most loudly of democracy are the very ones who would deny the circus to the masses!'[103] Once again, these fans evoked the notion of the circus as democratic, and during the war, the word took on a more urgent meaning than in the interwar years. Democracy connoted the polar opposite of authoritarianism, and the defence of the circus represented a defence of national values, including choice of leisure. Opposition to the circus was thus framed as a form of treachery equal to aiding and abetting the enemy. Yet despite the efforts of the fans and their strong words, the Liverpool holidays-at-home refused to feature circuses.[104] Nonetheless, circus performances remained an essential ingredient of wartime pleasure in many towns and cities. At the end of the war, not only were there more British circuses, there were more fans.

As the European war came to a close and the question of the physical and political reconstruction of Britain featured prominently in public discussion, some circus fans looked to international models for inspiration on improving the status of the circus as a national institution. As Parliament contemplated the nationalisation of major industries in Britain, CFA member Edward Graves discussed the merits of a 'state' circus. Looking to the Soviet model, Graves claimed the superiority of Russian circus performance rested on the treatment of the circus as a state institution, with a central circus school in Moscow.[105] 'Why', Graves asked, 'could this not work in Britain?'[106]

The idea of a state-promoted and protected circus paralleled the public discussion of 'nationalised culture' and publicly funded entertainment, recreation, and education through the arts. Historian Nick Hayes suggested two reasons for the sudden dialogue surrounding the wholesale financial support of the arts. The first entailed the belief that Britain fought to preserve what was 'best' in European civilisation, especially predominantly British forms of culture.[107] The second reason entailed the reconstruction of the nation and the 'good' citizen based on an appreciation of cultural roots and art forms. Nationalised culture in post-war Britain acted as a form of socially directed 'taste'.[108] According to Hayes, the new and powerful cultural establishment made clear distinctions between 'good' culture that, in turn, would generate 'good' citizens, and 'popular' culture that would not. Good culture was 'supported and validated through subsidy;' and 'popular' culture was left to follow 'the dictates and uncertainties of commercial viability' without government assistance.[109] The call for state intervention by some circus fans was an attempt to establish the circus as 'good' culture and distance the industry from threatening market forces.[110] Open competition and potential price restructuring presented a threat to the democratic underpinnings of the circus. Fans recognised that government policies during wartime like Holiday-at-Home helped sustain the industry, and this bolstered the fear that without similar support the peacetime circus might face insurmountable difficulties.

In 1945, despite these fears, circus audiences continued to enjoy performances in the sawdust ring. Princess Elizabeth claimed the recently reformed Royal George Sanger Circus was 'the best … ever seen'.[111] The Reco Brothers Circus enjoyed an unprecedented season and the Royal Imperial Circus broke all records and turned people away night after night.[112] Yet circus fans eagerly awaited the return of the Mills circus at Olympia. It was the return of the winter circus that most symbolised a return to normalcy after the disruptions of war and reconfirmed the capital as a site of cultural prominence. As if to demonstrate its allure, Olympia's box office sold 100,000 tickets on the day it opened.[113] The London press welcomed the Olympia circus back and declared the nation's 'accumulated tradition of the big top … [would never] … be lost' despite the war.[114] The *Illustrated London News* declared: '[the] circus came back to town' with 'all that implies' about British culture and character after the long years of war.[115] *The Sketch* affirmed the same sentiments and proclaimed that the Olympia show was back with all its 'pre-war glitter, thrills and suspense'.[116] As one London journalist claimed, the opening show at Olympia was truly a 'national event'.[117]

Despite an initial post-war boom, the revival of the British circus would not last. Circuses succumbed to market forces, new competition from television and renewed efforts on the part of the RSPCA to remove all animals from performances. By 1966, the Mills circus had closed, to the chagrin of fans, ending over fifty years of a commodity marketed by fans as continuous with, and an essential part of, British history.[118] Other new circuses formed after the Second World War, using new television technology to their advantage. Billy Smart formed his New World Circus in 1946. The following year, the BBC began to broadcast special programmes directly from Billy Smart's circus ring. The annual Billy Smart's Christmas Spectacular became a BBC winter holiday tradition until 1979, when once again, activists accused circuses of cruelty and pressured the BBC to withdraw sponsorship.

Conclusion

The circus industry as a whole survived the physical constraints of the Second World War, just as it survived economic depression, competition from other types of entertainment and opposition from animal welfare advocates.[119] The revitalisation of the circus industry between 1920 and 1945 came about as the result of successful promotion of the circus as an essential facet of a historic and essentially 'English' national identity. Fans and circus proprietors like Bertram Mills used novels, histories and advertising to endorse the circus as part of national heritage and found cultural resonance during a period of intense national anxiety. As politicians debated the end of empire and the establishment of the Commonwealth, as European nations moved further away from democracy and toward totalitarian states, as the world economic depression deepened and created massive unemployment, 'selling' the circus as part of the nation's more stable past acquired more importance for both circuses and their fans. The industry revived and expanded profitably and fans retained an entertainment they perceived as under threat. Together these entities constructed the modern circus as a facet of the 'national character', an important part of Britain's national heritage, and a symbol of British democratic values. At a time when much of Europe experienced political polarisation and social disintegration, circus advocates imagined the British circus as emblematic of national democratic unity. As with all advertising, the message conveyed was not always 'read' by the consumer in the way marketers intended. Nevertheless, the circus stood out as an older industry that prospered and gained popular support in Britain despite competition from modern, American-style entertainments like the cinema, and at a time when other forms of entertainment were declining.

The popularity of the circus was due in part to the concerted efforts of fans who published circus literature that emphasised the uniquely British origins of the modern circus and stressed the accessibility and affordability of what they believed to be democratic entertainment. Together with the business acumen of Bertram Mills, circus publications helped popularise, romanticise and, more importantly, market the circus as emblematic and continuous with a historical tradition of British leisure that championed British national values. Using the tools of democracy, fans became grassroots activists determined to influence both popular opinion and legislation. Like their adversaries, animal rights activists, fans organised and worked to lobby Parliament to preserve the circus as an emblem of national ideals.

In some ways circus fans were responding to the anxieties of the interwar years. The books and articles they wrote were sensitive evocations of an older English culture. However, while these authors lamented the loss of a more stable way of life, circus history gave fans a sense of belonging to a living tradition that was vital for the maintenance of a communal sense of identity fractured by modern life. While the interwar years marked the epilogue of an older social and economic order, circus fans like Disher, Bosworth and Furneaux-Smith attempted to arrest the social crisis and presented a 'bourgeois notion of Britishness and British history, as reified and authenticated through [the] circus'.[120] Historical figures like Philip Astley became the guardians of a British tradition of leisure and pleasure. Perpetuating the myth of Astley as the father of the modern circus formed part of a shared historicity that, for circus fans, emphasised the survival of an essentially British cultural form in an uncertain world.[121] That culture was also imagined as democratic. The idea of democracy in the interwar years was encouraged by a strong sense of middle-class self-confidence and the belief that English democracy would be defined in its own terms.[122] In the case of circus fans, this meant the appropriation of a visual symbol of democracy, dated to 1776, to coincide with the birth of the first 'democratic' nation, America.

Notes

1 William G. Bosworth, *Wagon Wheels: The Romance of the Circus* (London: Heath Cranton, 1935), 35.

2 M. Willson Disher, *Clowns and Pantomime* (1925; repr., London: Constable, 1955), *The Greatest Show on Earth* (1937; repr., New York: Benjamin Blom, 1971) and *Fairs, Circuses and Music Halls* (London: William Collins, 1942). Disher wrote novels and articles for the *Daily Mail, The Times, The Times Literary Supplement,* and the weekly *Sketch.*

3 Yoram Carmeli, 'The Invention of Circus and Bourgeois Hegemony: A Glance at British Circus Books', *Journal of Popular Culture* 29, no. 1 (Summer 1995): 213–21.

4 See Sandra Dawson, 'Working Class Consumers and the Campaign for Holidays with Pay', *Twentieth Century British History* 18, no. 3 (2007): 277–305.

5 See, for example, James Nott, *Music for the People: Popular Music and Dance in Interwar Britain* (Oxford: Oxford University Press, 2002) and Jeffrey Richards, *The Age of the Dream Palace: Cinema and Society in Britain, 1930–1939* (London: Routledge, 1990).

6 See Brenda Assael, *The Circus and Victorian Society* (Charlottesville, VA: University of Virginia Press, 2005) and Marius Kwint, 'Astley's Amphitheatre and the Early Circus in England, 1798–1830' (PhD diss., Oxford University, 1994).

7 Peta Tait, *Circus Bodies Cultural Identity in Ariel Performance* (London: Routledge, 2005); Helen Stoddart, *Rings of Desire: Circus History and Representation* (Manchester: Manchester University Press, 2000).

8 For a discussion of the growth of the popular press, see Adrian Bingham, *Gender, Modernity and the Popular Press in Interwar Britain* (Oxford: Oxford University Press, 2004). Lord Northcliffe owned the *Daily Mail* and *The Times.*

9 Willson M. Disher, *Clowns and Pantomime* and *The Greatest Show on Earth.*

10 See Robert Duncan Macleod (ed.), *Library Review* (MCB University Press, 1938),

136, and *The Publisher's Weekly,* vol. 138 (Philadelphia: R. R. Bower, 1940), 352.

11 Kwint maintains that Philip Astley was not the first to develop the modern circus; he was merely the first to close his performance off and charge admission. See Kwint, 'Astley's Amphitheatre'.

12 J. Michel Hogan, *Woodrow Wilson's Western Tour: Rhetoric, Public Opinion and the League of Nations* (College Station, TX: Texas A&M University Press, 2007).

13 P. T. Barnum is credited with the invention of American popular culture. See Bluford Adams, *E Pluribus Barnum: The Great Showman and the Making of U.S. Popular Culture* (Minneapolis, MN: University of Minnesota Press, 1997).

14 There were ten circuses in Britain in 1918. *King Pole,* Christmas and New Year Season, 1938/9. By 1945 there were over forty-five circuses in Britain. Hal Thomas, 'British Tenting Circuses 1940–1980', *King Pole* (Summer 1981).

15 See, for example, Victoria de Grazia, *Irresistible Empire: America's Advance Through 20th-Century Europe* (London: Belknap, 2005) and Gary Cross, *Time and Money: The Making of Consumer Culture* (London: Routledge, 1993).

16 'Mr. B. Mills on How He Entered Showland', *World's Fair,* 26 January 1935, 38.

17 'The Big Circus: Enraptured Audience of Children', *The Times,* 18 December 1920, 7; Bosworth, *Wagon Wheels,* 6; 'Sanger's Circus Centenary: 'Tiny' the Elephant', *The Times,* 25 June 1921, 7.

18 'The Charm of the Circus: Olympia Entertainment', *The Times,* 21 December 1923, 8. The Mills circus ring at Olympia seated 5,000 and the circus performed twice daily.

19 '"International Circus" at Olympia', *The Times,* 5 December 1925, 14.

20 Jan M. Brown, 'The British Expeditionary Force and the Difficult Transition to Peace, 1918–1919', *Journal of Strategic Studies* 19, no. 4 (1996): 89–104.

21 For a discussion of athletic ability, imperialism and masculinity, see Paul Deslandes, *Oxbridge Men: British Masculinity and the Undergraduate Experience* (Bloomington, IN: Indiana University Press, 2005), and Mrinalini Sinha, *Colonial Masculinity: The 'Manly Englishman' and the 'Effeminate Bengali' in the Late Nineteenth Century* (Manchester: Manchester University Press, 1995), 112.

22 See *Bertram Mills' Circus at Olympia, Official Programme, Dec. 1925–Jan. 1926,* 3–7, Toole-Stott Collection, Davidson Library, University of California at Santa Barbara (hereafter TSC), PA 2A/10B–15A.

23 'The Charm of the Circus: Olympia Entertainment', *The Times,* 21 December 1923, 8.

24 Stoddart, *Rings of Desire,* 13–33.

25 The Showman's Guild of Great Britain formed at the end of the nineteenth century to protect both the lifestyle and the culture of showmen. The weekly *World's Fair* is the official trade journal of the Showman's Guild.

26 'Mr. Bertram Mills Died Today', *Evening Standard,* 16 April 1938, 6.

27 Anthony Hippisley Coxe, *Grand Parade: A Survey of Bertram Mills' Circus,* unpublished paper, Theatre Museum, London (hereafter TM), GV 1821 B4 Folio.

28 'Crystal Palace Circus: Dick Turpin's Ride to York', *The Times,* 27 December 1922, 8 and 'Crystal Palace Circus', *The Times,* 24 December 1923, 8.

29 'Super-Circus at Wembley: Royal Visitors', *The Times*, 23 June 1925, 14.

30 'Circus for London: Mr. Bostock's Plans at Earl's Court', *The Times,* 11 October 1928, 14.

31 Hippisley Coxe, *Grand Parade*, TM, GV 1921 B4 Folio, 45.

32 Captain Edward G. Fairholme, Letter to the Editor, *The Times,* 30 December 1920, 6: C.

33 I am grateful to Christopher Stone for allowing me to view his private circus collection of ephemera (Bournemouth, UK, 21 December 2001).

34 'Christmas Circus at Olympia: Lord Lonsdale on Animal Training', *The Times*, 23 December 1922, 6.

35 Invitation to Maurice Willson Disher from Bertram Mills to Olympia pre-performance luncheon, 1928, TSC.

36 'Propaganda at Circus: Charge of Obstruction', *The Times,* 24 December, 1932, 6.

37 See, D. L. LeMahieu, *A Culture for Democracy: Mass Communication and the Cultivated Mind in Britain Between the Wars* (Oxford: Clarendon Press, 1988).

38 'A League of Equal Nations: Mr. Lloyd on Future of Empire', *The Times*, 29 June 1925, 9. See also 'Empire League of Nations', *The Times*, 28 April 1923, 7; 'British League of Nations: True Path to Peace, Mr. MacDonald's Address to Empire Press', *The Times*, 24 May 1938, 11.

39 Nott, *Music for the People,* 155.

40 Richards, *Age of the Dream Palace,* Ch. 1.

41 Nott, *Music for the People*, 157. Maurice Willson Disher wrote *Music Hall Parade* (London: Charles Scribner's Sons, 1938) to celebrate this older 'English' form of entertainment.

42 Hippisley Coxe, *Grand Parade,* TM, GV 1821 B4 Folio, 71–5.

43 'Passing of Bostock and Wombell's Circus', *The Times*, 1 December 1931, 12.

44 Dawson, 'Working Class Consumers', 277–305.

45 'Olympia Circus on Tour: Mr. Bertram Mills' New Enterprise', *The Times,* 3 April 1930, 12.

46 Letter from Cyril R. Mills to Christopher Stone, 2 August 1983, courtesy of Christopher Stone, Bournemouth, UK.

47 'Case Against Circus Manager Dismissed', *World's Fair,* 5 August 1933, 33; 'Circus Posters on Bridge: Case Against Traveling Show Dismissed', *World's Fair,* 19 August 1933, 32.

48 See David Matless, *Landscape and Englishness* (London: Reaktion, 1998).

49 'Disfiguring Circus Posters', *The Times,* 3 September 1932, 7.

50 'Circus Bills in Kent', *World's Fair,* 21 September 1935, 33.

51 'Circus Horse Ride – Charge of Cruelty Dismissed', *The Times*, 2 February 1926, 16.

52 'Mule Ill-Treated on the Stage – Circus Clown Fined', *The Times,* 30 June 1938, 11.

53 'Cruelty to Circus Horse', *The Times,* 31 August 1938, 8.

54 Hinton Stratton, 'Bertram Mills Circus: Fortunate Horses', *Hampshire Chronicle,* 18 April 1931.

55 'Training Circus Animals – Showmen's Answer to Charge of Cruelty', *The Times*, 15

January 1937, 9.

56 'Mule Ill-Treated on the Stage – Circus Clown Fined', *The Times,* 30 June, 1938, 11.

57 The Circus Fans Association of Great Britain advertised their new association in the *Paulo's Star Circus* program, c. 1938, TSC, PA 2A/10B-15A.

58 *Sawdust Ring,* subscription form / handbill, c.1935, TSC, PA Mss 14.

59 The CFA continued to meet annually at Olympia. See 'Rally of Circus Enthusiasts – Midnight Revelry in the Ring – Clowns as Guests', *Daily Telegraph,* 17 September 1934.

60 Bosworth, *Wagon Wheels,* 35.

61 A. Anthony (alias Edward Graves), 'C. F. A. of Great Britain: Inauguration Day a Success', *World's Fair,* 27 January 1934, 33.

62 Lady Eleanor Smith wrote *The Red Wagon* (London: Gollancz, 1930), *Satan's Circus and Other Stories* (London: Gollancz, 1932), *Life's a Circus* (London: Longman, 1939), and *British Circus Life* (London: Harrap, 1948).

63 *Sawdust Ring* 1, no. 1 (1934). See also *Sawdust,* subscription form / handbill, c.1935, TSC, PA Mss 14. The *Sawdust Ring* was published from 1934 to 1939, then replaced by *King Pole.*

64 Raymond Toole-Stott was the librarian and historian of the CFA. A civil servant, Toole-Stott worked for Bertram Mills for eight years before he opened his own circus in 1936. The tenting circus ran for two years, interrupted by the threat of war.

65 J. Russell Pickering, 'A German Circus', Letter to the Editor, *The Times,* 25 April 1932, 10.

66 'Gleich's International Circus – First Tour of Great Britain', *The Times,* 3 May 1932, 12.

67 Albert Anthony, 'Circus Notes', *World's Fair,* 7 January 1933, 32.

68 Quoted in 'Circus Notes', *World's Fair,* 7 January 1933, 32.

69 Albert Anthony, *World's Fair,* 7 January 1933, 13.

70 S. Constantine, 'The Buy British Campaign of 1931', *European Journal of Marketing* 21, no. 4 (1987): 44–59.

71 'Lady Smith Upholds Circuses', *World's Fair,* 21 January 1933, 34.

72 'Nazi Blow at Circus Artistes', *World's Fair,* 27 July 1935, 33.

73 'Italy Refusing Labour Permits', *World's Fair,* 14 December 1935, 1.

74 J. Crawford, Letter to the Editor, *World's Fair,* 6 April 1935, 39.

75 'Thrills of the Circus – English Talent at Olympia', *The Times,* 21 December 1935, 7.

76 Editorial, 'The Circus Revived', *The Times,* 21 December 1935, 11.

77 Vienna Correspondent 'Circus Elephant Eats 1,400 Doughnuts', *The Times,* 20 February 1937, 12.

78 New York Correspondent, 'A Circus Elephant's Fate: Death after Eating Boots', *The Times,* 17 June 1937, 16.

79 Berlin Correspondent, 'Escaped Circus Lions in German Village: Performing Donkey Eaten', *The Times,* 26 July 1937, 12.

80 This was also an argument made in the nineteenth century. See, Assael, *Circus and Respectable Society,* Ch. 4.

81 See, for example, Sandra Dawson, 'Busy and Bored: The Politics of Work and Leisure for Women Workers in WWII British Government Hostels', *Twentieth Century British History* 21, no. 1 (2010): 29–49.

82 'Traveling Showmen's Difficulties in War-time. Renewed Assurance of Support from MPs. Speeches at Guildhall Public Meeting', *World's Fair*, 27 January 1940, 8–9.

83 Edward Graves, 'Circus Renders Public Service', *World's Fair*, 11 October 1941, 12.

84 *World's Fair*, 14 August 1943, 1.

85 'Lord Provost and the Circus. 'Clean' and 'Wholesome' Fare', *World's Fair*, 22 July 1944, 1.

86 'Royal Children Visit Sanger's Circus', *World's Fair*, 29 May 1943, 1.

87 'Big Circus for Liverpool Parks', *World's Fair*, 27 June 1942, 1; 'Royal Allied Circus Starts Out', *World's Fair*, 20 June 1942, 1; 'Royal Britannic Circus. Harry Benet's New Show', *World's Fair*, 30 October 1943, 13.

88 Edward Graves, 'Circus Breaks Records', *World's Fair*, 6 February 1943, 12; B. Harris, 'BCR Notes', *World's Fair*, 3 April 1943, 12.

89 B. Harris, 'The Circus Season of 1943', *World's Fair*, 23 October 1943, 12.

90 *Ministry of Labour Report, 1939–1946* (HMSO: London, 1947), 120.

91 T. G. Hearney, 'Blackpool in War-time. Amusements in Full Swing', *World's Fair*, 17 August 1940, 7.

92 'Police at Mills Circus: Italian Clowns Detained', *World's Fair*, 22 June 1940, 17. The 1940 Treachery Act interned aliens who had lived less than 20 years in Britain by June 1940.

93 *World's Fair*, 13 July 1940, 14.

94 E. Grave, 'Sanger's After the War Plans', *World's Fair*, 13 September 1941, 12.

95 'Holidays at Home Scheme. Drawing Power of Showland Attractions', *World's Fair*, 7 March 1942, 1.

96 'Holidays at Home Fairs. Big Plans at Birmingham', *World's Fair*, 6 June 1942, 1.

97 'Circus for Croyden and Edinburgh? Holidays at Home Plans', *World's Fair*, 10 April 1943, 1.

98 'Reco Bros. Circus to Give Sunday Shows', *World's Fair*, 10 July 1943, 1. The ban on Sunday performances was lifted temporarily in some towns and cities in the war years, as was the twenty-eight day limit for itinerant entertainments such as fairs and circuses.

99 'Dicky' Bird, 'CFA Notes', *World's Fair*, 17 April 1943.

100 Mr. Malcolm, 'Killjoyism at it's Worst. Slashing Attack on Circus Critics', *World's Fair*, 19 June 1943, 1.

101 Arthur E. Peterson, letter to the editor, *World's Fair*, 10 July 1943, 13.

102 'In Defense of the Circus', *World's Fair*, 8 July 1944, 12.

103 B. Harris, 'The Circus Contributes to Democracy', *World's Fair*, 28 August 1943, 13.

104 'Liverpool Turns Down Circus Offer', *World's Fair*, 17 July 1943.

105 Edward Graves, 'The Circus in Russia', *World's Fair*, 5 May 1945, 12.

106 'Pegasus' and 'Should Circuses be State Controlled?' *World's Fair,* 23 June 1945, 16.

107 Nick Hayes, 'An "English War", Wartime Culture and "Millions Like Us"', in Nick Hayes and Jeff Hill (eds), *Millions Like Us?: British Culture in the Second World War* (Liverpool: Liverpool University Press, 1999), 1–32.

108 Becky Conekin, also discusses the post-war preoccupation with uplifting national taste. See *'The Autobiography of a Nation': The 1951 Festival of Britain* (Manchester: Manchester University Press, 2003).

109 Hayes, 'An "English War"', 28–9.

110 The idea of a nationalised circus continued to fascinate CFA membership. In a 1952 edition of the *King Pole,* E. M. Shears lauded Stalin's depiction of the circus as 'progressive democratic art' and described the numerical growth of static circuses in 'Mr. Stalin's Russia', *King Pole* (Summer 1952), 8–10.

111 'Royal Party's Visit to Circus: Young Duke Admires 'Buffalo Bill"', *World's Fair,* 8 September 1945, 1.

112 Edward Graves, 'Royal Imperial Circus Breaks all Records', *World's Fair,* 13 October 1945; 'Reco Bros. Good Season', *World's Fair,* 20 October 1945, 12.

113 Charles Graves, 'The Circus Come to Town', *The Sphere,* 21 December 1946, 408.

114 'The Circus – Welcome Back!' *Punch or the London Charivari,* 1 January 1947, 10.

115 'The Sawdust and Spangles Return to Town', *Illustrated London News,* 2 January 1947, 1.

116 'The Circus is Back at Olympia', *The Sketch,* 8 January 1947, 23.

117 Anthony Cookman, 'At the Circus', *The Tatler and Bystander,* 4 January 1950.

118 Cyril Mills' letter to Christopher Stone – Record of profit/loss of Bertram Mills Circus, 1935–1966. The Bertram Mills circus was a 'one-man-band' until the death of Bertram Mills in 1938. The circus was made a private limited liability company in 1935, and a public company in 1947. Nevertheless, the circus closed in 1966 on account of poor profits. Christopher Stone, Private Collection, Bournemouth, UK.

119 Between 1940 and 1945 there were over forty-five touring circuses in Britain as well as at least twelve static circuses. Hal Thomas, 'British Tenting Circuses 1940–1980', *King Pole* (Summer 1981).

120 Carmeli, 'The Invention of Circus and Bourgeois Hegemony', 214.

121 See Malcolm Smith, *Britain and 1940: History, Myth and Popular Memory,* (London: Routledge, 2000).

122 McKibben, *Classes and Cultures,* 530.

5

The western and British identity on British television in the 1950s

KELLY BOYD

Of the making of 'Westerns' there is no end and many of us who are long past the days of childhood still find pleasure in those celluloid evocations of the life of the range, the American stage-coach, and the grave though irascible Red Indians. (Unsigned review, *The Times,* 28 July 1952)[1]

British identity and culture was at the centre of schedules in the early days of British television, and most dramatic programming featured British protagonists. Schoolchildren and sailors, explorers and scientists, military men and missionaries peopled the airwaves. But the western adventure rivalled these narratives; by the latter half of the 1950s, scarcely a day went by without one being shown – an astonishing fact at a time when there were only two channels broadcasting only six to eight hours a day. Both cinematic and made-for-television fare were regularly scheduled, along with visits from cowboy stars and competitions for children on other shows. Although the western was recognised as essentially an American cultural form, it did not raise the spectre of Americanisation in the way that other imports – such as jazz, blues or rock-and-roll music – did from the rising superpower.[2] Instead, its popularity steadily grew, mirroring the genre's popularity around the world in this period. This essay will discuss the place of the western in British culture, establish the contours of early British television programming and culture, explore the extent of the

The author is grateful to Rohan McWilliam and Brett Bebber for their comments and patience during the writing of this chapter. She would also like to acknowledge the help she was given at the BBC Written Archives Centre by their archivists, but particularly Erin O'Neill, who guided her through the available documents there.

genre's popularity on British television in the 1950s and investigate the reasons why it was not viewed as a threat at a time when fears of Americanisation were being regularly articulated. While concerns about the negative influence of American westerns certainly existed, they were overcome by shared affinities for the genre and reinforced the unique association between Britain and America in the immediate post-war era.

In his examination of formula fiction on both page and screen, John G. Cawelti argued that the western invokes the symbolic landscape between civilisation and wilderness.[3] This allows the western to range beyond the nineteenth century and offer universal themes. The western was, of course, nothing new in the post-war period. Its roots are found in the literature of American westward expansion. Frontier stories were popular in antebellum America, for example in the Davy Crockett stories that Walt Disney would exploit in the 1950s.[4] By the end of the nineteenth century the cowboy hero had begun to emerge in the dime novel.[5] Many of these stories were reprinted in the penny dreadfuls and boys' story papers in England. These tales focused on the taming of the west and frequently were based on actual people like Wild Bill Hickok and Jesse James. The stories were somewhat cruder than the popular imperial fiction that British writers like H. Rider Haggard and G.A. Henty produced in the late nineteenth century. They also lacked the respect for nature and Native American culture that were the hallmarks of the German writer Karl May's tales of Winnetou and Old Shatterhand.[6] By far the most influential cultural figure that embodied the American West during the late nineteenth century was 'Buffalo Bill' Cody (1846–1917), who first brought his Wild West Show to Britain in 1887 for Queen Victoria's Golden Jubilee and later toured Europe.[7] Although this was not the first American cultural form to enliven the British stage in the nineteenth century (the minstrel show had earlier conquered the British public, and would also be very successfully resurrected on the BBC in the 1950s), the Wild West Show has been seen as an early agent of Americanisation in Europe.[8] Coming at the same time as the official closing of the American frontier in 1891 and Frederick Jackson Turner's articulation of the 'frontier thesis' of westward expansion as the defining fact of American character and nation, it also captured the romanticism of the 'winning of the west' perhaps best articulated in the popularity of Theodore Roosevelt during the same period. In fact, Roosevelt's 'Rough Riders' were eventually incorporated into the Wild West Show in the early twentieth century, although their field of battle had been Cuba, not the Great Plains. Kate Flint, however, argued that Buffalo Bill, and particularly his use of Native Americans, did not so much

Americanise Britain as offer it the opportunity to reinforce English identity.[9] The Indians served as proxies for the different native peoples within the British Empire. Their treatment under American strategies of expansion and control contrasted with imperial policy. This was perhaps most noticeable, Flint suggested, during Cody's first visit in 1887.

Buffalo Bill's Wild West Show's first venture outside the United States was only a little more than a decade after Custer's defeat at Little Big Horn; the Plains Indians were still being subdued. Geronimo's capture in 1886 could be characterised as a current event. Buffalo Bill's show emphasised the necessity of controlling and civilising the Indian, and Britons could see this as analogous to their responsibility in the empire. But they also could use this, Flint contended, to draw a line between the methods of Americans and those of the British, particularly in Canada. Whereas British identity meant making a measured and appropriate response to opposition from native groups, American identity was often seen as undisciplined and vengefully violent. Furthermore, by the time of Cody's final European tours in 1903–4, where spectacle had replaced verisimilitude, his showmanship was seen as typical of American sales practices, which Britons viewed as somewhat troubling. Flint's exploration of Buffalo Bill's influence on the British public's relationship with the American western suggests that it should be seen as a very direct connection, one that was enriched by Britain's attitude towards the United States as a former colony. This point was powerfully made by Louis S. Warren's forensic examination of Cody: *Buffalo Bill's America*.[10] Warren challenged the contemporary American interpretation of the first London tour as a triumph because Queen Victoria had 'bowed' to the American flag during a command performance. This was trumpeted as her first appearance since her widowhood in 1861, and her 'bow' entered the mythology of both the Wild West Show and the American rise to power as Britain's recognition of America's new status.[11] After demonstrating that Queen Victoria regularly held command performances, Warren noted that her acknowledgement of the flag may not have taken place. If it did, it might have been sparked by its musical accompaniment, the satiric 'Yankee Doodle Dandy', which Britain had employed to ridicule its opponents during the Revolutionary War.[12] He suggested that the British interpretation was rather different, seeing the show in more neutral terms, as an example of the 'regeneration of the Anglo-Saxon race on the American frontier'.[13] The American western thus functions as an alternative narrative to British history, one that is rooted in many of the same traditions. The western's popularity was enhanced by this shared past, but it was also reinforced by the large numbers of British subjects who continued to migrate there.[14] The western, then, is a cultural artifact of the interwoven history of Britain and America.

Buffalo Bill's Wild West Show was not unique in offering the American west to the British for their cultural consumption. It was helped by the ubiquity of the western tale in the best-selling genre fiction of writers like Owen Wister and Zane Grey, the creation of the popular character of 'Hopalong Cassidy' by Clarence E. Mulford in 1904, and in early cinema. Movies, of course, have been seen as one of the primary sites of Americanisation in the twentieth century as Hollywood's fare was widely sold around the globe.[15] Cowboy films, by virtue of their action and their simple stories of good guys and bad guys, were popular worldwide. Although they quickly became more popular in rural areas in the United States because of the simplicity of their narratives, they also sold well in other global settings. The stories were easily understood, and in the silent era were not hampered by the need for proper accents or multiple title cards. By the 1920s and 1930s they were used systematically to draw juvenile viewers into the cinema-going habit. Special screenings for children on Saturdays regularly included cowboy movies, and after the coming of sound, singing cowboys drew girls to the genre as well as boys.[16] The link between Britain and North America was reinforced in the Amalgamated Press boys' story paper *Wild West Weekly*, which was launched in 1939.[17] The tales often mimicked the cinema, but also created their own stock characters in the vein of the Lone Ranger. Each issue serialised the novelisation of a recent cinematic western and included complete tales. Additionally, bits of western history were included – for example, recounting the history of the Pony Express. Importantly, there were tales of the Canadian West, reinforcing this important imperial link. General interest boys' story papers also included western tales. D. C. Thompson's *The Wizard*, probably one of the most widely read papers of the period, regularly sent its British heroes to visit the American frontier where they aided the process of settling the west. One series of stories featured 'Thick Ear Donovan', a British schoolmaster who tames a class of American schoolboys in Poison Valley, where 'in the little cemetery behind the school lay the remains of half a dozen school teachers who had been bumped off'.[18] Donovan brings order to the town by basically acting as sheriff. Thompson's papers frequently used the western setting for its stories and always treated its American inhabitants as in need of taming and guidance.[19] The reading of westerns was not confined to youngsters, however. In his 1931 'Hop-Picking' diary, George Orwell noted that 'down and out people seem to read exclusively from books of the Buffalo Bill type. Every tramp carries one of these, and they have a type of circulating library, all swapping books when they get to the spike.'[20]

Comedic western films relied on audiences' knowledge of cultural stereo-types in drawing humour from prospecting in films like Charles Chaplin's *The Gold Rush* (1925), Buster Keaton's *The Paleface* (1922), or *Go West!* (1925). In an era when all films needed to be suitable for all audiences, the western appealed to adults more through spectacle by the mid-1920s. John Ford's *The Iron Horse* (1924) celebrated the building of the transcontinental railway, while Raoul Walsh's remarkable early talkie, *The Big Trail*, employed wide-screen and location shooting to depict antebellum western migration. But the western as a mature cinematic art form did not really emerge until 1939 with the appear-ance of John Ford's *Stagecoach*, which introduced cinema-goers to the beauties of Monument Valley.[21] The maturation process speeded up in the post-war years with more depth from Ford, but also in films from Howard Hawks, Sam Fuller, Fred Zinnemann, Anthony Mann, Budd Boetticher and many others. Many of these films featured a psychological complexity unseen in earlier works.[22]

It was inevitable that this genre would transfer to the small screen and the 1950s was the period when more television westerns were broadcast than at any other time. In the United States the astute cowboy actor William Boyd recognised the coming popularity of television and purchased the rights to the name of the character he played on the big screen and all of the films he had appeared in. The re-edited Hopalong Cassidy films were amongst the earliest hits on American television. New productions, now tailored for televi-sion, were filmed. Similarly shrewd cowboy actors Gene Autry and Roy Rogers (who both also sang) transformed themselves from B-movie actors to television stars. All three produced their own television series that played for decades in syndication.[23] They also adeptly exploited their screen personas with licens-ing deals, public appearances and clear-eyed visions of exactly what they were selling and to whom. Amongst others, *The Lone Ranger* emerged out of radio, where it enjoyed immense popularity from its creation in 1933. As well as defining a certain kind of American attitude that prefigured unilateralism, it boasted a regular Native American character in Tonto, memorably played by the Canadian Mohawk actor Jay Silverheels.[24] Also notable in the immediate post-war period was the adaptation of the Mexican caballero, the Cisco Kid, into the first Hispanic hero on American television. Unusually, this series was filmed in colour in a period when all television broadcasts were in black and white.[25] Another odd thing to note about the juvenile westerns was that they were not all set in the old west, and many had, if not quite a contemporary feel, modern features like airplanes (*Sky King*, 1951–62), jeeps (Roy Rogers' side-kick Pat Brady's 'Nellybelle'), and, of course, telephones for communication and radio for the singing cowboys to perform on. Stories were liable to focus on bankers trying to foreclose on worthy ranchers, which probably owed more to the recent economic depression in the 1930s than to the settling of a newly opened frontier. These shows would soon be joined by dozens more westerns as the studios recognised their profit potential and that an adult audience also appreciated the genre.

By the mid-1950s, with the crystallisation of American television into a set of rigidly scheduled national broadcasters, the adult western had been created. *Gunsmoke* had originally been devised for radio (1952–61), but its television version ran for a record twenty years, from 1955 to 1975.[26] These new dramas were not as simplistic as their cinematic ancestors, but sought to reflect some of the complexity achieved in recent flicks. They aimed to examine different aspects of westward expansion. *Wagon Train* (1957–62) explored the reasons why different groups and individuals made the journey. *Rawhide* (1959–65) depicted the role of the cowboy driving cattle to market. Anthology series like *Death Valley Days* (1952–75) shifted emphasis from week to week but filmed on location in Death Valley, California. *Have Gun, Will Travel* (1957–62) followed a gentleman gunfighter for hire on his travels around the west. *Sugarfoot* (1957–61) practised law, *Frontier Doctor* (1958–59) cured folks and *Frontier Circus* (1961–62) entertained isolated audiences. *Bonanza* (1959–73) was a family saga set in Nevada near Lake Tahoe just after the Civil War. Dozens more variations on these themes were evident in the other westerns that emerged in this period.[27]

The American high-water mark was reached in 1959 when twenty-six separate westerns were scheduled for evening viewing each week. Not all of these were shown in Britain, but the western was a central part of both BBC and commercial television schedules in these years. Although both broadcasters restricted the amount of imported programming shown, the western was the most popular genre purchased for broadcast. In order to appreciate its popularity it is necessary to explore the context in which early British television schedules were created, as well as the philosophies behind the creation of both public-service and commercial television in Britain.

Regularly broadcast television came to Britain earlier than anywhere else in the world, with the BBC providing daily viewing to the London area from 1936 until the declaration of war in 1939.[28] As with its senior service, radio, it provided education, information and entertainment to the small group of viewers wealthy enough to own a television set. After the war it recommenced broadcasting in 1946 with few changes. It was committed to live broadcasting, and most of the accounts of British television are hindered by this fact, as little of the programming has survived. Television funding came out of the monies received by the BBC from the collection of an annual tax on radio and television ownership.[29] The amount of money spent on the television service was low in the immediate post-war years, focused on the live dramas, talks programmes, musical interludes and outside broadcasts which made up the bulk of the four to six transmission hours per day. The emphasis on live broadcasts echoed radio broadcasting but also reflected the high cost of using filmed material. Neither filming nor, eventually, video-recording could be afforded in more than a very restricted number of programmes.

In the mid-1950s, a second channel was launched in Britain.[30] This channel was split between several regional broadcasters and was funded by commercials. Much of the discussion preceding its launch centred on the amount of foreign content which it would be permitted to broadcast. This question had not arisen when the BBC was the lone source of television because it was clearly dedicated to the creation rather than the importation of content. But by the mid-1950s, American television was beginning to crystallise as an industry and its salesmen were urging British commercial broadcasting to import the latest American television hits.[31] In order to alleviate worries about foreign product dominating the British market, the independent television companies agreed to limit foreign programming to fourteen per cent. The BBC, although not required by law to do so, said it would also adhere to this restriction. This appeased most of the critics, many of whom were animated by the possibility of lost jobs for British performers and technicians if imported filmed entertainment crowded out British productions. American programming was often belittled, which was not unexpected at a time when the rise of television was making the cinema seem under threat and the economic health of Britain was under pressure.[32]

From 1948, westerns began to enter the British schedules. This happened in several phases. First, feature-length westerns began to be broadcast. In the earliest years, these were mainly programmers, the B-films which occupied the lower half of a bill and might feature a character whose adventures were retold in a series of films. These can be seen as the precursors to television series. The second phase began with the broadcasting of made-for-television series set in the west but aimed at a juvenile audience. This second group was increasingly confined to the Children's Television slot before 6 p.m. At the launch of independent television in 1955, several of these series would be seen on the new channel as well. The third phase comprised the new made-for-television 'adult' westerns. Appearing on both the BBC and independent television, they entered the weekly schedules in 1955, with more and more being introduced during the rest of the decade. Finally, there were adult westerns made for the cinema. They were transmitted sparingly and were generally shown on holidays, when most people might be able to enjoy them. Each group will be discussed below.

A peek at the television schedules up to the end of the 1950s reveals that British-originated shows predominated but that an increasing number of American shows were being transmitted, especially after the launch of independent television in 1955. Comedies, thrillers and current affairs all appeared, but the most popular genre throughout this entire period was the western. But this enthusiasm did not begin suddenly with the opening of the second network. Its roots lay in the programming choices made at the BBC in the late 1940s. Although the schedulers have left no indication about why they chose the films they did, it is apparent that the western ticked several boxes. They were suitable entertainment for both adults and children. They reflected a certain type of moral universe where good triumphed over evil. They were cheap to acquire and fitted comfortably into schedules.

On the afternoon of 15 January 1948, the BBC home audience was offered *Fighting Mad*, a film starring James Newill as Sargeant Renfrew of the Royal Canadian Mounted Police. Its setting on the border allows crimes initiated in America to be resolved in Canada by the hero, a singing Mountie. Reflecting the American film industry's desire to sell films beyond its national borders (and perhaps the recent popularity of the Canadian-set *Rose-Marie* starring Jeannette MacDonald and Nelson Eddy), the plots and the story of establishing order on the frontier put the Renfrew films clearly at the centre of the western film tradition. Made in 1937 by Grand National Pictures, this was the third of seven Renfrew movies filmed between 1937 and 1940. By the end of 1952 these seven films were screened forty-four times in total and had become a staple of afternoon television. But they were not alone. The more conventional cowboy film became a regular feature in the schedules for the next few years. Renfrew was quickly joined by Tex Ritter, Tom Keene, Ken Maynard, George O'Brien and the Range Busters, which featured Ray 'Crash' Corrigan, in 1948 alone. In that year, an examination of the *Radio Times* reveals that fifty-seven slots were filled by westerns.

The introduction of this genre to viewers merited significant coverage in the *Radio Times* and also engendered a flurry of letters in its occasional correspondence columns. At this time the *Radio Times* had a separate television edition which one had to order specially from one's newsagent in order to receive it. Programme listings predominated, and usually four pages were dedicated to listings and short descriptions of new programmes on offer, generally focusing on the plays that week or personalities appearing on variety shows. 'Viewers' Views' appeared only sporadically, often only once a month. Most viewers wrote in to congratulate the BBC on a particular play or programme. There was some debate on the advisability of repeating dramatic productions. While some viewers lamented that this prevented the appearance of other, fresh shows, others were thankful that they could go out some evenings and still see the play from that week. *Renfrew*, unusually, received two columns in April and June signalling its popularity.[33]

Of more interest, perhaps, was the correspondence that emerged around cowboy films. The first thing to note is that these were certainly not the westerns from masters of the genre like John Ford, but humble programmes which had been made to fill out bills and had always been perceived as more popular with kids, in rural areas, and in the United States. They emerged from production companies like Monogram and their stories were simple morality tales with clear demarcation of the good guys and the bad guys. Although their appearance on weekday and Sunday afternoons clearly indicates that they targeted a young audience, these films had a broader appeal. In September George Bentley of Addlestone in Surrey wrote in to complain: 'Why do you always put cowboy films on in the afternoon when most people are at work? I personally think they are among the best shows you put on – a proper's man's show. As I like some good riding and shooting I should like to see the films in the evening.'[34] Two weeks later, five more letters appeared on the topic, each agreeing that an evening slot would be welcome, although one viewer made the request because he worked nights and had no desire to watch them as they were 'a disgrace to a man's intelligence'.[35] More letters arrived in subsequent editions on both sides of the debate, but what became clear was that the cowboy film had become a staple of the service.

In 1949 Hopalong Cassidy, Buck Jones and Bob Steele joined the others, as well as a twelve-part serial featuring Rin-Tin-Tin and Rex the Wonderhorse, while the Christmas holiday serial was the sixteen-part *Custer's Last Stand*. In 1949 fifty-two cowboy films or serials were shown, but the numbers halved in 1950 to twenty-six, fluctuating at around that number for the next few years. The cowboy film was a staple of early television, due to its availability, its relatively short length of around an hour and the generally uncontroversial nature of its content at the time. Only one letter in 1949 in the *Radio Times* voiced any disquiet about its suitability and its 'distinctively bad influence' on children.[36] However, the BBC continued to include westerns as part of their weekly schedule. In 1950, Hopalong Cassidy appeared more than any other star but was joined by, amongst others, Richard Arlen, Ricardo Cortez and George O'Brien. Laurel and Hardy's *Way Out West* (1937) was also screened for the first time. By 1952, the Rangebusters and Tex Ritter enjoyed multiple showings, while in 1953 a new group of Hopalong Cassidy movies entered the schedules. Almost everything was repeated a couple of times, so viewers had ample opportunity to see each programme. *The Cisco Kid* dominated the schedules in 1954. This Hispanic hero had been created by O. Henry in 1907 as an outlaw, but on screen, in movies and television as well as on radio, he was translated into a Mexican caballero. In 1928, Warner Baxter won the Best Actor Oscar in this role in the film *In Old Arizona*. Television's Cisco Kid, Duncan Reynaldo, had appeared in the role on the big screen as well and was one of the few examples of a non-Anglo-Saxon cowboy hero. The Cisco Kid programmes were made for television, as was the Range Rider series that also began to screen that year. All of these shows were made in the United States.

The frontier story was so popular that in 1954 the BBC took the unusual step of commissioning and producing its own American frontier drama, the five-part *The Cabin in the Clearing*, which was adapted by Felix Felton and Susan Ashman from a novel by Edward Sylvester Ellis. First published in 1899, it was subtitled a 'Tale of the Frontier' and aimed at the youth market. Set in Wyoming, it has all the excitement of living on the edge of civilisation and centres on survival in the face of opposition from the local Indian tribe. The BBC's adaptation was performed live, and therefore no longer exists, but the excitement of the production was recalled in an oral history interview with Dame Peggy Mount, who remembered the scene when the Indians were encircling the cabin and shooting flaming arrows at it. The fire extinguishers failed to control the blaze so the actors had to soldier on.[37] The production was revived with a new cast in 1959 and again performed live. That it was chosen for production demonstrates how BBC children's television producers looked beyond Britain's shores for tales to televise, and with this drama they tapped into the popularity of westerns.[38] However, the western that was to dominate both the BBC and commercial television were the cowboy series created specifically for the new technology.

The western's popularity was such that when commercial television began to broadcast, there was no question that these series would be included. Unsurprisingly, the first two appeared in the late afternoon slot aimed at children, although with the hope that parents might be watching as well. On the first Sunday of commercial broadcasts, viewers were offered *The Roy Rogers Show*, which had been shot for US television from 1951 onward. Directly followed by what would become the popular *Adventures of Robin Hood*, it offered an hour of viewing for the entire family. The made for television *Hopalong Cassidy* programmes inhabited a similar slot on Thursday afternoons throughout the autumn.[39] On Saturday, 7 December 1955 they were joined by the first episode of *Gun-Law* (better known as *Gunsmoke* in the United States). Initially, it would be shown weekly on Saturday nights. Although the night of broadcast changed, it was a weekly part of the viewing schedule for many years. The drama had premiered in the United States only in September and was the first 'adult' western on American television. It was pitched at an adult audience and had a nine o'clock transmission time in Britain, clearly not a time when kids were meant to watch. Although when viewed today it seems less than complex, it was bringing to the small screen some of the themes masters like Ford and Hawks had begun to explore in their own pictures. It even hinted at sexual matters, and the violence was more lethal. Over the next few years, the adult television western blossomed, and these shows were not ignored by British programmers. They were popular in the United Kingdom as well as the United States. By 1958, *Gunsmoke/Gun-Law* had been joined by former BBC shows *Hopalong Cassidy*, *The Cisco Kid* and *Rin-Tin-Tin* for the kids and *Zane Grey Theatre* and *Cheyenne* for adults. Over the years many of the popular American television westerns would grace British small screens. In April 1956 commercial television added *The Adventures of Rin-Tin-Tin* to its late Wednesday afternoon line-up. The marketing of these westerns was enhanced by personal appearances. Both Gene Autry and Roy Rogers reinforced their popularity by appearing on live children's television programmes. The latter made an appearance on an ITV Christmas Day live broadcast from Paddington Green's Children's Hospital. A few months later, he sponsored a nationwide road-safety contest whose finale was broadcast live on Sunday, 22 April 1956.

The BBC did not concede the genre entirely to its new rival. Almost immediately it began weekly showings, generally on a Friday afternoon, of one of the most popular westerns of the period, *The Lone Ranger*. Unlike the singing cowboys Autry and Rogers, who dominated their competitors' schedules, *The Lone Ranger* was explicitly set in the period of westward expansion. The hero had been a Texas Ranger who had been in a posse betrayed by a renegade Indian. Discovered half-alive by Tonto, he is nursed back to health and vows to secretly work for justice. Unlike a vigilante, he forswears killing and always turns criminals over to the nearest sheriff for trial and punishment. In his exploration of this moral world, analyst John Shelton Lawrence isolated the qualities *The Lone Ranger* embodies. These include its 'bipolar moral world' of starkly defined good and evil, and the projection that the hero is licensed to take up his crusade due to his initial experience, which was his 'call to destiny'. Furthermore, Lawrence explored the way the 'supremacy of the caucasian male' is underlined by Tonto's continued subordinate position, signalled by his failure to master the English language. In terms of its importance as an inspiration for Americans, the Lone Ranger emerges only when required by the failure of institutions, where he generally works in secret in response to evil, always successful in a way proportionate to the challenge he has faced.[40] Lawrence's analysis focused on the importance of the character for adult Americans, especially in terms of foreign policy. Whether British viewers imbibed the same lesson is questionable. John Cawelti's interpretation of the figure's appeal took a Freudian approach as he examined its potency for an adolescent audience. For him, 'the Western expresses the conflict between the adolescent's desire to be an adult and his fear and hesitation about the nature of adulthood.' This hinges on the hero's ability to step in and out of his role (by use of the mask), his fight against corrupt powers like greedy bankers, and his success at punishing and exposing evildoers, while holding himself apart from society. Cawelti wondered: 'is [it] stretching it too much to suggest that [the hero riding into the distance] evokes a childish wish to be free to spurn parental love as something no longer needed? In short, to be a Lone Ranger means to escape from the restrictiveness and helplessness of childhood without incurring any sense of guilt or adult responsibility.'[41] Although this undoubtedly overstated the potency of the Lone Ranger, it suggests that westerns were consumed as moral tales in a way that transcended national boundaries.

Clearly, the adult television western did not have a simple, well-defined message, but its increasing popularity in these years also needs attention. On commercial television, *Gun-Law* was soon joined by *Frontier Doctor* in 1956 and the UK/Canadian co-production *Hawkeye and the Last of the Mohicans*, Dick Powell's *Zane Grey Theatre*, and *The Sheriff of Cochise* in 1957. The following year, they were supplemented by *Wagon Train*, *Cheyenne*, *The Grey Ghost* (set during the American Civil War on the western frontier), *The Life and Legend of Wyatt Earp*, and *The Sheriff of Cochise*. Meanwhile children's television had been supplemented with *Brave Eagle*, *Buffalo Bill, Jr.*, *Annie Oakley*, *Steve Donovan Western Marshal*, and *The Cisco Kid*, as well as the animal hero stories

The Adventures of Rin-Tin-Tin and *Fury*. Not to be outdone, the BBC broadcast *Champion the Wonder Horse* in their late afternoon slot, and added *Wells Fargo* to their Saturday evening schedule. During the last full week of August 1958 only Tuesdays featured no western adventure. A devotee of the genre could have seen *Wyatt Earp*, *The Sheriff of Cochise*, *Wagon Train*, *Rin-Tin-Tin*, *The Lone Ranger*, *The Grey Ghost*, *The Cisco Kid*, *Gun-Law* [*Gunsmoke*], *Boots and Saddles*, and *Cheyenne*. In 1959 both the BBC and commercial television added more westerns to their schedules: *Frontier*, *Maverick*, *Have Gun – Will Travel*, *Bronco*, *Rawhide*, *The Deputy*, *Tombstone Territory*, *Union Pacific* and *Laramie*. Almost all were added to evening viewing and the earlier westerns were only occasionally alternated with them or withdrawn.[42]

That these programmes were popular is not disputed. In 1956 Associated Television took out a full-page advertisement in *The Times* to attract advertisers that mentioned the high viewing figures for both Roy Rogers and *Gun-Law*.[43] Playing cowboys and Indians does not seem to have diminished in this period. If anything, Graham Dawson suggested it increased, fed by the imagery offered on screen. Writing about the formation of masculinity in the twentieth century, he saw the American cavalry officer as another candidate to join the repertory of pretend figures that boys might imagine themselves to be. This was reinforced by the addition of American armies to the array of toy soldiers offered by British manufacturers. Dawson confided that he 'dressed up and imagined [himself] as a cowboy, a cavalier, a US cavalryman and a Second World War British commando'.[44] He described at length (and shared pictures of) his appearance in cowboy hats and explained how this proceeded to more elaborate costumes until he gave them up as a teenager. Dawson's engagement with the Wild West was part of his quest to become a man, to understand masculinity. At no time did he suggest that the western encouraged him to become an American. It was simply another narrative of growing up.[45] Other authorities echoed this. A *Times* editorial in 1952 noted that research suggested that cowboy films had 'a psycho-therapeutic effect on the mind' for all boys, rejecting the recent worries about their suspected 'subversive' influence.[46]

Other events also underline the continued popularity of the genre. Although Buffalo Bill was long gone, Wild West Shows continued to circulate around Britain. *The Times* reviewed one at Haringey in 1952, which it opined would 'delight the heart of every small boy'.[47] In 1958, Hugh O'Brian, star of the *Wyatt Earp* television programme, was the central attraction at a less well-reviewed show at the Odeon in London's Tottenham Court Road. Knife-throwing and singing were more in evidence than horses at the latter,

which *The Times* characterised as 'unfocused'.[48] By far the greatest phenomenon which touched on the genre was the craze sparked by the wide release
of Walt Disney's *Davy Crockett, King of the Wild Frontier* in 1956. The marketing machine shifted into gear and Davy's coonskin cap became the must-have
item in Britain as in other parts of the world. In Derby, it was reported that
cats were being hunted for their pelts in order to fashion a homemade cap, and
on the Welsh borders a housing dispute led to taunts to the tune of the Davy
Crockett theme song.[49] The hit song spread around the world with youngsters everywhere making it their own.[50] Crockett's popularity was worrying to
some. *The Times* triumphantly reported that Hackney Libraries Committee
had detected a clear preference of young British readers for Robin Hood over
Davy Crockett. Three days later, an editorial trumpeted: 'it is good to hear that
[Hackney's] young clients patriotically prefer Robin Hood to the American
hero Davy Crockett.'[51] Although the American hero did enter the pantomime
repertoire that Christmas in a production of *The Adventures of Davy Crockett* at
the Queen's Theatre, Hornchurch, it has not remained there.[52]

With the increasing spread of commercial television, fears about the negative influence of the western simmered, but the worries were generally within
the context of more generalised fears about television's influence which were
echoed by elites in other countries, including the United States.[53] Perhaps the
most perspicacious commentator was F. S. Milligan, chairman of the National
Advisory Committee on Television Group-viewing, who noted that 'it might
need a new generation before the social implications of television were fully
realized'.[54] Perhaps the most telling testimony of the popularity of the western
came during the General Election in October 1959, when the Labour Party
unsuccessfully argued that the evening's transmission of *Rawhide* be cancelled
as it would almost certainly tempt voters to skip going to the poll. As Labour
voters generally voted after work, the Party feared it would affect them neg-
atively. Although Labour lost, a review of the figures did not support their
analysis.[55]

The bulk of this chapter has focused on the television offerings of the early
post-war period, but other cinematic westerns did appear. They were very rare,
not because of their subject matter or unpopularity but because up until the
end of the 1950s, the film studios and distributors withheld their recent and
most popular films from television transmission. Nevertheless, some popular,
critically lauded westerns were among the handful of films transmitted. *Stage-
coach* (1939), which is seen as a turning point for the western in its treatment of adult themes, was shown twice in 1956, including on Christmas Eve.

High Noon (1952) played on Christmas Eve 1959. Other less well-known but critically lauded westerns were also occasionally screened. Few other Academy-Award nominated films had been shown by this time, the exceptions being some of Katherine Hepburn's or Fred Astaire's films from the mid-1930s, which came as part of a deal to acquire the RKO library. Despite difficulties in the industry, the western continued to be a preferred choice for programmers.

What was the significance of this, especially in a period of international unsteadiness when the Cold War was residing in the background of many of the debates on British cultural strength? The inclusion of American television programmes on British television, but especially westerns, reinforced certain ideas about the ties between Britain and the United States. Many of these shows made explicit links between the two nations, often depicting them as cousins. This was made most explicit on the programme *Maverick* when Roger Moore joined the cast as the English cousin of the stars.[56] But other shows also peppered their episodes with British characters, even if their accents were not always quite believable. This was a cultural reinforcement of the 'special relationship' between the nations, which mirrored national efforts to strengthen this tie. In the United States it may have reflected the familiarity many servicemen had gained with their British cousins in the late war, but these programmes underlined the similarities rather than the differences between the two nations. Other television series imported into Britain also stressed some of the same commonalities, but the western also had the advantage of being set outside the present day. For British audiences it recalled a time when adventurous men explored and settled the world outside Europe. In an age when the British empire was shrinking, British home-grown series turned to historical heroes from myth, fact and fiction, from Robin Hood and Prince Valiant to the Scarlet Pimpernel. These tales were not set in the further reaches of the British Empire as these were now problematic places. The American western offered a place where viewers could more easily fantasise about the conquest of new worlds. Indeed, the British would make two westerns for the big screen in the next few years. First came *The Sheriff of Fractured Jaw* (1958), starring Kenneth More as an Englishman who is accidentally appointed sheriff of a rough town whose major asset is saloon owner Jayne Mansfield. Although this was a comedy, it was directed by one of the masters of the western, Raoul Walsh. The second was *Carry On Cowboy* (1966), illustrating the deep engagement of British audiences with the western as it lampoons them all.

In the great debates emerging in the 1950s about Americanisation, the western did not seem to offer much harm. In some ways it was too late for that, as tales of the frontier had been popular for well over one hundred years. The cowboy was also emblematic of youth culture, and it did not seem a bad idea for the children of the 1950s to be allowed to enjoy what their fathers had liked a generation earlier on cinema screens. These simple tales for kids and more challenging ones for adults, tales that often dealt with questions about the treatment of native Americans or the corrupting power of big business, offered a place where ethical issues could be weighed up. They were also part of a transatlantic culture that, with the constant improvement of communications and travel, would continue to cross-fertilise. As the film historian Roger Manvell noted in an essay entitled, 'How Deep Does American Influence Go?': 'America and Britain remain totally different countries, as any visitor from one to the other will see almost immediately.'[57] The western is just a small part of the story of how both cultures thrived and grew.

Notes

1 Unsigned review, 'The Wild West: Cowboys and Red Indians at Harringay', *The Times*, 28 July 1952, 8.

2 Victoria de Grazia, *Irresistible Empire: America's Advance Through Twentieth-Century Europe* (Cambridge, MA: Belknap Press of Harvard University, 2005) and Richard Pells, *Not Like Us: How Europeans have Loved, Hated and Transformed American Culture since World War II* (New York: Basic Books, 1997). Both persuasively demonstrate the extent to which Europe has resisted Americanisation in the twentieth century.

3 John G. Cawelti, *Adventure, Mystery and Romance: Formula Stories as Art and Popular Culture* (Chicago, IL: The University of Chicago Press, 1976), 193; some of these ideas are also developed in his earlier *The Six-Gun Mystique* (Bowling Green, OH: Bowling Green University Press, 1975).

4 Carroll Smith Rosenberg, 'Davey Crockett as Trickster: Pornography, Liminality and Symbolic Inversion in Victorian America', *Journal of Contemporary History* 17 (1982): 325–50; Mark Derr, *The Frontiersman: The Real Life and Many Legends of Davy Crockett* (New York: William Morrow, 1993); Mandy Merck, 'Davy Crockett', *History Workshop Journal* 40 (Autumn 1995): 185–9; J. Fred MacDonald, *Who Shot the Sheriff? The Rise and Fall of the Television Western* (New York: Praeger, 1987), 39–43.

5 See 'The Western: A Look at the Evolution of a Formula', Ch. 8, in Cawelti, *Adventure, Mystery, Romance*.

6 Christopher Frayling, *Spaghetti Westerns: Cowboys and Europeans from Karl May to Sergio Leone* (1980; repr., London: I. B. Tauris, 2006).

7 Sarah J. Blackstone, *Buckskins, Bullets, and Business: A History of Buffalo Bill's Wild West* (New York: Greenwood, 1986); Alan Gallop, *Buffalo Bill's British Wild West* (Stroud: Sutton, 2001); Louis S. Warren, *Buffalo Bill's America* (New York: Alfred A.

Knopf, 2005); Tom F. Cunningham, '*Your Fathers the Ghosts': Buffalo Bill's Wild West in Scotland* (Edinburgh: Black and White), 2007.

8 Robert W. Rydell and Rob Kroes, *Buffalo Bill in Bologna: The Americanization of the World, 1869–1922* (Chicago: Chicago University Press, 2005).

9 Kate Flint, *The Transatlantic Indian, 1776–1930* (Princeton, NJ: Princeton University Press, 2009), esp. 226–55.

10 See 'Wild West London', Ch. 11, in Louis S. Warren, *Buffalo Bill's America: William Cody and the Wild West Show* (New York: Knopf, 2005), 282–339.

11 Gallop, *Buffalo Bill's British Wild West*, 100.

12 Warren, *Buffalo Bill's America*, 286.

13 Warren, *Buffalo Bill's America*, 328.

14 Rowland Tappan Berthoff, *British Immigrants in Industrial America, 1790–1950* (Cambridge, MA: Harvard University Press, 1953), 1–11; Charlotte Erickson, *Leaving England: Essays on British Emigration in the Nineteenth Century* (Ithaca, NY: Cornell University Press, 1994); Colin Pooley and Jean Turnbull, *Migration and Mobility in Britain since the Eighteenth Century* (London: UCL Press, 1998), 275–98; Ian Whyte, 'Migration and Settlement', in Chris Williams (ed.), *A Companion to Nineteenth-Century Britain* (Oxford: Blackwell, 2004), 281–2.

15 There is a large bibliography on the western film, although most of it centres on the adult western from Ford onwards.

16 The singing cowboy had emerged in the first decade of radio. Cowboys, of course, had sung around campfires to entertain themselves, and this music became a durable part of the country music industry. See Douglas B. Green, *Singing in the Saddle: The History of the Singing Cowboy* (Nashville, TN: Country Music Foundation Press, 2002). Peter Stanfield, *Horse Opera: The Strange History of the 1930s Singing Cowboy* (Urbana, IL: University of Illinois Press, 2002), dates the film genre from 1934 to 1956 (p. 1). He argues that westerns were used by the studios to target rural and immigrant filmgoers with their heroes mediating between capital and labour, modernity and tradition, industry and agriculture, urban and rural lifestyles (p. 4). The singing cowboy films retained this formula, but they were also used by the rising music industry to market a more 'benign, respectable *and* modern rural identity than did more vulgar vernacular music styles' (author's italics, p. 5). They and their music especially appealed to women (p. 5).

17 *Wild West Weekly* was published between March 1938 and February 1939 at the price of 2 pence per issue. *Boy's Cinema Weekly* (1919–39) also featured westerns.

18 'Thick-Ear Donovan – Tinhorn Toole', *The Wizard* no. 604 (30 June 1934): 343 and 346–62.

19 For a fuller exploration of some of these themes, see Kelly Boyd, *Manliness and the Boy's Story Paper in Britain: A Cultural History, 1855–1940* (London: Macmillan, 2002),

20 George Orwell, *The Collected Essays, Journalism and Letters of George* Orwell, vol. 1, *An Age Like This, 1920–1940*, ed. Sonia Orwell and Ian Angus (Harmondsworth: Penguin), 76.

21 Kathleen A. McDonough, 'Wee Willie Winkie Goes West: The Influence of the

British Empire Genre on Ford's Cavalry Trilogy', in Peter C. Rollins and John E. O'Connor (eds), *Hollywood's West: The American Frontier in Film, Television, and History* (Lexington, KY: University Press of Kentucky, 2005), 99–114, argues that making a film which focused on the traditions of the British Empire, of loyalty to the sovereign, the army and the imperial mission caused Ford to re-examine the role of the American army in American westward expansion in his Cavalry trilogy: *Fort Apache* (1948), *She Wore a Yellow Ribbon* (1949) and *Rio Grande* (1950). In these films the individualist is no longer the hero, but threatens the larger goal of the taming of the West.

22 The literature on the western in cinema is immense. A good annotated bibliography is provided by Jack Nachbar and Ray Merlock, 'Bibliography – Trail Dust: Books about Western Movies, Selected Classics and Works since 1980', in Rollins and O'Connor (eds), *Hollywood's West*, 322–44.

23 The years of active production and number of episodes made for each were as follows: *Hopalong Cassidy* (1952–54; twenty-six 30-minute episodes; twenty-six 60-minute episodes), *The Gene Autry Show* (1950–55; ninety-one 30-minute episodes) and *The Roy Rogers Show* (1951–57; 100 episodes); all information from Internet Movie Database (www.imdb.com).

24 *The Lone Ranger* starring Clayton Moore appeared from 1949 to 1957. See John Shelton Lawrence, 'The Lone Ranger: Adult Legacies of a Juvenile Western', in Rollins and O'Connor (eds), *Hollywood's West*, 81–96.

25 Christopher H. Sterling and John Michael Kittross, *Stay Tuned: A History of American Broadcasting*, 3rd edn (New York: Lawrence Erlbaum, 2001), 864. As late as 1966, less than ten per cent of American households had colour television.

26 Suzanne Barabas and Gabor Barabas, *Gunsmoke: A Complete History* (Jefferson, NC: McFarland, 1990).

27 Donald H. Kirkley, Jr., *A Descriptive Study of the Network Television Western during the Seasons 1955–56 - 1962–3* (New York: Arno, 1979); Richard Aquila (ed.), *Wanted Dead or Alive; The American West in Popular Culture* (Urbana, IL: University of Illinois Press, 1996); Gary A. Yoggy, *Riding the Video Range: The Rise and Fall of the Western on Television* (Jefferson, NC: McFarland, 1995); Gary A. Yoggy (ed.), *Back in the Saddle: Essays on Western Film and Television Actors* (Jefferson, NC: McFarland, 1998).

28 Asa Briggs, *The History of Broadcasting in the United Kingdom*, vol. 4, *Sound and Vision* (Oxford: Oxford University Press, 1979); Andrew Crisell, *An Introductory History of British Broadcasting* (London: Routledge, 1997); Valeria Camporesi, *Mass Culture and National Traditions: The BBC and American Broadcasting, 1922–1954* (Fucecchio: European Press Academic Publishing, 2000); Tim O'Sullivan, 'Post-War Television in Britain: BBC and ITV', in Michelle Hilmes (ed.), *The Television History Book* (London: British Film Institute, 2003), 30–5.

29 The tax on radio ownership began in 1921, and only ended in 1970. The way the new technology was incorporated into the home is treated in Tim O'Sullivan, 'Television Memories and Cultures of Viewing', in John Corner (ed.) *Popular Television in Britain: Studies in Cultural History* (London: British Film Institute, 1991), 159–81,

and 'Researching the Viewing Culture: Television and the Home, 1946–1960', in Helen Wheatley (ed.), *Re-Viewing Television History: Critical Issues in Television His-toriography* (London: I.B. Tauris, 2007), 159–69. Jack Williams, *Entertaining the Nation: A Social History of British Television* (London: Sutton, 2004) has little to say on this period.

30 Bernard Sendall, *Independent Television in Britain,* vol. 1, *Origins and Foundation, 1946–62* (London: Macmillan, 1982).

31 Kerry Segrave, *American Television Abroad: Hollywood's Attempt to Dominate World Television* (Jefferson, NC: McFarland, 1998).

32 Francis Williams, *The American Invasion* (London: Anthony Blond, 1962), 36–7.

33 Unfortunately, the files at the BBC Written Archive Centre contain no records which discuss the film's broadcast on the BBC. The files focus on BBC-created program-ming, its popularity and the balance between different types of shows. The *Radio Times*, which solicited brief items from the schedulers and programme-makers, is the best source of information on how external programming was integrated into the schedules and the value assigned to them from time to time.

34 'Viewers are Saying, Evening on the Range', *Radio Times* 100/1301 (17 September 1948), 24.

35 'Viewers are Saying, Evening on the Range', *Radio Times* 101/1303 (1 October 1948), 25. The letter is from D. Hurley, Leyton E10.

36 'Viewers are Saying, Rough Stuff for Children', *Radio Times* 102/1322 (11 February 1949), 25. The letter is from E. W. Morris, Palmer's Green N13.

37 Kate Dunn, *Do Not Adjust Your Set* (London: John Murray, 2003), 118–19.

38 Nineteenth-century American novels cropped up regularly as the source of BBC children's productions. Probably the most popular were Louisa May Alcott's, includ-ing, but not limited to, *Little Women*.

39 Weirdly, both the BBC and commercial television screened Hopalong Cassidy shows in the last week of September 1955. At 5.30 p.m. on Thursday, 29 Septem-ber, commercial television broadcast *The Devil's Playground* while the next day the BBC transmitted *Stagecoach War* at 5 p.m. These were feature-length films which continued to play intermittently, particularly on the BBC. By November, commer-cial television had switched over to the made-for-TV fare.

40 Lawrence, 90–1.

41 Cawelti, *Six-Gun Mystique*, 81–3.

42 All information here is drawn from *The Radio Times*, 1946–59, *The TV Times* 1955–59, The TVTimes Project, 1955–85 online database, and *The Times*. I am grateful to the British Film Institute for allowing me access to their printed copies of *The Radio Times* (which contained all of the London television pages in the early days) and *TVTimes*.

43 *The Times*, 22 June 1956, 5. A half-page advertisement with the same information also appeared on 5 July 1956, 9.

44 Graham Dawson, *Soldier Heroes: British Adventure, Empire and the Imagining of Masculinity* (London: Routledge, 1999), 240.

45 Ralph Brauer with Donna Brauer, *The Horse, The Gun and the Piece of Property;*

Changing Images of the TV Western (Bowling Green, OH: Bowling Green University Press, 1975), 30–3, suggested that for American boys watching in the 1950s they were the rough equivalent of the fairy tale. He focused on the way boys could read westerns in two ways, one which underlined moral behaviour, but another which suggested subversive ways of dealing with problems. This book was a meditation on Brauer's attempts to define and understand the genre.

46 'Editorial: The Soothing Six-Shooter', *The Times*, 7 April 1952, 7.

47 'The Wild West: Cowboys and Red Indians at Harringay', *The Times*, 28 July 1952, 8. Harringay is in northeast suburban London.

48 'Wild West Show Lacks Emphasis: Routine Variety Bill', *The Times*, 27 December 1958, 9.

49 'Cats 'Killed for their Skins': Warning on 'Davy Crockett' hats', *The Times*, 9 May 1956, 7; 'Feud on the Welsh Border: Taunts to the Tune of Davy Crockett', *The Times* 27 April 1956, 6. The housing dispute was about differential rents imposed by Abergavenny Rural District Council, and the alderman taunted was a supporter of the unpopular measure.

50 Iona and Peter Opie, *The Lore and Language of Schoolchildren* (1959, repr. New York: New York Review of Books, 2001), 6–7 and 118–20.

51 'Children Tiring of Science Fiction: Staunch Support for Robin Hood', *The Times* 6 November 1956, 6; 'Editorial; Robin Beats Davy', *The Times*, 9 November 1956, 11.

52 'Review: Queen's Theatre, Hornchurch [Essex]: '"The Adventures of Davy Crockett"', *The Times*, 24 December 1956, 10. The review was very positive, and the cast included an Oxonian Indian chief!

53 'Television Competitors for the Child's Attention: Need to Safeguard a Suggestible Audience', *The Times*, 8 October 1958, 6, outlines fears in America. 'Television's Impact on Taste, Habits, and Politics: Mr Mayhew Lists His Four "Failings" of Commercial Service', *The Times*, 16 October 1958, 2, summarises Christopher Mayhew, MP's speech to the National Council on Social Services. Under a subheading 'Pleasure in Cowboys' the chair, Sir John Wolfenden, admitted that 'he did not mind seeing his own television screen "littered with dead cowboys." It was what Aristotle might have called "one of the purest of pleasures" (Laughter).'

54 'Television's Impact on Taste', *The Times*, 16 October 1958, 2.

55 Joseph Trenaman and Denis McQuail, *Television and the Political Image: A Study of the Impact of Television on the 1959 General Election* (London: Methuen, 1961), 94–5. See also Lawrence Black, *The Political Culture of the Left in Affluent Britain: Old Labour, New Britain?* (London: Palgrave, 2003), 167–9, to see the thinking behind the Labour Party's worries.

56 Moore replaced James Garner in the third season. Sean Connery also tested for the part. See Roger Moore, *My Word is My Bond* (London: Michael O'Mara Books, 2008), 141; Michael Feeney Callan, *Sean Connery: His Life and Films* (London: W.H. Allen, 1983), 113.

57 Roger Manvell, 'How Deep does American Influence Go?' *The Times*, 22 August 1956, xiv.

6

'The misuse of leisure': football violence, politics and family values in 1970s Britain

BRETT BEBBER

From the late 1960s forward, violence at professional football matches generated concerns about the security of the national pastime, forcing British politicians to attempt to rework the public image of football. Rooted in broad social and economic transformations, football violence could not be easily explained, and produced anxieties about the security of sports spectatorship and leisure generally. Both Labour and Conservative representatives used the budding problem as an opportunity to gain political capital. Casting themselves as protectors of the national working-class sport, members of both parties aimed to ally themselves with local football communities in their constituencies by safeguarding football from the imposition of social violence. In addition, as the problem proliferated across the nation, garnering the attention of the Home Office and the Department of the Environment (DOE), politicians aimed to engender national party favour by restoring order in a supposedly declining and degenerative social milieu. After years of political debate and guidance from both parties, Labour passed the Safety at Sports Grounds Bill in 1975, which directed and subsidised architectural changes to stadiums as a preventative measure against disorder in professional football. Importantly, both parties hoped that attempting to clean up professional football would also promote sports participation on the local level, further mustering popularity for their party's associations with sport and leisure provision generally. Using the Bill as a key moment in government intervention into British leisure, this article reveals how football violence occasioned one of the first acts in the gradual and piecemeal intervention of state regulation in the football industry.

The regulation instituted by the Bill also constituted an early step in a long process of modernisation and commercialisation of professional football. Years before the mandate for all-seated stadiums and the creation of the English Premier League – both substantial moments in football's commercialisation – state agencies couched government intervention as necessary for public security and the future of one of the nation's most popular activities. In order to justify state involvement, both parties romanticised football spectatorship as reminiscent of a more stable period when families attended matches together. Calling on the nostalgia of the immediate post-war period, politicians elevated nostalgia for the 'pre-hooligan' era and promised that football reform would reinstitute watching football as a safe leisure activity for women and children. Thus, the debates engendered by the Bill provide a unique window onto the intersections of state, leisure and family in post-war Britain.

Though several others have discussed the connections between politics and sport, few have understood the ways in which political parties advocated the participation and supportership of football and other forms of leisure as integral to political strategy in the post-war period. Football violence forced politicians to re-evaluate the relationship between leisure and the state. State intervention in sport and leisure has a long history dating back to the medieval period, but the creation of the Central Council of Recreative Physical Training in 1935 was a key moment in the state's provision of leisure for citizens in the twentieth century.[1] Expansion of state funding for leisure, including the creation of the Arts Council in 1946 and the National Parks Commission in 1949, increased in the post-war period as the welfare state attempted to provide opportunities for personal and healthful development.[2] The Wolfenden Committee, established in 1957, also investigated how the government might best expand and develop British sport in light of growing popularity, resulting in recommendations to build a central Sports Council.[3] In addition to provision for sports and leisure participation, the state has also intervened to legislate and protect the social order, as well as to encourage international diplomacy.[4] However, the roles played by the state in developing sport and leisure and regulating them were intimately intertwined. British politicians in the 1970s often perceived the overlap between participation in sports on the local level and the protection of sports spectatorship as a leisurely activity. Assuming both roles allowed them to maintain a close relationship with local voters while also promoting football as emblematic of national values.

In the main, politicians expressed increased interest in football regulation and intervention at moments of perceived decline and crisis, including disasters caused by overcrowding and unstable architecture at stadiums and seasons when violence escalated from the mid-1960s forward. Early reports, like the Shortt report on the first Wembley FA Cup final in 1923 and the Molewyn-Hughes report on the crushing of thirty-three supporters in Bolton in 1946, addressed overcrowding and hinted at future changes in policing. Official inquiries and 'panic-law' legislation became the tools used to convey a sense of seriousness about addressing football violence and the industry generally.[5] For example, the later Popplewell and Taylor inquiries resulted in the transition from terrace spectating to all-seated stadiums in the early 1990s.[6] Though these reports often resulted in drastic changes to the football industry and the experiences of football spectating, these official inquiries lacked specificity and consistently served to assuage public calls for government action. Dozens of official reports and working parties have been commissioned since the emergence of football violence in the mid-1960s, nearly all of which presented safety as the dominant standard, calling for increased punishment and swift justice in a society that increasingly valued law-and-order principles.[7] I contend that the Safety at Sports Grounds Bill, first presented under Edward Heath's Conservative administration and finalised under Labour in 1975, was a key moment in the state intervention of football. Long before Margaret Thatcher labelled disorderly football fans the 'enemy within', both parties staked their claim to protecting British football from the blight of social violence by battling over the Bill that ushered in significant architectural modifications to most stadiums and grounds. Analysis of debates and public discourses surrounding the Bill's long consideration reveals how politicians employed popular public sentiments to justify state intercession in the protection and promotion of leisure.

State intervention increased at a time when the role of football in British society was paradoxical. On the one hand, professional football as an industry was in decline. After the stunning World Cup victory of 1966 concretised football as 'the people's game', declining attendances, dilapidated stadiums and football violence contributed to waning popularity in the 1970s.[8] From 1971 to 1986, Football League attendances dropped from 28.2 million to 16.5 million, and from 4.2 million to 2.5 million between 1964 and 1986 in Scotland.[9] On the other hand, participation in the sport massively increased. Youngsters and adults turned out for weekend clubs in unprecedented numbers, totalling more than 1.5 million participants by 1980.[10] Increased coverage of matches on television and radio, as well as the acceleration of sports coverage in the media, meant that football, 'was probably more pervasive than ever before in British social and cultural life'.[11] It's not surprising that politicians were attracted to intervening in both professional football and ground-level participation and often saw them as components of a common approach to providing leisure.

Most academic studies of football 'hooliganism' have focused on its working-class origins, subcultural connections, interpersonal dynamics, and role in larger macrosociological models.[12] As strong historical and anthropological studies have demonstrated, football violence emerged in the mid-1960s as a result of economic deprivation, working-class community building, and masculine identity formation. Conflicts between rival groups of fans, often sensationalised by the media, were rooted in reclaiming working-class community, aggressive territoriality and club loyalty.[13] Fan antipathies also reflected broader social and cultural changes in postcolonial Britain and became a site for debates about the ethnic and economic framework of the nation.[14] Though a complete review of this literature is not possible here, these researchers have effectively shown how football violence, because of its deep associations with group and ethnic identity, partisan devotion, and resistance to authority, cannot be easily explained or eradicated. Rather than further interrogating fan subjectivities or the group dynamics of social violence, I examine the opportunities football violence presented to British politicians keen to court those interested in watching or participating in football. By emphasising the moral depravity of football violence, condemning it publicly, and casting themselves as the redeemers of British football, Labour and Conservative politicians capitalised on opportunities to gain local and national support for both their parties and themselves. They made use of a deeply embarrassing political problem to present themselves as leaders in promoting safe, family-oriented leisure opportunities for their constituents.

Both parties aggressively incorporated considerations about sport's popularity into their larger discussions of provision of leisure for British citizens. Three main discursive threads emerged, all of which emphasised the primary role of government in imparting security for both participation and spectatorship in football. First, the general promotion of safety featured in government discussions as both parties aimed to position themselves as the providers of a better, reliable form of entertainment in the midst of perceived national degeneration and the threat of social violence. Football violence contributed to ongoing concerns about subcultural youth violence and permissiveness in an era of emerging 'law-and-order' mentalities. Second, government authorities imbued football with import for national and local communities, emphasising its value to working-class Britons. In particular, the Labour party recast football as a form of leisure necessary to industrialised urban life and emphasised their role in defending the national working-class pastime for both local participants and supporters of the professional sport. These ideas reflected a shift from earlier socialist approaches to leisure that emphasised the degenerative effects of mass culture on working-class life, though both groups stressed the idea that leisure offered solace from the industrial working environment.[15] Third, legislators romanticised football as the epitome of family recreation, invoking idealised family entertainment from earlier periods in football's history as evocative of a better future for working-class leisure. The discussion of family values, the promise to protect local football, and assurances to reduce anxieties about youth violence justified government-mandated changes to sports administration and policy. In sum, promoting leisure had become so integrated into parliamentary political culture that elected officials courted votes based on the primacy of sport in Britons' lives and the government's mandate to defend it.

The political uses of sport

In January 1968, shortly after football violence emerged at some London and Scottish clubs, Arthur Davidson (Labour MP for Accrington) commented on the lack of government attention on sport in British society: 'We seldom seem to discuss sport, whether as it affects very young people, or as it affects those of us who are not quite so young. This topic is discussed more than any other by the man in the street, in pubs, and elsewhere, and when people open their newspapers in the morning, the first page that most of them read … is not the front page, but the back one.'[16] Davidson's assessment of the high popularity of sport and the government's infrequent discussion of it was correct. Before the 1960s, government agencies had only intermittent and infrequent interactions with sport.[17]

After England hosted and won the World Cup in 1966, both of the main political parties courted constituencies that valued sport and leisure. Labour representatives, however, more explicitly identified their voters' associations with these recreations. Throughout the 1960s and 1970s they devoted more money to sports funding and recognised the relationship between sports and the working-class backgrounds of the majority of their voters. As leader of the party, Harold Wilson made several attempts to identify himself as an avid lover of football, including joining the England team for its victory celebration on the balcony of the Royal Garden Hotel in London.[18] In 1964, Labour had established the position of Minister of Sport as a Parliamentary Under-Secretary of State to project the party's seriousness about addressing sport as a national institution.[19] The first man Wilson selected for the position was former Football League referee and Birmingham MP Denis Howell. Howell played an exceptional role in the coming debate over football violence, spearheading Labour's effort to reform professional football and promote sport at both local and national levels. Howell understood that 'the followers of sport compose[d] a substantial section of the rank and file of the Labour Party'.[20] In maintaining this relationship with working-class constituencies, Howell wanted to protect supporters at stadiums across the country from the growing threat of football violence. Yet just as important was Labour's continued commitment to funding local sports initiatives that encouraged participation, good health and recreation. To this end, Labour constructed the first Advisory Sports Council to collect information and distribute national funds to local sports initiatives.[21]

Because football violence emerged at a time when both parties began to formalise their approach to sports funding and sports administration, discussions of football spectatorship and funding for sports and leisure through local initiatives often intersected. Prime Minister Harold Wilson acknowledged the need to pursue sport for his working-class voters specifically. In a letter to the Chancellor of the Exchequer, he wrote, 'There is no doubt that those involved in sport are genuinely concerned. Unless we can show that we have some ideas about this the pressure is likely to grow.' Noting that Labour had satisfied middle-class lobbyists calling for greater funding for the arts, he said, 'We have provided more help for the arts where it was also needed, and, as you know, I supported that decision. If we do not show that we have done something for sport, we shall hear the criticism that we have discriminated against the area which is of greatest interest to the majority, including those among who our political support is concentrated.'[22] In fact, many of the debates about funding sport were carried out in the context of funding leisure generally, and politicians often cast arts against sports funding in battles for limited resources. Though neither party wanted to neglect any part of the populace, these discussions were coded with class distinctions as Labour championed sports funding for its working-class voters and the Tories favoured arts funding for its middle-class constituents.

Howell consistently lobbied his own party to recognise the need to support sports initiatives in working-class districts. In one party memorandum he noted that 'a Labour government must deal fairly with sport in relation to the arts'. Noting large discrepancies in the budget he inherited from his Conservative predecessors, he argued, 'It is absurd that the grant to the Sports Council should be only one-third of that to the Arts Council, bearing in mind the number of devotees of these two fields.' Howell concluded by justifying further funding: 'leaving political considerations aside, it is clearly in the *national* interest that the Government should do more to promote sport'. He added, 'In many other countries the Government explicitly recognises the importance of sport in promoting improved health and physical fitness, reducing loss of time at work and above all in making a valuable social contribution to the reduction of hooliganism. There is no doubt that there would be positive benefits to the community in providing increased funds for sport.'[23] For many Labour representatives, sport served a dual purpose. First, it encouraged a healthy vitality for working citizens, preparing them for the physicality of labour and helping them to avoid leave from work that slowed economic production. Such attitudes remained from Victorian perceptions of sport as beneficial activity in preparation for vigorous imperial adventure and industrial administration.[24] Second, sport initiatives could possibly prevent boredom and idleness, the supposed contributors to youth violence in post-war Britain. Thus, funding sports took precedence over the arts for most Labour politicians.

Yet Labour representatives consistently presented sport not only as a conditioning activity but also as a leisurely diversion from the stresses of factory work and deprived urban areas. As a Birmingham representative, Howell was quick to assert sport's therapeutic qualities: 'Those of us who know the large cities are aware of the sort of problems to be found in them. We know all about the misuse of leisure in our society and the lack of facilities for a good leisure service. This is the root cause of much of the difficulty in our urban communities; this is the most pressing of all the needs.'[25] In several debates, Howell used his familiarity with working-class communities to criticise the Opposition, noting that Tories were willing to cut funding for leisure because they failed to appreciate urban deprivation. He remarked that Conservatives did not 'understand the problems in our cities':

> They do not appreciate the problems which face a youngster who comes from an indifferent home with overcrowded conditions and who works, day in and day out, in a factory on the same job. He comes home to enjoy his leisure, and has only the street corner, because there are no adequate leisure facilities in the town. That is the prospect facing millions of young people.[26]

Underlying these comments were the assumptions that idle time for young working-class men often led to outbreaks of social violence, and that the state must be the provider. Alan Lee Williams (Labour MP for Hornchurch) worried about looming decreases in working hours, theorising that unoccupied time led to the recent emergence of football violence: 'It arises from the extra leisure time which young people now have, and which will increase in the years ahead. In spite of the excellent sentiment of the "Back Britain" movement to work an extra half hour a day, as time goes on the working week will be shortened.'[27] Clearly, Labour members correlated sports funding with both stimulation for boredom and release from the stresses of factory life for workers.

Politicians also linked sports funding with the promotion of industrial harmony in other ways. Some Labour officials feared that industrial financiers would only choose British cities as sites for industrial investment if proper leisure and sports funding sustained the labour force. Labour MPs who represented industrial districts also spent time and money recruiting new industrial development to keep their constituents employed. For many, leisure had a role to play in their recruitment. Tom Dalyell, a Scottish Labour member from West Lothian, noted that 'in a development area, I would again say that, in the decision-making of great industrial firms, it really matters whether they think sports facilities and arts facilities will be available for their employees.' He strategised that it was 'a factor in deciding whether to bring industry to an area of under-employment'.[28] Denis Howell used the demand for industrial recruiting to promote his own party's sport agenda. He established a commission of local industrialists to advise the Sports Council on where to invest sports funding to achieve maximum value for investment. Allowing that 'the biggest source of underused sports facilities was in the industrial sports sector', Howell and the commission requested input from local businessmen on how 'industrial facilities should be developed in future, not merely for the use of [their] workpeople, although that would be their prime importance, but also for the benefit generally of the neighbourhood'. Accordingly, Labour justified sports funding as a necessary alternative to work, but also as a crucial factor in recruiting industrial investment. Researching the benefits to both industrialists and local communities would, 'set the pattern for future co-operative efforts needed among all such organizations'.[29]

Clearly, football violence presented a threat to working-class leisure, as politicians also feared that football violence in professional settings could threaten local sports initiatives as the general perception of football and working-class youth soured. In fact, football violence certainly drove down attendance at professional matches as many chose to avoid the growing inconveniences and possible dangers of spectating. Thus, many politicians from both parties worried about the losses of football clubs as principal contributors to economic vitality in their local communities. An Inland Revenue report was requested as part of the research for the upcoming Sports Grounds Bill. It stated that only 16 of 126 clubs avoided financial losses during the 1972/73 season. Forty-three clubs showed losses of between £100,000 and £200,000, another 31 clubs demonstrated losses above £200,000, and all of the clubs accounted for over £17 million in total accrued debt.[30] Most attributed the decline in financial revenue to decreased attendance, a result of increased football violence. Burnley Labour representative Dan Jones said, 'Soccer affords a tremendous amount of therapeutic treatment for our young people, and although we complain, quite properly, about the degree of hooliganism amongst them, I fear that if this sport were to decline or were allowed to drift away through lack of financial support those problems would grow.'[31] Hooliganism not only threatened the reputation of the national sport, it also threatened to remove possibilities for leisure and economic development in local communities.

Conservatives, conversely, defended free-market principles in accounting for the financial circumstances of football clubs. Eldon Griffiths, the Minister of Sport under Edward Heath's Conservative administration from 1970 to 1974 and Howell's chief opponent in debates over leisure funding, 'forecast that, except on gala occasions, there was unlikely to be any return to the record attendances of previous years'. He felt that 'in the longer term football must live with "the sea change taking place in the public's leisure habits". There was a massive shift from spectator sports to participation sports.' Furthermore, 'the size of football gates would increasingly be affected by television, the spread of car ownership, [and] the movement of population from city centres to suburbs.'[32] In competition with other forms of leisure, and in light of the growing anxieties about football violence, football clubs struggled in the early 1970s to contribute to the economic strength of local communities.

Though Labour certainly proved more aggressive in promoting sports provision and the protection of the football industry, some Tories also showed concern. In particular, Griffiths became the mouthpiece for Tory policy on sport, capitalising on the social consensus that sport and security of the football industry benefited British society. In 1973, he recognised that society 'now confront[ed] an explosion of demand for more recreational facilities. Millions of people who were previously content to stay at home, or watch other people play games, [we]re now demanding both the space and the facilities in which to take part in sports themselves'. Tory sports reform centred on the idea that they were responding to increasing demand. But their funding for sports provision was lacking, with bleak prospects for increased expenditure under the harsh economic conditions of the mid-1970s. Griffiths admitted: 'at constant prices our national investment in new sports facilities is still lower in the 1970s than it was in the early 1960s – despite a great leap in demand'. With little money to spend on sports development, Griffiths worried that Britain would provide less for its citizens than its global competitors. Griffiths lamented: 'Compared with our main partners in the EEC and with Japan, the USA and all the main Communist countries, our provision of sports facilities is falling further and further behind.' His report noted that the United Kingdom spent 50p per head of population on sports funding, while Germany, France and the Netherlands spent £1.27, £1.35 and £1.78, respectively.[33] Such concern reflected Griffiths' and other Conservatives' anxiety about remaining competitive in the provision of leisure in shifting economic circumstances.

But Tory apprehensions were fed more by political strategy and potential embarrassment than by well-thought-out approaches to leisure provision and sports participation. In the same report, Griffiths asked, 'Does this really matter? Personally I see no reason why we should strive to keep up with the sporting Joneses … The first responsibility clearly rests with the individual. It is not the duty of the State to pay for people's leisure.' Conservatives feared political embarrassment, often encouraged by Labour members who brought Conservatives' scanty sports funding to light, but would not transgress their party's commitment to individualism and reducing the size of government. Their attention to sports funding was determined by voter interest and increased worries about criminal delinquency related to sports, particularly football violence. Griffiths noted, 'I have little doubt (though no-one can prove it) that in most of our constituents' minds there is an assumed relationship between sport and good health; between more sport and a higher standard of living and education; and between more sport and a counter-attack against boredom, frustration and delinquency. It is a better than average bet that more and better sports provision is what most people want.'[34] For Griffiths and other Conservatives, greater sports funding, and thus greater participation, could potentially conjure perceptions of British prosperity and therefore more votes. More importantly, sport could act as a remedy for a variety of social stresses.

In fact, Conservative discourses frequently aped Labour sentiments when they invoked the idea that sports provision helped to alleviate criminality in urban environments. In a memorandum for consideration by other ministers, and in effort to convince them of the necessity of a meagre £500,000 increase in sports expenditure in 1973, Griffiths reminded his party colleagues, 'Sport promotes physical and mental health; counters boredom and heads off delinquency; and helps engender sound social relationships.'[35] Conservative discourses on sport, though, lacked discussions of benefits specifically for work-ing-class districts and industrial productivity that marked Labour commentary. Instead, Conservative notions of sport as an opportunity for physical and psy-chological relief coincided with perceptions of urban life as damaging and anti-social. Conservatives reinforced these notions by perceiving football violence as the outcome of the growth of boredom and mechanisation in large cities. Most Conservative sport authorities also believed that local sports initiatives could only flourish apart from state intervention. Thus, the Tories refashioned the Sports Council under Royal Charter as a quasi-autonomous agency, ruled by an advisory board of government appointees in 1972.[36] Geoffrey Rippon, Secretary of the State for the Environment, declared at the opening ceremony of new Sports Council facilities, 'It is entirely right that the Sports Council should be an independent body free to make its own executive decisions.' But, he interjected, 'Government can and does encourage the development of sport; something that is good and healthy in a society that needs relief from the over-mechanized and pre-packaged life too many of us have to lead.'[37] Here again, sports participation was perceived as reprieve from automated routines and droning industrialisation which supposedly debilitated urban Britons.

Clearly, the articulations of the functions of sport by each party were patently different, revealing how each perceived its role for their targeted voters. Labour authorities continuously expressed the need for sports participa-tion as preparation and provision for industrial development, as a cohesive and leisurely counterpart to work in labourers' lives. The opportunity to support local professional clubs also provided good recreation and stimulated local eco-nomic vitality. Alternatively, Conservatives communicated that sports, both as welfare provision and as professional entertainment, generally offered physical and mental relief, but were most worried about the public's perception of their unwillingness to get serious about sports provision and football regulation. Such discourses left them prone to public disapproval for not understanding the leisure needs of working-class men and women. In fact, Griffiths worried that Conservatives were at risk of oppositional criticisms that they completely ignored working-class sporting interests, arguing, 'The intrinsic case for such an expanded programme is reinforced by political considerations.' Explicitly recognising the class dimensions of leisure provision, he told his peers, 'There is an impression throughout the country … that the provision which the Government makes for sport, described by some as working men's pleasure, is niggardly compared with the level of grant in aid to the Arts Council, for what some choose to regard as chiefly for middle class benefit.' He also worried that his party's expenditure on sport in the early 1970s paled in relation to its continental counterparts, further weakening his party's position on sport: 'Nor is it possible to escape the very debatable contrasts drawn, to the Government's disadvantage, between this and other countries' levels of public investment in sport, per head of population.' For Griffiths, the answer was slightly more funding, but he faced an uphill battle wresting it from other ministers, making only slight increases to the Sports Council budget over three years.[38] The Conservatives' most assertive intervention into sports issues, though, was the policy advancement on the regulation of football stadiums.

The Safety at Sports Grounds Bill

Though not directly related to sports on the ground level, the Safety at Sports Grounds Bill afforded the opportunity for politicians to appear to safeguard the cherished weekend leisure of sports spectatorship. The Bill was initially the outcome of government investigations into the Ibrox stadium disaster at Glasgow in January 1971, and it followed the Chester Report, which aimed to rectify football's troubled finances. Prime Minister Edward Heath commissioned Lord Wheatley, a Scottish solicitor, to manage the inquiry. The resulting 'Wheatley Report' recorded several failures in architectural design and crowd control, providing an opening for Conservatives to mediate sports policy at an opportune time.[39] But Heath's administration was voted out of office before finalising the Bill, allowing Harold Wilson's Labour administration to further focus their efforts on sports policy. The Bill was ultimately passed in 1975, presenting sports governors with a law-and-order victory in troubling times for sports. State and party documents reveal that not only was the Bill intended to create a stadium licensing scheme and update architectural standards, but it also provided opportunities for politicians to tackle the growing problem of football violence by allowing examinations of club security and policing practices. In the process, both parties jostled to be seen as the protectors of sports recreation and sports spectating in a purportedly declining social milieu. In the end, the Bill also represented the first in a long line of legislative interventions into the football industry, pre-dating later changes to seating accommodation and other commercialising forces. The Bill's recommendations and policy standards represented an early imposition of government power on private sports business in an effort to project a sense of security and stability for the nation's beloved pastime.

The struggle over stadium regulation began with the Ibrox stadium disaster, which encouraged governmental intervention into stadium management at a time when British football, and British society generally, was on the verge of a fiscal crisis. Government officials from both parties had already commissioned several inquiries into the growing problem of football violence and the declining financial state of many British football clubs.[40] But the importance of architectural integrity and crowd management was elevated when a stairwell collapsed at the massive Glasgow stadium, killing 66 and injuring 517 people. After inquiry director Lord Wheatley published his report and suggested that state agencies inspect, recommend, and perhaps fund stadium renovations, Conservatives failed to act in a timely fashion. One Conservative was afraid that 'The Government would be extremely vulnerable if no action were taken on the report and next football season brought another serious accident.'[41] But with ongoing concerns about the final technical proposals and financing details, Conservatives slowly developed the Bill throughout 1972 and 1973 and failed to act decisively through preliminary readings before being voted out of office in March 1974.

The long delay in Conservatives' legislative efforts for stadium improvement can be attributed to a declining economy and a polarised political climate. The development of both government policy on sport and patterns of sport spectatorship were conditioned by these broader economic trends and political debates, and should be understood in this context. Increased economic fluctuations, including the 1973 OPEC oil crisis, continuous social divestment, the devaluation of the pound and high inflation rates left many working Britons with less disposable income and private businesses with lower real profits.[42] The so-called 'golden age of affluence' was already in decline by the late 1960s, and the state slowly sinking into deficit, resulting in Britain requesting an unprecedented $3.9 billion loan from the International Monetary Fund in 1976.[43] Both Labour and Conservative administrations oversaw a drastic decrease in public spending, declines in industrial production, and the overall decay of the British economy during the 1970s. In addition, a falsified yet pervading sense of crisis about youth crime and moral degeneration led to widespread political fervour for the supposed restoration of law-and-order.[44] All of these challenges squeezed the professional football industry and, coupled with the emergence of football violence during the same period, placed football clubs in dire financial circumstances. All but the biggest football clubs faced frightening fiscal insecurity at the same time that the image of British football was marred by youth violence.

Conservatives feared that mandating regulation and stadium modernisation would bankrupt some clubs, compounding their negative reputation amongst some sporting communities. Government funding for sport recreation would have to be supplemented by state subsidies for stadium improvements, both to keep football clubs alive and to ensure the sense of social security in football that both parties championed. Yet, with a commitment to decreased expenditure and wildly uncertain economic conditions, Conservatives were loath to actually dole out funds to private football clubs. As one party official noted, football clubs, like 'anyone who offered entertainment to the public[,] should be prepared to pay for measures necessary to ensure their safety'.[45] Most Conservatives advocated the principle that 'the costs of securing standards acceptable to society should be borne by those who put those standards at risk'. Considering subsidies for security improvements, both for architectural and crowd management purposes, would also tax already tight budgets for sports provision. The Department of the Environment considered having the Sports Council administer loans to football clubs, for they already had experience of building sporting facilities for recreational use. But Griffiths and other sports governors adopted 'the view that the resources available for the development of sporting facilities [we]re already inadequate to meet demands and that such funds as there [we]re should be deployed not towards the assistance of spectator sport, but towards the development of participation in sport'.[46]

Griffiths floated the idea of licensing only the largest clubs with the highest risk for potential human damage, therefore eliminating the need to fund stadium modernisation for all clubs. 'Scaling down the Bill in this way would … go a long way towards removing much of the criticism we are otherwise bound to meet', he argued. Mandating changes for all clubs would, in his opinion, 'unnecessarily stir up a political hornets' nest.'[47] Without government subsidisation, he estimated that the costs of modernisation would bleed dry all but the top twenty clubs and further reduce attendances across the board. Even worse, it would 'make it necessary for them to put up admission charges'.[48] Playing a role in eliminating smaller, community-oriented football clubs and helping to raise the price of football spectating would be a political disaster at a time when both parties aimed to concretise their party's perception as favourable to the public's sporting interests.

Though the Bill made it through three readings in the House of Lords and two in the Commons, Conservatives delayed long enough to prevent its enactment under their watch. When Labour won the next general election in March 1974, Prime Minister Harold Wilson tasked Denis Howell with the job of carrying out the Bill. Howell proved ready to pass the Bill and accept the credit for redeeming football from the blights of increased violence and poor management. He immediately established a working party to finalise the Bill's details and hoped to eliminate the persistence of football violence. By the mid-1970s, Howell had spent the better part of a decade overseeing the football industry's decline and the increase in football violence. Upon establishing his extensive committee, Howell told the *Daily Mail*, 'Indeed we have had too much talking. What we want now is action.'[49] From the outset, Howell used the Bill as an opportunity to cast himself and his party as the only capable governors willing to stamp out youth criminality and social violence plaguing the professional sport. Howell transformed the initial licensing scheme intended to modernise stadium architecture and prevent possible disasters into a full-fledged moral panic that demonised young working-class spectators participating in football violence. Howell and his working party used the pretext of the Bill as the means to carry out changes to the football industry that would attempt to prevent rowdy spectating.

In his initial declarations of the working party's purpose, Howell made it clear that football violence must be considered in any potential legislation aimed at intervening in the football industry. Howell adopted generalised discourses of safety and security to legitimate this expansion of his inquiry. In an outline of his committee's charge, he wrote, 'there is a collective responsibility on all concerned with the health of football to devise some means whereby behaviour problems can be checked, controlled and eliminated as far as possible'. Rather than merely preventing future fatalities, Howell now aimed to 'consider the question of behavioural motivation, communication, containment and control' of fans.[50] Over the next three years, Howell and a wide range of assistants from the DOE, the Home Office and the Metropolitan Police Office investigated a wide variety of practical challenges, behavioural theories and policing strategies in efforts to lessen football violence. The working party travelled across England and Scotland talking to football authorities and police experts, considering a wide range of tactics that included restricting crowd mobility, maintaining crowd control, preventing pitch invasions, properly managing egress and ingress, establishing emergency evacuation procedures, expanding facilities for policing, elevating police authority, limiting the travel capacity of away fans, and erecting architectural barriers and pens to segregate opposing groups of violent fans.[51]

Howell became the leading government authority on sports violence and used the Safety at Sports Grounds Bill as the legislative means to enact tough law-and-order policies for his party against rowdy spectators in a highly publicised setting. Decades before all-seated stadiums were introduced to control and protect spectators, government officials manipulated the architectural composition of grounds and terraces in order to implement controls against interactive violence in football. Howell continuously asserted the need for this wide-reaching mediation of the football industry: 'The danger to the public from hooliganism is, with the passage of time, likely to be greater than the danger to the public resulting from disasters such as the one which gave rise to the Bill.'[52] Conservative MP Neil Macfarlane agreed, and emphasised, 'When structural alterations are made to grounds to comply with the forthcoming code, other measures should be taken to make them hooligan-proof.'[53] In the Bill's final stages, the original licensing scheme had become an afterthought.[54]

Howell's aggressiveness troubled his colleagues at the Home Office, who fretted about the wide range of policing and judicial responsibilities regarding football violence assumed by Howell's office.[55] But David Lane, a member of Howell's working party and agent for the Home Office, admitted, 'the line between measures for crowd safety and those for combating hooliganism can be very thin'.[56] By 1975, several different practical problems in professional football had been conflated into a general discourse on safety that aimed to satisfy public appeals for tougher measures against football violence.

Howell and the Labour party also wanted to finally capitalise on the political opportunity the Bill presented to link their party to the broad favourability of sport. After berating Conservatives for delaying the passage of the Bill, Home Office officials 'agreed that the Government would be vulnerable' if the Bill was not advanced immediately.[57] Roy Hughes, chairman for the Labour Party Sports Group, lamented to Prime Minister Wilson that Conservatives were gaining political capital as long as Labour failed to follow through on a bill that Tories reluctantly initiated. The Party risked losing its strong associations with working-class favour for sport. 'I hope therefore that you will give this matter your personal attention to ensure that sport in this country is seen to be having a fair deal from the Labour Government.'[58] Shadow Sports Minister Hector Monro also catalysed a Conservative press campaign that vilified Labour both for ostensibly preventing the passage of a bill Conservatives authored and for neglecting their duty to faithfully oversee sports funding.[59] The *Daily Mail* chastised the ruling party for their 'miserly interest in sport and recreation' generally, introducing a 'Fair Play for Fair Sport' column that outlined Labour's continuous mishandling of sports-related affairs. The column again raised the issue that the Sports Council 's £7.85 million budget paled in comparison to the Arts Council's proposed £26.15 million in funding.[60] The article aimed to make Labour sports ministers appear out of touch with their working-class base of voters. Though the fundamentals of this budget appropriation were inherited from the previous Conservative administration, Labour clearly faced their own political obstacles in establishing themselves as the party for sport.

Howell was more successful in leading Labour to pass the Bill than his Conservative predecessors because he elevated anxieties about football violence. His aggressive and ambitious campaign to stamp out football hooliganism elevated the role for governance in sport, increased his personal political profile, and established a problem for which he ostensibly produced a hard-nosed and workmanlike series of solutions. Throughout his working party's investigation, Howell intermittently released recommendations and adjustments to policing policies and crowd management strategies that projected an air of control and calculated discipline to counteract young vilified football rowdies. In the summer of 1974, shortly after taking control of the office, Howell concluded a series of stadium site visits by demanding that football clubs make several inexpensive changes within a month to shore up policing and architectural control before the 1974–75 season began. In it he proposed 'that movement on terraces should be restricted as much as possible' to prevent supporters from communing, interacting and fighting. Crowd segregation was also a priority, as 'less problems occur where the terraces are divided as far as possible into sections by the use of railings or barriers, both vertically and horizontally'. The working party also recommended the construction of large walls, fences or moats around the pitch to prevent disorderly spectators from invading the playing field.[61] Articulating a broad range of architectural controls fused the two elements of the Bill – crowd control and stadium modernisation. The recommendations and mandated changes also had the effect of elevating the issue, dehumanising and abstracting communities of supporters, and creating a space for successful government intervention into a troubled area of sports policy. From 1974 forward, he also addressed every publicised outbreak of football violence, both at home and in international competitions on the continent, with strong public statements of rebuke. Howell's aggressive campaign clearly positioned Labour responses as the toughest challenge to allegedly growing levels of youth violence and social disintegration, and their manifestation in football.

Labour sports ministers also advocated creative financial management to avoid charges that the government would ruin football by mandating expensive grounds modifications without necessary subsidies. The Home Office created another working party, this one to assess financing changes to sports grounds. The group estimated that the minimal changes required to comply with a new licensing scheme would cost roughly £45,000 per stadium for sixty-two different clubs, at a total cost of £2.8 million.[62] An Inland Revenue report confirmed that many clubs were indeed financially vulnerable, informing both parties that the 'taxable capacity' of English and Scottish football league clubs was marginal.[63] Several clubs threatened to withdraw their support and promised to crush the Bill should no financial help come from the government.[64] While Conservatives had considered levies on a variety of different sporting events, Howell and Football League authority Alan Hardaker proposed that funds be raised through a 'Spot the Ball' betting competition organised by the Pools Promoters Association. A recent football photograph, usually with several players in action, was airbrushed to remove the ball from the image. Participants then paid a nominal fee to cast their best guess for where the ball might have been in the original photograph.[65] The projected income from the lottery competition secured the passage of the Bill by eliminating the challenge of financial subsidies.

In the end, the Safety at Sports Grounds Bill became a major political boon for Labour sports governors for many reasons. First, the long debates and sports policy decisions that occurred throughout the Bill's creation expanded a relatively minor licensing scheme into a substantive new direction in eliminating social violence and protecting the nation's favoured working-class sport. Through Howell's leadership, the Bill came to embody a policy of social rectification through sporting environments. Whereas earlier some politicians had lamented that football remained the only entertainment industry without government regulation, the Bill enabled Howell and Labour to test and implement new strategies to deter football violence and display their political capacity for ostensibly remaking a safer Britain.[66] Labour concretised themselves as the party in favour of sports participation and spectating as popular leisure for working-class citizens, while providing a performance of discipline and order to supposedly neutralise the chaotic violence and mercurial economies of the football industry. Second, the party funded the architectural changes they mandated without reducing the funding for sports provision. Since most citizens and many politicians collectively aggregated sports participation and professional sports spectating into similar categories of leisure, they avoided the appearance that they would reduce expenditure to sports on the ground level. Third, many MPs championed the Bill as a success for the football clubs in their constituencies, casting themselves as local campaigners for law and order. When incidents of violence emerged at their local club, MPs called upon the

Bill as evidence of progress on the matter.[67] Finally, Labour also avoided the eminent threat of another football disaster caused by failing architecture and mishandled crowd management. Though Labour enacted the bill, and though several investigative committees pre-dated it, both parties worked to establish the foundations for the first large-scale legislative intervention into the football industry. In response to insecure social and economic conditions, preventing the possible demise of both local football and the professional industry proved a popular political accomplishment.

Family values and football policy

Before summarising the importance of this series of government interventions into the football industry, one other thread of political discourse should be noted and analysed. In addition to projecting calculated discipline to counteract the indiscipline of fans, sports regulators also advocated strong family values and nostalgic depictions of earlier eras of football spectating to convince voters of their competence in governing sport. With the passage of the Safety at Sports Grounds Bill, Howell argued that government must 'conquer the problem and make football, a great sport, once again safe for any man to take his wife and family to see.'[68] Recalling notions of football as peaceful family entertainment aimed to both restore the tarnished image of the sport and imagine a harmonious alternative to the current state of professional football. From the mid-1960s forward, football spectating came to be dominated by working-class men, and other groups of spectators were forced to experience the match within spatial arrangements and increased levels of policing that aimed to minimise the impact of outbreaks of football violence. By the mid-1970s spectating football seemed far different from the pleasant weekend entertainment that had marked the sport in the interwar and immediate post-war periods. Politicians from both parties purposefully invoked nostalgic reminiscences of harmonious football leisure to convince the public of the necessity of the Safety at Sports Grounds Bill and its attending costs. The symbol of the family loomed large in these discourses, figuring centrally in discussions of how to restore football to a golden age of safe entertainment.

Discussions of the family's role in football, and the impact of football on the family, transpired as soon as the phenomenon of youth violence emerged. The 1967 Harrington inquiry, one of the first government investigations into football violence, found the absence of families at football grounds to be troubling. Conducted by a group of University of Birmingham psychologists led by J. A.

Harrington, the report suggested that part of the impetus for football violence among young men could stem from improper family relations. Though noting that football 'hooligans' came from a variety of different family backgrounds, the report added that many offenders' families showed 'the usual patterns of rejection, hostility and inconsistency'. 'In one London area where hooliganism is rife', the report stated, 'we found evidence of the combination of a strict authoritarian father and an indulgent and protective mother.' Apart from conditioning the lives of their children, fathers could also bring frustration from the match home, for 'wife beating is said to be linked with a football game. Some wives apparently live in dread of Saturdays ... If the local side loses a wife may fear her husband will return home worse for drink and give her a thrashing to get rid of the anger he feels about the lost game.' The report also noted that several young psychiatric patients described being terrified about their father's behaviour on match days.[69] For the Birmingham researchers, abnormal family conditions led by dominant men not only created havoc on match days but also spilled over into the household. Though not entirely conclusive, the researchers forwarded the idea that football violence, as both outcome and cause, played a role in a reciprocating cycle of family distress. Such perceptions display the initial thinking on the emerging problem among both academics and the public.

The researchers added that the acts of rowdy fans also disrupted otherwise pleasant family entertainment for the majority of supporters. In a section addressing the incendiary effects of obscene chanting, the group singled out one interview response: 'One man wrote, "No man with any sense of responsibility would bring his wife and family to a match today." Such views ... undermine the ideal of the football ground as a suitable place for the entertainment and enjoyment of the whole family.'[70] Clearly, both the researchers and many supporters regarded football as a place lacking decency, where the ideal family leisure activity had been overtaken by a minority group of irresponsible fans. Rowdy supporters made it impossible for men to provide this form of leisure for their families, threatening their ability to pass on local and national pride for British football to their kin. John Watkinson (Labour MP for Gloucestershire West) argued that football rowdyism tarnished the magnetism of the national sport for women and children: 'I remember the grip that the 1966 World Cup had on the people of this country. It was claimed that this was a sport that could attract the whole family, but any man who took his wife or girl friend to see a football match in this country, would be endangering that woman if he took her on to the terraces, such is the state of behaviour and hooliganism that we have to endure.'[71] Both politicians and other supporters assumed the family as the perfect setting for harmonious leisure, with the husband at the helm, and worried about the safety of women and children. But a growing number of young supporters obviously rejected such sentiments, preferring the camaraderie, interaction of their peers, and more physical and possibly threatening football settings. Nonetheless, as the nature and experience of watching football and attending a match drastically evolved in the post-war period, many men longed for a return to pleasantly ordered stadium environments where they could bring their families to attend games with them. Such sentiments not only intimated that previous eras of football spectating were far more pleasant but also framed the football match as a place for men, ordered by accountability and mutual respect, where children and women needed male protection and could only be invited in proper circumstances.

In order to address this glaring issue, both the Department of the Environment and the Home Office closely monitored the establishment of 'family enclosures' as they carried out their investigations of sports grounds during the early 1970s. In the ongoing tweaking of stadium organisation, some clubs experimented with segregated areas for families, women and boys that aimed to protect family spectating. A 1969 working party made the suggestion that boys be separated, as many football violence offenders were adolescent boys.[72] But the group also imagined practical difficulties in instituting these measures. Namely, some group members were concerned that separate boys' enclosures might actually have a negative effect on family values, discouraging fathers from attending with their sons. In the end, the inquiry recommended to clubs that only unaccompanied schoolchildren be separated.[73] Arsenal F. C. had already created an exclusive 'enclosure for schoolchildren at 2s per head' at the start of the 1964–65 season, but eventually modified the plan because, 'some parents [wanted] their children with them in the ground rather than have them in the special enclosure.' Nevertheless, unaccompanied children were, 'restricted to the special enclosure because of the considerable damage they cause[d] to [Arsenal's] property when allowed to roam the stadium'.[74] The establishment of segregated family spectating could be perceived as divisive, but it became a practical reality allowing for the separation and close policing of adolescents without attending family members.

Other clubs experienced more rapid success with family enclosures, and the idea became a mainstay of most clubs throughout the late 1970s and 1980s. Club executive Eddie Plumley remembered that the family enclosures at Watford sold out in the first year. The club eventually removed the 500 seats and restored the terraces within the enclosure, not only to increase the capacity to 1,500, but ostensibly to re-establish the community-oriented feel of free-moving and standing spectators.[75] Leicester City developed a family enclosure 'to encourage parents and children to come back. Here was an area in which people said they were safe: 'All I've got to be is a member, buy a ticket and I know nobody else will go into that section other than a member.'[76] Advocates of family enclosures contributed to the broad discourses on safety and overlapped notions of security with the restoration of family-oriented football. Creating a safe place for family entertainment also contributed to the projection of control and order to counteract the chaotic perceptions of football rowdyism. By 1989, family enclosures had been adopted by eighty-four clubs, and the Football League began giving seminars to inform clubs of opportunities for restoring a family atmosphere after another horrible football disaster at Hillsborough stadium in Sheffield in 1989, where ninety-six supporters died.[77]

In addition to providing spaces for families at matches, some politicians also advocated punishing families for failing to be responsible for adolescents involved in football violence. In a parliamentary debate on football violence, Conservative Neil Macfarlane (MP for Sutton and Cheam) noted that he was pleased to hear that several clubs and magistrates were reportedly attempting to 'enlist parental involvement' of offenders. In particular, Macfarlane raised the idea of increasing fines and asking parents to accept partial responsibility: 'The parents might well be asked to make a greater contribution when the magistrates consider what fine to levy … I believe that if fathers were invited by the magistrates to pay the fines on behalf of their wayward sons we would have a great deal of success.'[78] Again, Macfarlane assumed the father as the head of the family, in charge of chastising disobedient sons and accepting responsibility for their actions. In this suggestion, the fine would serve as a corrective for the supposed declining role of the father in the football family by increasing their 'parental involvement'.

Denis Howell also conjectured about the connection between deteriorated family models and football violence. In 1977, after many changes from the Bill had been instituted, yet with no substantial decline in football violence, Howell frustratingly admitted, 'none of us knows the answers or even the reasons … To date we have had all sorts of inquiries.' He elaborated, 'I have my own prejudice. In most working-class homes the mother is the disciplinarian. A lot of this trouble can be traced back to the time when mothers began regularly to go out to work. Now mothers have three jobs … [and] the easy way to get the children away from under their feet is to give them 50p to go out.' Howell called on well-worn discourses of working-class family decline and suggested that violent working-class adolescents had money for leisure but no internal family regulation, no mutually shared time with other family members, and no discipline from 'disciplinarian' mothers. Unlike other commentators, Howell placed the mother at the centre of the working-class family and intimated that economic conditions and a failure to provide higher wages prevented mothers from inculcating respectable behaviour and community responsibility. Breakdowns in family structure supposedly contributed to the erosion of family-oriented leisure in professional football.

Throughout these multiple articulations of the role of the family and the status of family football leisure, women spectators appear only as abstractions. They are notable for the absence of their voices and opinions and only appear as 'wives' of football men in discussions of football violence, further emphasising the presence of male-ordered family values. Most politicians and the press lumped all types of unruly acts into a general category of 'hooliganism' and aggregated any offenders as demonised 'hooligans' with few attempts at specificity. But records of the experiences of women spectators in this period are particularly deficient. In reviewing hundreds of government records, police documents, witness statements and press accounts, I found that women supporters appeared in very few. One notable exception captured at least one group of women's experiences. Several young women supporters of Leeds United, aged eighteen to twenty years old, wrote a letter to Denis Howell to complain about new policing strategies and the general aggressiveness of stadium authorities and constables at matches. 'We undersigned girls are Leeds United fanatics and we are sick and tired of being treated as second-class citizens just because we go to football matches.' In a long letter, they never asserted their experiences as different from other Leeds fans, but wrote as a collective to complain that 'the one ones who pay our money week in, week out' should not be treated like those perpetuating violence, who 'deserve what they get'. Instead, they complained about brutal treatment from police, including being trampled by a constable's stomping horse despite adhering to police orders and stadium rules. They concluded, 'Nothing resolute is ever done about hooliganism only talk.'[79] Though ignored by government agencies and press coverage, many young women certainly supported football and challenged the popular perception that women only attended as invitees of their husbands in an imagined, idealised setting.

Politicians' invocations of family helped them to justify changes to football policy. By discussing the deterioration of the working-class family as part of the origins of football violence, as well as the danger that rowdyism posed to family-oriented leisure, politicians and researchers justified further interventions into the football industry. Lamenting the loss of working-class men's ability to take their families to a match suggested that young working-class offenders were not only ruining the sport but also debilitating their communities by perpetuating urban deprivation and the breakdown of their own community ideals. Many of these comments on making working-class family members more responsible, and providing safe entertainment for working-class families, were structured by gender and class. Of course, discourses of family values were certainly well tested and resilient in providing justification for any policies centred around safety and security. When applied to subtly recalled earlier periods of peaceful, undisturbed football entertainment, these arguments gained strength and allowed extensive interventions into professional football.

Conclusions

In the 1960s, the affluence of many Britons certainly created increased opportunities for leisure. Though the extension and persistence of this affluence can be overstated, it coincided with a large increase and reorganisation of the state's investment in sports and recreation. From the mid-1960s through the 1970s, each of the two main political parties forged their sports policy, attempting to curry favour with potential voters by positioning themselves as providers of local sports funding and protectors of beloved professional football clubs. As sports and leisure generally increased in popularity with a wide variety of constituents, Labourites and Conservatives articulated different reasons for funding sports on a local level, but they produced similar arguments about safety, security and family entertainment to justify piecemeal interventions into the private football industry. In doing so, they coordinated a wide range of policing strategies to prevent football violence and engineered architectural improvements to control physical spaces within stadiums. In the end, few of the interventions staved off football violence and most certainly failed to instill discipline amongst aggressive supporters. Physically oriented and violent forms of football spectatorship continued well into the 1980s and 1990s, though they adapted to new circumstances as the regulation of football evolved. The long debate and eventual passage of the Safety at Sports Grounds Bill provides a window onto the popular and political perceptions of sport during this crucial period in the development of leisure and recreation policies, and this affords an opportunity to see how both parties faced practical and legislative obstacles in spreading their rhetoric and enacting their goals. Ultimately, government struggles with sports policy in this period reveal the growing importance of forms of leisure in political strategy, and they demonstrate the mutually reciprocating relationship between sports and leisure and the social, political and economic contexts from which they emerged.

Notes

1 See Peter Borsay, *A History of British Leisure: The British Experience since 1500* (London: Palgrave, 2006), Ch. 3; Howell Justin Evans, *Service to Sport: The Story of the CCPR, 1935–1972* (London: Pelham, 1974).

2 Martin Polley, *Moving the Goalposts: A History of Sport and Society in Britain since 1945* (London: Routledge, 1998), 16–18; Ian Henry, *The Politics of Leisure Policy* (Basingstoke: Macmillan, 1993); Jeffrey Hill, *Sport, Leisure & Culture in Twentieth-Century Britain* (London: Palgrave, 2002), Chs 9 and 10.

3 *Sport & the Community: The Report of the Wolfenden Committee on Sport* (London: Central Council of Physical Recreation, 1960).

4 See Polley, *Moving the Goalposts*, Ch. 1. For more on the 'modes of intervention' delineated by sociologists and historians, see John Hargreaves, *Sport, Power and Culture: A Social and Historical Analysis of Popular Sports in Britain* (New York: St. Martin's Press, 1986).

5 Steve Greenfield and Guy Osborn, 'When the Writ Hits the Fan: Panic Law and Football Fandom', in Adam Brown (ed.), *Fanatics!: Power, Identity and Fandom in Football* (London: Routledge, 1998).

6 Anthony King, *The End of the Terraces: The Transformation of English Football* (Leicester: Leicester University Press, 2001), especially Ch. 1.

7 Steve Greenfield and Guy Osborn, *Regulating Football: Commodification, Consumption and the Law* (London: Pluto Press, 2001).

8 James Walvin, *Football and the Decline of Britain* (Basingstoke: Macmillan, 1986); Matthew Taylor, *The Association Game: A History of British Football* (New York: Pearson Longman, 2008), Ch. 5.

9 Taylor, *The Association Game*, 264.

10 *Ibid.*, 253. See also Sports Council, *Digest of Sports Statistics for the UK* (London: Sports Council, 1991).

11 Taylor, *The Association Game*, 274–5. On television, see Garry Whannel, *Fields in Vision: Television Sport and Cultural Transformation* (London: Routledge, 1992).

12 For an entrée into this growing body of literature see the reviews of research in Megan O'Neill, *Policing Football: Social Interaction and Negotiated Disorder* (London: Palgrave, 2006), and Steve Frosdick and Peter Marsh, *Football Hooliganism* (Portland, OR: Willan, 2005). See also Norbert Elias and Eric Dunning, *Quest for Excitement: Sport and Leisure in the Civilising Process* (Oxford: Blackwell, 1994). The terms 'hooligan' and 'hooliganism' have been used persistently by press outlets and some academics, perpetuating the criminalisation of football fans. The term

'football violence' as a descriptive phrase is preferred here.

13 See Ian Taylor, 'Soccer Consciousness and Soccer Hooliganism', in Stanley Cohen (ed.), *Images of Deviance* (New York: Penguin, 1976); Ian Taylor, 'Class, Violence and Sport: The Case of Soccer Hooliganism in Britain', in Hart Cantelon and Richard Gruneau (eds), *Sport, Culture and the Modern State* (Buffalo: University of Toronto Press, 1982); Gary Armstrong, *Football Hooligans: Knowing the Score* (Oxford: Berg, 1998); Richard Giulianotti, *Football: A Sociology of the Global Game* (Cambridge: Polity Press, 1999).

14 See Brett Bebber, *Violence and Racism in Football: Politics and Cultural Conflict in Britain, 1968-98* (London: Pickering & Chatto, 2012); Les Back, Tim Crabbe and John Solomos, *The Changing Face of Football: Racism, Multiculturalism and Identity in the English Game* (Oxford: Berg, 2001).

15 See Jeffrey Hill's discussion of interwar socialism in Chapter 1 of this volume.

16 Davidson, House of Commons, 19 January 1968, Parliamentary Debates, vol. 756, col. 2186.

17 John Coghlan and Ida Webb, *Sport and British Politics since the 1960s* (London: Falmer Press, 1990).

18 Richard Holt and Tony Mason, *Sport in Britain, 1945–2000* (London: Wiley-Blackwell, 2001), 165.

19 Quintin Hogg served as the first Minister with Special Responsibility for Sport from 1962 to 1964, but the position was given a wider range of responsibilities and formalised after Harold Wilson's victory in 1964.

20 Denis Howell, Department of the Environment to John Gilbert, Financial Secretary, Department of Treasury (13 January 1975). In Public Record Office (hereafter PRO), AT60/37, file 1.

21 See Polley, *Moving the Goalposts*, 20–3.

22 Harold Wilson to Chancellor of the Exchequer (24 February 1975). PRO, AT60/11, file 22.

23 Denis Howell, Department of Environment to John Gilbert, Financial Secretary, Department of Treasury (13 January 1975). PRO, AT60/2, file 49. Emphasis mine.

24 See Patrick McDevitt, *May the Best Man Win: Sport, Masculinity and Nationalism in Great Britain and the Empire, 1880–1935* (London: Palgrave, 2004) and Mike Huggins, *The Victorians and Sport* (London: Hambledon and London, 2007).

25 Howell, House of Commons, 19 January 1968, Parliamentary Debates, vol. 756, col. 2178.

26 Howell, House of Commons, 15 July 1971, Parliamentary Debates, vol. 821, cols 823–4.

27 Williams, House of Commons, 19 January 1968, Parliamentary Debates, vol. 756, col. 2187.

28 Dalyell, House of Commons, 19 January 1968, Parliamentary Debates, vol. 756, col. 2180.

29 Howell, House of Commons, 19 January 1968, Parliamentary Debates, vol. 756, cols 2196–7.

30 M. McDonald, Inland Revenue Secretary's Office, to J. McEntyre, Home Office (18 July 1974). PRO, HO300/123, file 2.

31 Jones, House of Commons, 19 June 1975, Parliamentary Debates, vol. 893, col.

1765.

32 Department of the Environment Press Notice (18 September 1973). PRO, AT49/90, file 18.

33 Eldon Griffiths, Memo on Expenditure on Sport (2 April 1973). PRO, AT60/1, file 10, 1–2.

34 *Ibid.*, 3.

35 Eldon Griffiths, Memo on Increased Expenditure in Sport (15 February 1973). PRO, AT60/1, file 6.

36 See Polley, *Moving the Goalposts,* 21–3.

37 Geoffrey Rippon, Secretary of State for the Environment, Speech at the Official Opening of the Extensions to the Sports Centre (16 November 1973). PRO, AT60/1, file 12.

38 Eldon Griffiths, Paper for Consideration of Ministers, The Case for a Substantial Increase in Spending by the Sports Council (15 February 1973). PRO, AT60/1, file 6.

39 Lord Wheatley, *Report of the Inquiry into Crowd Safety at Sports Grounds*, Cmnd. 4952 (London: HMSO, 1972).

40 See J.A. Harrington, *Soccer Hooliganism* (Bristol: John Wright, 1968); Sir John Lang, *Crowd Behaviour at Football Matches: Report of the Working Party* (London, HMSO, 1969).

41 Phillip Allen, Memo on Crowd Safety at Sports Grounds (7 December 1972). PRO, HO300/93, file 2.

42 See Wim Meeusen, 'European Economic Integration: From Business Cycle to Business Cycle', in Rosemary Wakeman (ed.), *Themes in European History since 1945* (London: Routledge, 2003), 240–2.

43 Kenneth O. Morgan, *The People's Peace* (New York: Oxford University Press, 1990), 277–280.

44 Stuart Hall, *et al.*, *Policing the Crisis: Mugging, the State and Law and Order* (London: Palgrave Macmillan, 1978).

45 J. H. Waddell, Home Office, in Cabinet Meeting Minutes, Group of Officials on Safety at Sports Grounds (2 April 1971). PRO, CAB130/508, file 3.

46 Joint Memorandum by the Secretary of State for the Home Department and the Secretary of State for Scotland, with the Home and Social Affairs Committee, on Crowd Safety at Sports Grounds (29 June 1973). PRO, HO300/99, file 13.

47 Eldon Griffiths, Department of the Environment to David Lane, Home Office (19 June 1973). PRO, HO300/99, file 4.

48 Eldon Griffiths to Robert Carr (July 1973). PRO, HO300/99, file 16.

49 *Daily Mail*, 20 March 1974.

50 Working Party on Crowd Behaviour, Note by the Department of the Environment (undated, probably March 1974).

51 This wide range of strategies and their outcomes have been addressed in detail. See Bebber, *Violence and Racism in Football.*

52 Howell, House of Commons, 18 January 1974, Parliamentary Debates, vol. 867, col. 1091.

53 Macfarlane, House of Commons, 19 June 1975, Parliamentary Debates, vol. 893, col. 1783.

54 *Daily Mail*, 30 August 1975.

55 See S. G. Norris, Private Secretary at the Home Office, to Mr Graham-Harrison (20 March 1974). PRO, HO300/112, file 3.

56 David Lane to Mr Shuffrey (4 September 1974). PRO, HO300/113, file 3.

57 Minutes of a Meeting on the Safety of Sports Grounds Bill, Home Office (4 April 1974). PRO, HO300/112, file 14.

58 Roy Hughes to Harold Wilson, 9 March 1975. PRO, AT60/37, file 3.

59 J.J. Rendell, Department of the Environment, to Mr. Leavett. PRO, AT60/2, file 66.

60 *Daily Mail*, 5 March 1975.

61 Ministerial Working Party on Crowd Behaviour, First Recommendations (23 May 1974). PRO, HO300/112, file 35.

62 Working Paper, Working Group on Financing Improvements at Sportsgrounds, Home Office (8 May 1974). PRO, HO300/122, file 12.

63 M. McDonald, Inland Revenue Secretary's Office, to J. McEntyre, Home Office (18 July 1974). PRO, HO300/123, file 2.

64 Note of a Meeting at the Home Office on Safety at Sports Grounds (1 May 1974). PRO, HO300/122, file 9.

65 For the documents on this resolution, see PRO, AT60/11, especially files 15, 17, 20, and PRO, AT60/37.

66 See Tam Dalyell's (Labour: West Lothian) comments in Dalyell, House of Commons, 18 January 1974, Parliamentary Debates, vol. 867, col. 1137.

67 See the local concerns of Peter Blaker (Conservative: Blackpool South) and James Johnson (Labour: Hull West) in House of Commons, 4 December 1974, Parliamentary Debates, vol. 882, cols 1533–5.

68 Howell, House of Commons, 19 June 1975, Parliamentary Debates, vol. 893, col. 1803.

69 Harrington, *Soccer Hooliganism*, 23–4.

70 *Ibid.*, 52.

71 Watkinson, House of Commons, 19 June 1975, Parliamentary Debates, vol. 893, 1776.

72 Working Party on Crowd Behaviour at Football Matches, Report of a Meeting (16 June 1969). PRO, HO287/1500, file 3.

73 Lang, *Crowd Behaviour at Football Matches*, 8.

74 Announcements from Arsenal Football Club Programme, 11 April 1964 and 29 August 1964, in Tom Watt (ed.), *The End: 80 Years of Life on Arsenal's North Bank* (London: Mainstream, 1993).

75 Andrew Ward and Rogan Taylor (eds), *Kicking and Screaming: An Oral History of Football in England* (London: Robson, 1998), 364.

76 Jack Curtis, discussing his employment at Leicester City F. C., in *Kicking and Screaming*, 364.

77 The information on Football League seminars can be found in Note on Family Initiatives, PRO, HO397/81.

78 Macfarlane, House of Commons, 19 June 1975, House of Commons, vol. 893, col. 1786.

79 Heidi Gleissner, Sue Isherwood, Carole Parkhouse, Linda Crosby and Violet Wright to Denis Howell (3 September 1975). PRO, HO287/2053 (Part 1).

7

Permissive claptrap: cannabis law and the legacy of the 1960s

CHAD MARTIN

In 1995, a *Lancet* editorial called for the liberalisation of cannabis laws, stating: 'The smoking of cannabis, even long term, is not harmful to health'. However, the editors were not hopeful that the proposed changes would occur. 'Cannabis has become a political football,' they wrote, 'and one that governments continually duck.'[1] How did cannabis use become an intractable political issue? It first came to widespread public attention during the time of the Permissive Society in the 1960s. During this period of cultural liberalisation, an attempt was made to loosen the restrictions on cannabis use, but the window of opportunity closed, drug law reform stalled, and the permissive era ended as drug laws proved to be the one issue too polarising for reform. During the 1970s and 1980s, 'permissiveness' became a term of abuse, and even as cannabis use became increasingly common and other European countries liberalised their laws, politicians refused to consider decriminalisation. Despite a lack of substantial legal reform, cannabis use became so widespread that it overwhelmed policing efforts, and the laws against it often fell into disuse. This chapter looks at how the era of the Permissive Society led to an attempt to change the drug laws of Britain, and how debates over the legacy of those years has shaped drug policy since the 1960s.

The 1960s Permissive Society

In 1967, the *Guardian* ran a series of articles entitled 'The Permissive Society' in an attempt to catalogue the rapid social and cultural changes of the period.

The articles dealt with several different topics, including music, censorship and sex. The conclusion was the same in every case: the moral conservatism rooted in the Victorian era was rapidly decaying and being replaced by a new spirit of tolerance. As one of the newspaper's editors wrote, it was 'a widespread public acquiescence in the dissolution of the old accepted standards' that occurred 'with unexampled suddenness, in the space of a few years'.[2] The driving forces behind this shift were the young avant-garde. The articles quoted from fashion designer Mary Quant, musicians John Lennon and Mick Jagger, anti-psychiatrist R. D. Laing, representatives of the youth subculture known as the 'underground' or 'counterculture', and others.[3] The growth of popular culture combined with post-war affluence to give these cultural leaders and bohemians a national, and often international, voice. The result of this pressure from below was not only a change in folkways, but also institutional change.

While some members of older generations were resistant to what they saw as the decline in morality inherent in the Permissive Society, others were enthusiastic about challenging traditions. There were some upper-middle-class Britons born in the first decades of the twentieth century who, influenced by the Bohemianism of the Bloomsbury group, were receptive to the challenges to what they saw as lingering Victorian orthodoxy. The most significant member of this generation, in terms of promoting institutional changes in line with the idea of the Permissive Society, was Labour politician Roy Jenkins. From 1955 to 1959, while Labour was out of power, Jenkins worked to push through a new Obscene Publications Act, which liberalised censorship laws. The Labour Party won the 1964 General Election, and in December 1965, Prime Minister Harold Wilson appointed Jenkins as his Home Secretary.

The time was right for change. The Labour government of 1945–51 had been concerned with post-war rebuilding and the establishment of the welfare state. The following thirteen years saw rule by a Conservative party uninterested in social reform legislation. Throughout this period, extra-parliamentary pressure groups such as the Divorce Law Reform Union (founded in 1906), the Abortion Law Reform Association (founded in 1936), and the Homosexual Law Reform Society (founded in 1958) agitated for their causes and formulated specific recommendations for reform.[4] These organisations could now work with a sympathetic Home Secretary to bring about change.

Within the next three years the National Health Service was instructed to provide birth control to women regardless of age or marital status, with a provision that it could be offered free of charge.[5] Homosexuality was decriminalised in the Sexual Offences Act of 1967. Abortion services were legalised the same year.[6] Censorship of the theatre was abolished with the Theatres Act of 1968. Racial discrimination in housing, employment and public services was banned through the Race Relations Act. The Family Law Reform Act and Divorce Reform Act of 1969 respectively lowered the age of majority from twenty-one to eighteen and introduced no-fault divorces. The resultant rapid pace of change seemed especially striking compared to the lack of action on these issues in the previous decades, and it is unsurprising that the *Guardian* began their Permissive Society series in the lead up to final passage of the Abortion Bill.

Cannabis

It is in this context that members of the underground brought laws pertaining to cannabis use to the government's attention as an issue worthy of reform. Cannabis was illegal in Britain from 1928, and yet there was no significant use of the drug until the wave of post-Second World War colonial immigrants.[7] Sociologist Jock Young noted that in the late 1950s and early 1960s 'the occurrence of marijuana-smoking was minute and largely limited to first generation West Indian immigrants'.[8] As the Government noted, in the immediate post-war period, customs agents found the drug 'in ships from Indian and African ports and thought to be destined for petty traffickers in touch with coloured seamen and entertainers in London docks and clubs. By 1950 illicit traffic in cannabis had been observed in other parts of the country where there was a coloured population.'[9] However, with the growth of the underground in the mid-1960s, the use of cannabis spread to the white, native-born community and dramatically increased in scale.

The number of people convicted of marijuana possession increased as the underground grew. There were 663 convictions in 1963, and only 45% of those convicted were white, at a time when non-whites amounted to only 2% of the population. In 1967, the number of convictions had risen to 2,393, and 73% of those convicted were white. Among all convictions that year, 65% of the offenders were under the age of twenty-five.[10] By the end of the decade, some health officials estimated that 15% of the students at the University of London had tried hashish.[11]

Unlike the immigrant community, which wanted to avoid confrontations with the authorities, the counterculture was made up of many articulate and well-educated Britons who felt no hesitation about challenging the status quo. From 1966, the most popular underground newspaper – the *International*

Times (IT) – regularly advocated the use of cannabis. In 1967, John 'Hoppy' Hopkins, one of the newspaper's founders, also organised the first 'Legalise Pot' rally in London after he was arrested for the second time on cannabis charges. These changes were noticed by politicians. That same year, Conservative MP Paul Channon said on the floor of the House, 'there are large numbers of respectable people with good jobs, or students, who are taking [cannabis], and they represent an intelligent section of our society'.[12]

Steve Abrams, an American pursuing doctoral work at Oxford University, wrote a newspaper article in early 1967 about soft drug use at Oxford that caused a national stir and made him something of a celebrity in the underground. He claimed: 'there are at least 500 junior members of the University who smoke cannabis when it is available. In addition, the drug is now being used by a few dozen of the younger Dons.'[13] Because of this public attention, Abrams founded the organisation *SOMA* to research the biological and psychological effects of cannabis and to advocate for its decriminalisation.[14] Later in 1967, others in the underground formed the group *Release* to provide legal aid and advice for those arrested on drug charges. These spokespeople for the counterculture began to coalesce into what would later be called the 'pot lobby', and during the ensuing debates they played a role similar to that of earlier extra-parliamentary pressure groups.

Wootton Committee

Following Abrams' article on cannabis use at Oxford, the Vice-Chancellor of the university asked Roy Jenkins 'for an urgent national inquiry into the medical dangers of drug taking' because although there was 'little evidence of student addiction to "hard" drugs ... they were concerned at reports of the numbers who might be experimenting with cannabis'.[15] As a result, the Hallucinogens Sub-Committee of the standing Advisory Committee on Drug Dependence was formed on 7 April 1967 at the request of the Home Secretary. It was chaired by Baroness Wootton of Abinger, a renowned social scientist, a governor of the BBC and a life peer. The ten other members included psychiatrists, pharmacologists, a magistrate (who was also chair of the Poisons Board) and a senior officer from Scotland Yard. Just as the Departmental Committee on Morphine and Heroin Addiction (the Rolleston Committee) of the 1920s and the Inter-departmental Committee on Drug Addiction (the Brain Committee) of the early 1960s had successfully recommended reforms for the laws dealing with heroin and other hard drugs, the Wootton Sub-Committee was to investigate cannabis and LSD use and advise Parliament on appropriate legislation, with the assumption that its report would carry substantial weight.[16]

In June 1967, leading members of the British counterculture met at the Indica bookshop in London to discuss the recent sentencing of Hoppy to nine months in prison on a cannabis charge. There Abrams put forward the idea of taking out an advertisement in the *Times* calling for the decriminalisation of cannabis in order to influence the Wootton Committee.[17] Indica's owner Barry Miles was a friend of Paul McCartney, and the Beatle offered to put up the £1,800 needed to pay for the full-page advertisement.

The advertisement was designed to appeal to mainstream sentiment. Published on 24 July, it was headlined 'The Law Against Marijuana Is Immoral in Principle and Unworkable in Practice' and concluded that cannabis was 'the least harmful pleasure-giving drug, probably much safer than alcohol or tobacco'.[18] The sixty-five signatures included journalist (and future Tory MP) Jonathan Aitken, playwright Peter Brook, Nobel laureate Francis Crick, author Graham Greene, artist David Hockney, Francis Huxley, Young Liberal leader George Kiloh, television presenter David Dimbleby, George Melly, Kenneth Tynan, Labour MPs Tom Driberg and Brian Walden, anti-psychiatrists David Cooper and R.D. Laing, all four Beatles and manager Brian Epstein, and several prominent physicians.[19]

The efforts of the underground had an immediate effect on the course of the Sub-Committee's investigations.[20] As the Sub-Committee's report noted:

> Our first enquiries were proceeding without publicity into the pharmacological and medical aspects when other developments gave our study new and much increased significance. An advertisement in *The Times* on the 24th July 1967 represented that the long-asserted dangers of cannabis were exaggerated and that the related law was socially damaging, if not unworkable. This was followed by a wave of debate about these issues in Parliament, the Press and elsewhere … This publicity made more explicit the nature of some current 'protest' about official policy on drugs; defined more clearly some of the main issues in our study; and led us to give greater attention to the legal aspects of the problem.[21]

The Sub-Committee met seventeen times in preparation for its report on cannabis, and several underground figures – including Abrams, *IT* editor Bill Levy and artist Martin Sharp – gave testimony. The Sub-Committee's report made it obvious that the underground witnesses had strongly argued their libertarian viewpoint. It stated that 'adult men and women, it is said, ought to be free to make their own decisions, in accordance with their personal tastes, and their own moral judgments, as to what substances they think it proper to consume.'[22]

The Sub-Committee had started its investigation burdened by popular myths surrounding cannabis use, and the testimony of the members of the underground was completely successful in dispelling these illusions. The report concluded:

> There is no evidence that in Western society serious physical dangers are directly associated with the smoking of cannabis ... It can be clearly argued on the world picture that cannabis use does not lead to heroin addiction ... In the United Kingdom the taking of cannabis has not so far been regarded even by the severest critics, as a direct cause of serious crime ... All in all, it is impossible to make out a firm case against cannabis as being potentially a greater personal or social danger than alcohol.[23]

The report was submitted to the Home Secretary in October 1968 and published on his authority in January 1969. In general, it was balanced between the views of the underground that cannabis was essentially harmless and the reservations some committee members had about decriminalisation. The conclusion was 'that the existing criminal sanctions intended to curb its use are unjustifiably severe'.[24] The Sub-Committee recommended amending the Dangerous Drugs Act of 1965 to reduce the maximum penalty for the summary conviction of cannabis possession from a £250 fine and one year in prison to a £100 fine and four months in prison. Likewise, they suggested the maximum penalty for the indictment of cannabis possession to be changed from a £1,000 fine and ten years in prison to an unlimited fine and two years.[25] There were two dissenting opinions, one by Peter E. Brodie (an Assistant Commissioner of Scotland Yard) arguing that the indictable offences should have a maximum five-year sentence and one by sociologist Michael Schofield (one of the signatories of *SOMA*'s 1967 *Times* advertisement), who thought both penalties should be lower than the majority recommendation. In short, all of the Sub-Committee members thought the penalties should be lower than those provided in the 1965 act, though none was prepared to support decriminalisation.[26]

Although most Sub-Committee members had seen through the predominant myths around cannabis use, these were still common currency among large sections of the public. When the report was published, the tabloid press practically howled with outrage. Headlines included 'Dangers in this conspiracy of the drugged', 'It's a junkies charter', 'Russian Roulette – with a fully loaded revolver – we must fight drugs lobby', and 'Lady Wootton's Committee have a lot to answer for – now the drugs flood in'.[27] One tabloid concluded, 'If there has been pressure it has come from the legalise pot lobby ... The best thing to do with this report is to dump it in the wastepaper basket.'[28] In the professional press, the verdict was split, with the *British Medical Journal* attacking the report and *The Lancet* supporting it.

It was inevitable that the report would receive a hostile reception from some members of Parliament. In a response to the 1967 *Times* advertisement, that year's Conservative Party Conference passed a resolution that 'it disapproves strongly any move towards a more permissive attitude to the so-called "soft" drugs.'[29] During the debate over this resolution, Shadow Home Secretary Quintin Hogg, a leading figure in the Conservative party's 'law and order' campaign, claimed that cannabis use was 'confined to a few corrupt and corrupting centres of moral degradation' and that 'in the course of its disreputable career, it has given the name "assassin"'.[30] He went on to say that publishing the *SOMA* ad was 'a heavy responsibility which [*Times* editor William Rees-Mogg] will have to carry with him during the rest of his professional life. But far worse is the responsibility to those who signed that advertisement.'[31] Hogg received a standing ovation for his address, and the motion was passed overwhelmingly. Parliament first took up discussion of the Wootton Report in late January, after the negative press coverage had already broken. During the debate, Hogg reiterated the Conservative party's position on soft drugs, as well as perpetuating many myths about cannabis that were dismissed by the Wootton Report. He claimed that cannabis caused aggressive behaviour, that it was addictive, and that its use led to heroin addiction and criminal activity (including murder). He also said that lawyers and doctors agreed that 'although they [could] not always give figures which prove[d] these facts ... this drug [wa]s associated in their minds and professional experience with crime, violence and abnormality of one sort or another'.[32] Hogg also used the opportunity to make an attack on the underground, saying, 'the question of cannabis and its use has been the subject of a considerable propaganda campaign'.[33]

Any thoughts that the Labour Government might support the findings of a committee that it had appointed were quickly dispelled when Home Secretary James Callaghan rose to reply to Hogg's speech and said: '[it] represents my own approach completely, I feel like pronouncing the benediction ... I congratulate the right hon. and learned Gentleman on the moral force, passion and conviction with which he put his views, with which I find myself wholeheartedly in agreement.'[34] This represented perhaps the most unfortunate aspect of the timing of the report, because while the Sub-Committee was conducting its research, the office of Home Secretary passed from Roy Jenkins, who in many ways had been the architect of the 'permissive society', to the much more conservative Callaghan.

As Kenneth O. Morgan noted, 'The abrupt government rejection of permissiveness and libertarianism associated with the youth counter-culture was a historic landmark in British social experience.'[35] Callaghan's hostile reception to the report was motivated by several factors. His Baptist upbringing and trade-union background gave him a different outlook from Jenkins. He represented the conservative element in the Labour party that was concerned with wages, hours and working conditions, but was content with the cultural status quo and frightened of what he saw as the socially destabilising agenda of student radicals and the underground. As one of *Release*'s solicitors, who gave testimony to the Wootton Sub-Committee, said, 'If one had had a more liberal Home Secretary [the Wootton Report] would have been taken up. ... [Callaghan] didn't have the dimension of Jenkins – didn't have the understanding of modern liberal issues.'[36] Another factor was that Callaghan had close ties to the police. He was the paid parliamentary consultant of the Police Federation from 1955 to 1964, and the union opposed the Wootton Report's claims that officers were abusing their powers of search and arrest when enforcing drug laws.[37] Indeed, he told members of the Federation, 'I am not ready to take the risks of permissiveness.'[38]

There were political considerations as well. Many were never comfortable with the changes brought by permissiveness. For example, Mary Whitehouse founded her 'clean up TV campaign' in 1964.[39] Likewise, the Labour government was aware that Jenkins' policies were not universally popular. In 1967, cabinet minister Richard Crossman noted in his diary after the bill to legalise homosexuality was passed, 'certainly working-class people in the north jeer at their Members at the weekend and ask them why they're looking after the buggers at Westminster instead of looking after the unemployed at home.'[40]

Crossman's reference to unemployment underscored the transition from unmitigated prosperity to economic hardship that occurred in the middle of the decade. The pound had been devalued in November 1967 (partially due to Callaghan's incompetence as Chancellor of the Exchequer) and as the cost of living rose and imports became dearer, the government's rhetoric changed from the 'white heat' optimism of the early Wilson years to talk of the 'hard slog' and shared sacrifice. The *Guardian* had noted that '"Permissiveness" as a social trend came in with full employment', and as this affluence ebbed the public mood shifted.[41] The working-class base of the Labour party had been willing to accept a government that pushed for social change when the cost of living and unemployment rates were relatively low, but by the time the Wootton Committee reported, both of these economic indicators were on the rise. A related problem was the way that mainstream media portrayed the underground. While members of the counterculture were often successful in attracting the notice of politicians and having their issues taken seriously, they also attracted the reprobation and ire of the tabloid press and conservative social commentators. As the economy weakened, members of the older generations became less tolerant of moral relativism, sexual experimentation and drug use associated with the unconventional and supposedly workshy youth movement, leading to attacks on permissiveness. In July 1969, Roy Jenkins thought that 'the forces of liberalism and human freedom [we]re now to some extent on the defensive': 'The permissive society – always a misleading description – has been allowed to become a dirty phrase.'[42] Given this shift in public opinion, and with an election expected in 1970, the Conservatives politicised the Permissive Society by promoting themselves as the party of 'law and order'.[43]

For all these reasons, Callaghan not only dismissed the Sub-Committee's findings, saying 'this is not the time either to legalise the drug or to reduce the penalties', he also used the opportunity to attack the underground:[44]

> I think that it came as a surprise, if not a shock, to most people, when that notorious advertisement appeared in *The Times* in 1967, to find that there is a lobby in favour of legalising cannabis. The House should recognise that this lobby exists, and my reading of the Report is that the Wootton Sub-Committee was over-influenced by this lobby ... The existence of this lobby is something that the House and public opinion should take into account and be ready to combat, as I am. It is another aspect of the so-called permissive society, and I am glad if my decision has enabled the House to call a halt in the advancing tide of so-called permissiveness. I regard it as one of the most unlikeable words that has been invented in recent years.[45]

As a result, the Wootton Report and the Permissive Society were buried in the same coffin.

The Baroness Wootton stated that she found Callaghan's statement 'insulting', and the *Sunday Times* concluded that 'no committee set up by the government of the day has seen its work devastated so brusquely'.[46] Wootton refused to admit defeat, and arranged a meeting with Secretary of State for Health and Social Services Richard Crossman for 14 August 1969.[47] His department was in charge of preventing and curing addiction, and Wootton hoped to have all matters relating to drugs transferred there from the Home Office in order to have the committee's report implemented. This would have redefined drug use as an issue of health care rather than law enforcement and removed it from

Callaghan's purview. Unfortunately, Crossman's knowledge of the issue was lacking. After meeting with Wootton he wrote in his diary that her report dealt with, 'oh, what's it called, not heroin but one of the other drugs', and he concluded that Callaghan's position was correct and told Wootton that it was too late to do anything.[48]

The Misuse of Drugs Act

In January 1970, the Home Affairs Committee of the Cabinet agreed on the outline for a new Misuse of Drugs Bill. The Committee proposed to lower the maximum penalty for indictment for cannabis possession from ten to three years – one year more than the Wootton recommendation. However, when news of the bill leaked to the press, Callaghan attempted to remove the provisions dealing with cannabis at a cabinet meeting on 26 February.[49] This was unusual, given that issues were usually only brought to the Cabinet if there was disagreement in a committee. Evidently, Callaghan was afraid of being portrayed as reversing his position on the Wootton Report, and according to Minister of Technology Tony Benn, 'Jim had come to the conclusion that, with the strong Tory attacks over law and order and the permissive society, he should not now ease the law.'[50]

Callaghan considered cannabis 'perhaps the most widely publicised and certainly the most controversial of the drugs dealt with by the Bill'.[51] This may seem somewhat strange, because the legislation also dealt with heroin, cocaine, LSD and amphetamines, but the statement gave some idea of how the debate over the Wootton Report and the activities of the underground had focused public attention on the drug. Since he did not want to appear to be weakening on the issue, Callaghan proposed having no legal differentiation between types of drugs. He wanted maximum penalties of either seven or ten years (he was uncertain which was best) for possession and fourteen years for trafficking of everything from cannabis to heroin.

Benn thought that the ensuing debate was 'very vulgar stuff because the real argument in favour of easement is of course strong'.[52] Indeed, the main point made in support of Callaghan was that easing the restriction on cannabis would be seen as an 'apparent concession to the permissive tendencies in society ... and the Government might be at considerable political risk as a result'.[53] Those on the other side argued that it was wrong to legislate solely on political considerations. No one claimed that cannabis was as harmful as heroin or other hard drugs. No one offered a moral or legal basis for maintaining tough penalties for cannabis. Cannabis law was a political consideration more than a matter of health or public safety. Crossman wrote that 'The discussion was particularly fascinating because no one really doubted the rightness of … the reduction of the penalties for possession … Nobody denied this, they simply said that the public wouldn't understand it and that we now couldn't afford to alienate people on this issue.'[54]

Eventually, a vote was called on whether to accept the proposals of the Home Affairs Committee or Callaghan's alternative plan, which highlighted the cultural divide in the Cabinet. As Crossman recorded, 'we had for the first time a sociological vote, that is to say, every member of the cabinet who had been to university voted one way [to differentiate between drugs and lower the cannabis penalties] and everyone else voted the other'.[55] The only exception to this was the Oxford-educated Prime Minister, who voted with his Home Secretary. Even with Wilson's support, Callaghan was outvoted. He then insisted that the maximum penalty upon indictment be changed from three years to five, and the cabinet allowed this amendment. As a result, the Misuse of Drugs Bill was published on 11 March.[56]

The bill did not die when the Labour Government was voted out of office on 18 June 1970 but was re-introduced by Tory Home Secretary Reginald Maudling and became the Misuse of Drugs Act 1971. It seems ironic, given Callaghan's concern that the bill would provide Conservatives with political ammunition during the election, that the Tories reintroduced the Labour legislation without alteration. However, this also highlighted the fact that, electioneering aside, the two parties were not far apart on the issue.[57] The act, which remains the basis of British drug law to the present, divided drugs into three categories, labelled in descending order of seriousness as class A, class B and class C. Class A included heroin, cocaine, and LSD. Class B included methamphetamine and cannabis. The result was that the maximum penalty for the summary conviction of cannabis possession in a magistrate's court went from a £250 fine and one year in prison to a £400 fine and six months in prison.[58] The maximum penalty for the indictment of cannabis possession changed from a £1,000 fine and ten years in prison to an unlimited fine and five years.[59] Also, a separate charge for drug trafficking was introduced for the first time, with the court left to decide whether or not the accused was a dealer, regardless of the amount of drugs confiscated. The maximum penalty for a summary conviction for trafficking was a £400 fine and a year in prison and for indictment an unlimited fine and fourteen years in prison, with no distinction being made between trafficking in cannabis and trafficking in hard drugs such as heroin.

The political legacy of the 1960s

During the parliamentary debate over the 1971 bill, MP Norman St John-Stevas said, 'the danger is that the whole issue will be debated as part of a blanket condemnation … of the permissive society'.[60] That is exactly what happened, not just in the early 1970s but also in subsequent debates. As political arguments over drug use became inextricably linked to the legacy of the 1960s in general, as well as to the underground and permissive society in particular, the two were often conflated.

Despite the calls for decriminalisation both inside and outside of Parliament – many using the Wootton Report for support – and despite moves toward decriminalisation in Europe and parts of the United States, British law ossified.[61] One reason was that the very idea of permissiveness was vilified. The Permissive Society died with post-war affluence, as Great Britain lurched from one economic crisis to another in the next two decades. During these years, no serious Labour politician wanted to be associated with libertarianism, much less libertinism, and during the eighteen years of Tory rule from 1979 to 1997, the party vilified the 1960s as one of the roots of Britain's problems. Prime Minister Thatcher famously summed up her view, saying, 'We are reaping what was sown in the 1960s when fashionable theories and *permissive* claptrap set the scene for a society in which the old values of discipline and self-restraint were denigrated.'[62] Tory party chairman Norman Tebbit reiterated this position, stating that 'British society must regain a sense of order … Order in our streets. Order in schools and order in the home' so that it could overcome 'the poisoned legacy of the permissive society'.[63]

Of course, Thatcher did not believe in either permissiveness or society, stating in 1987, 'There is no such thing as society.'[64] Her ideology was one of individual responsibility and moral restraint. As a result, drug policy was considered as part of a larger plan of enforcing public order so that the complete 'legacy' of the 'profits of the permissive society' could be overcome. In 1989, Thatcher boasted, 'That's why we've toughened the law on the muggers and marauders. That's why we've increased penalties on drink-driving, on drugs, on rape. That's why we've increased the police and strengthened their powers … For there can be no freedom without order. There can be no order without authority.'[65] This attitude fundamentally defined the Conservative Government's drug policy, as exemplified in the harsh Drug Trafficking Offences Act in 1986. Defending this position in the face of both increasing cannabis use in the United Kingdom and broader European debates about liberalising cannabis laws, Thatcher said, 'you cannot beat drug-taking by legalising drugs! That is the way to destroy young lives, ruin families and undermine society itself. Our task is to protect young people, not deliberately to expose them to danger. I can assure you that our Government here will never legalise illicit drugs, hard or soft.'[66] After Thatcher's departure, Conservative party policy continued a hard line on soft drugs. In 1995, under John Major, there was a five-fold increase in the maximum fine for cannabis possession.

In order to take his party from the political wilderness to power, Tony Blair fashioned New Labour by jettisoning many elements that had provided the Conservatives with their main points of attack on the party, from a commitment to socialism to a liberal approach on social issues. Blair wanted to use the image of the 1960s, and he did not mind it circulating that he played guitar in a rock band at Oxford, or the publication of photos of him with long hair and bell-bottoms.[67] However, he was unwilling to take political risks on social issues.

In 1995, Clare Short, then a member of the Labour shadow cabinet, suggested that cannabis could be decriminalised. Blair publicly reprimanded her and warned other Labour leaders not to 'make personal statements that c[ould] be used against [them] by the media and [thei]r political enemies'.[68] New Labour was aware of how cannabis policy could be used as a political weapon. In a 1995 by-election, the Liberal Democrat candidate was repeatedly attacked as 'soft on drugs' by the Labour party, in a campaign managed by Peter Mandelson, for having called for a Royal Commission to study cannabis decriminalisation.[69] The result of these policies was a 'cross-party consensus on law and order' that 'occurred largely because New Labour accepted many of the policy changes of the Thatcherite years in law and order'.[70]

Once in power, Blair launched a campaign to reform law enforcement by declaring the 'end of the 1960s liberal, social consensus on law and order'.[71] He also took an opportunity to praise James Callaghan, saying: 'he powerfully opposed calls to legalise cannabis. And he described his commitment to order and authority in ways that at that time seemed old-fashioned but in 2007 seem remarkably close to where the consensus is.'[72] This was mostly political theatre, but it also demonstrated a lack of support for legal reforms. As Italy, Switzerland, Spain and Portugal decriminalised cannabis and the coffee shops in Amsterdam remained a favoured destination of British travellers, the UK government did nothing.[73]

Enforcing cannabis law

Despite the fact that the laws regarding cannabis have not been substantially altered since 1971, the enforcement of the law is radically different. The rapid growth in cannabis use was a topic in the debate over the 1971 Act. Tory MP Bill Deedes said, 'marijuana can no longer be regarded as a wayward habit of young nonconformists … it has become a widely accepted social habit.'[74] Cannabis use started out in small amounts in immigrant enclaves, but the counterculture brought it into regular use among significant numbers of Britons. As this subculture spread beyond its London roots, it brought cannabis use to the urban centres of the country. Even after the underground ceased to be a dominant youth subculture, its influence transcended its demise. As several historians have pointed out – the fashions, music and drugs of the 1960s counterculture became mainstream youth culture by the 1970s.[75] The Wootton Report estimated in 1968 as many as 300,000 people were using cannabis. By 1972, the estimate was up to 2,000,000.[76]

In 1963, sociologist Howard Becker claimed that marijuana use was enough to result in the user being identified as a deviant by mainstream society. This label subjected the user to sanctions from those who considered marijuana use immoral or the result of psychological problems. These sanctions could be both formal, such as imprisonment, and informal, such as social ostracism.[77] As cannabis use spread and became more acceptable, legal sanctions remained while social sanctions disappeared. Already by 1970, a *New Society* article claimed that among schoolchildren, 'Drug taking seemed often to be yet one more element in the behaviour of a lad who wants to grow up quick, who smokes cigarettes young and bluffs his way into the pub underage.'[78] Given the nature of modern consumer capitalism, laden with the concept that consumers can maximise their pleasure by the exercising of free choice in the market place, it seems inevitable that cannabis would eventually become yet another recreational commodity. Once cannabis came to be seen in this light by a large stratum of society, the laws against its use became increasingly irrelevant anachronisms. Even those who did not smoke cannabis often accepted its use by their peers as a normal part of social life. Especially for young people, it ceased to be a mark of deviant behaviour and became another lifestyle choice, much like the use of legal drugs such as tobacco and alcohol.[79] In the 1990s, *Release* claimed that 'more people smoke cannabis than go to football matches, visit art galleries or go to church on Sunday', and sociologists stated that 'the availability of drugs is a normal part of the leisure-pleasure landscape'.[80]

This process of normalising cannabis use did not have an immediate effect on law enforcement. Following the Conservative party's 1979 victory, Thatcher's attacks on permissiveness encouraged officers who wanted to employ a more aggressive form of policing, and the result was a series of zero-tolerance campaigns aimed at young, urban offenders.[81] The primary tool of this aggressive policing was the 'sus' law, which allowed police to stop, search and arrest anyone on suspicion of criminal activity.[82] Given the ubiquity of cannabis use in certain communities, the police could argue that a person's appearance, and possibly ethnicity, was enough to justify a stop on suspicion of possession. Police regularly abused this power in order to contest the control of public spaces, especially in primarily Afro-Caribbean neighbourhoods.[83]

This abuse of police powers was a significant factor in the riots that broke out in several cities – including Leeds, Liverpool and London – beginning in 1980.[84] These disturbances, coupled with a rise in heroin use, forced the police to rethink their approach to cannabis.[85] It seemed impossible to enforce the laws against cannabis rigidly while at the same time maintaining public order. Problems that were more serious demanded police resources while cannabis use continued to increase. The police dealt with 15,000 cannabis offenders in 1980 and more than 40,000 in 1990.[86]

The Misuse of Drugs Act set maximum penalties but not minimum penalties. Rather than try to imprison cannabis users, police increasingly turned to formal cautioning. Of the over 40,000 people arrested for cannabis offences in 1990, only 1,126 were imprisoned for cannabis possession, some of the rest being fined but most merely cautioned.[87] In 1995, the drugs sub-committee of the Association of Chief Police Officers called for the use of cautions rather than prosecutions for the first arrest of drug dealers.[88] Another approach was simply to turn a blind eye to cannabis possession. Alex Marnoch, the police commander placed in charge of Brixton after the 1981 riot, strongly discouraged his officers from making arrests for the possession of cannabis for personal use.[89] This view eventually spread to other urban police forces. A 1991 survey in Sussex showed that 20 per cent of the officers there did not even bother with a formal caution and ignored cannabis possession, claiming, 'some officers feel that they are manufacturing criminals and dealing with a victimless crime'.[90] A further study at the end of the 1990s showed that less than one third of police officers surveyed always arrested people for possession.[91]

Conclusion

Despite changes in how cannabis use was policed, the laws regarding its use remained largely unchanged from the 1970s. The government's Advisory

Council on the Misuse of Drugs (ACMD), which was established by the 1971 Act, published reports in 1979 and 1982 that called for cannabis to be reclassified from a class B to a class C drug.[92] A 1991 report by Justice – the British section of the International Commission of Jurists – and the Police Foundation's Runciman Report of 2000 agreed.[93] Both Conservative and Labour governments repeatedly ignored this advice.[94]

By 1999, 40 per cent of fifteen- and sixteen-year-olds had tried the drug, and 29 per cent of Britons had used it in the past year.[95] Despite having the harshest cannabis laws in western Europe, Britain had the highest rate of cannabis use in the European Union. In 2001, a high-ranking Scotland Yard officer stated the obvious, 'Arresting people for smoking dope is pointless … It's a waste of time, the war is lost.'[96] In the same year, Scotland Yard's commander in Lambeth, south London, publicly instructed his men to no longer arrest cannabis users.

There was a brief attempt to politically capitalise on the lax enforcement of cannabis laws. At the 2000 Conservative Party Conference, shadow home secretary Ann Widdecombe called for a 'zero tolerance' policy toward cannabis that would end cautioning and impose a mandatory £100 fine for possession.[97] This proposal backfired when the Police Superintendents' Association came out strongly against it, eight other members of the Tory shadow cabinet admitted that they had smoked cannabis, and Charles Kennedy of the Liberal Democrats took the opportunity to become the first party leader to call for decriminalisation.[98] A year later, Tory MP John Bercow, who was soon brought into the shadow cabinet, called for cannabis decriminalisation in a letter to his colleagues, saying it would allow the Conservatives to 'reconnect with millions of people who consider the present law to be an ass'.[99] This dissention within Conservative ranks over cannabis seemed to give Labour room to manoeuvre on the issue. Following another ACMD report in 2002, Tony Blair's Labour administration decided to reclassify cannabis as a class C drug (the same class as ketamine, GHB and some tranquilisers) in January 2004.[100]

This change proved to be short-lived. Gordon Brown became prime minister in 2007 with low poll numbers and with a growing concern in the country over crime rates. With an election fast approaching and Conservative leader David Cameron eager to portray him as soft on crime, Brown decided to return cannabis to class B, over the objections of his scientific advisors, in May 2008.[101] Professor David Nutt, chair of the ACMD, was forced to resign for claiming that the decision of Brown and Home Secretary Alan Johnson was politically motivated.[102]

These changes in the law made very little difference in the lives of cannabis users. A former Assistant Commissioner at Scotland Yard wrote, 'the police and courts take a more lenient view towards users of cannabis because they deem it as less harmful than other drugs … Reclassification will change nothing[; it] hints more of a political ping-pong match than anything more serious.'[103] Indeed, of more than 160,000 people found with cannabis in 2008–9, almost 67 per cent were simply given a verbal warning, 16 per cent were officially cautioned, and only 17 per cent were formally charged.[104] Governments are unwilling to accept responsibility for regulating and managing illegal drugs as a health issue. Instead, both Conservatives and Labour continue to ignore the reality of the normalisation of cannabis use and to support criminal prosecution for possession. However, the reality of enforcement is very different, and in many urban areas simple possession is effectively decriminalised.[105]

While it remains politically impossible to make the laws of Britain match the reality of modern European drug use, cannabis use has become 'Britain's most popular crime', and those who lobbied the Wootton Sub-Committee achieved most of their goals.[106] This came about not through legislative victories but from cultural change. Cannabis use is no longer exclusively associated with the Afro-Caribbean community or with deviant youth subcultures. Instead, it is an acknowledged, and widely accepted, part of the cultural landscape of modern Britain.[107] It is a part of rock music mythology that in 1965, when the Beatles went to Buckingham Palace to accept their MBEs from the Queen, they first went into a palace bathroom to smoke a joint.[108] Whether to calm their nerves or as a subversive gesture in the heart of the Establishment, it was clearly a rebellious act.[109] In 2002, it was revealed that the Queen's 16-year-old grandson, Prince Harry, smoked hash.[110] The news was greeted as a minor bit of bad public relations for the Royal Family.[111] As the Bishop of Edinburgh said when admitting his own past cannabis use, it was widely accepted that, 'For anyone under 45 it is just a part of growing up.'[112] In the end, while the Permissive Society became a term of political abuse, permissiveness won the day.[113]

Notes

1 *Lancet*, 11 November 1995.

2 *Guardian*, *The Permissive Society: The Guardian Inquiry* (London: Panther, 1969), 10.

3 Laing, aged forty at the time, may seem out of place, but he was considered a 'guru to so many young people in London, a necessary presence when inner space is dis-

cussed'. *IT* (London), 16 January 1967. 'Underground' was the preferred British term, although the American 'counterculture' was sometimes used, especially in the mainstream media. The terms refer to a specific youth subculture that evolved out of the earlier beat (or beatnik) subculture during the early to mid-1960s in both countries.

4 Jeffrey Weeks, *Sex, Politics & Society: The Regulation of Sexuality Since 1800, Second Edition* (London: Longman, 1989), 265.

5 National Health Service (Family Planning) Act, 1967.

6 Abortion Act, 1967.

7 For the story of cannabis in Britain until 1928, see James H. Mill, *Cannabis Britannica: Empire, Trade and Prohibition* (Oxford: Oxford University Press, 2003).

8 Jock Young, *The Drugtakers: The Social Meaning of Drug Use* (London: Paladin, 1971), 11.

9 Home Office, *Cannabis: Report by the Advisory Committee on Drug Dependence* (London: Her Majesty's Stationery Office, 1968), 8. The report, though clearly indicating that cannabis use was a product of immigration, went on to say, '[i]n 1950, however, police raids on certain London jazz clubs produced clear evidence that cannabis was being used by the indigenous population.'

10 Young, 12.

11 Donald Louria, *The Drug Scene* (New York: McGraw-Hill, 1968), 66.

12 Channon, House of Commons, 28 July 1967, Parliamentary Debates, vol. 751, cols 1152–3.

13 *People* (London), 29 January 1967, and *Cherwell*, 1 February 1967. Abrams claimed that after investigating the various colleges of the university, he 'came to the conclusion that it was roughly 10 per cent of the 10,000 junior members in the university – 1,000 – then I cut it in half and made it 500 to be on the safe side'. David Black, *Acid: The Secret History of LSD* (London: Vision Paperbacks, 1998), 70.

14 *Ibid*. Soma is both a hallucinogen from Vedic mythology and a drug in Aldous Huxley's 1932 dystopian novel *Brave New World*.

15 *Times*, 4 April 1967.

16 The only other government study of cannabis was the 1897 report of the Indian Hemp Drugs Commission (seven volumes). Cannabis remained legal in India until 1948. Caroline Coon & Rufus Harris, *The Release Report on Drug Offenders and the Law* (London: Sphere, 1969), 114–5.

17 Abrams got the idea from an article Allen Ginsberg wrote for the book *The Marijuana Papers*. Jonathon Green, *Days In The Life: Voices from the English Underground, 1961–1971* (London: William Heinemann, 1988), 192.

18 *Times*, 24 July 1967.

19 The advertisement was entirely conceived and organised by the underground, and the actual layout was handled by Mike McInnerney, the art & graphics designer of *IT*.

20 They also sparked debate in Parliament. On 28 July 1967, there was an interesting discussion on the floor of the Commons in response to the *Times* advertisement. Alice Bacon, Minster of State at the Home Office, asked, 'What sort of society will

we create if everyone wants to escape from reality?' Labour MP Tom Driberg, one of the two MPs to sign the *Times* advertisement, replied, 'They want to escape from this horrible society we have created.' Driberg, House of Commons, 28 July 1967, Parliamentary Debates, vol. 751, col. 1164.

21 Home Office, *Cannabis*, 1.

22 Home Office, *Cannabis*, 4.

23 *Ibid.*, 7 and 13–5.

24 *Ibid.*, v.

25 Young, 199. Summary convictions were for minor offences tried in a magistrate's court. Indictable offences were more serious and tried before a jury. The accused could opt for jury trial, though with the possibility of an increased penalty.

26 Lady Wootton said '[e]ven those who wanted to legalise [cannabis], even those people who signed the *Times* advertisement, admit that immediate legalisation is not practical.' *Sunday Times*, 12 January 1969.

27 *Daily Mirror*, 28 November 1968; *Evening News*, 8 January 1969; *Daily Express*, Jan. 13, 1969; *News of the World* (London), 12 January 1969.

28 *Daily Sketch*, 8 January 1969.

29 *Times*, 21 October 1967.

30 *Ibid.* and *Guardian*, 21 October 1967. The words 'assassin' and 'hashish' can both be traced back to the Islamic cult leader Hassan I Sabbah (also known as Hassan ibn al-Sabbah and Sayyidna Hasan bin Sabbah), who died in 1124.

31 *Ibid.* Rees-Mogg replied, saying '[w]e believe that people who want to change the law have a right to put their case to the public … Mr. Hogg thinks that the subject of drugs is so dangerous that free discussion cannot be allowed, that those who disagree with him have no right to be heard.' *Times*, 23 October 1967.

32 Hogg, House of Commons, 27 January 1969, Parliamentary Debates, vol. 776, col. 958.

33 *Ibid.*, 947.

34 *Ibid.*, 958.

35 Kenneth O. Morgan, *Callaghan: A Life* (Oxford University Press, 1997), 321.

36 David Offenbach, unpublished interview with Jonathon Green c.1987. In possession of author.

37 Geoffrey Alderman, *Pressure Groups and Government in Great Britain* (London: Longman, 1984), 64. These accusations of police misconduct were later corroborated when Detective Chief Inspector Victor Kelaher, the head of the Drug Squad, was indicted for a variety of abuses along with five of his officers. Three officers were convicted and imprisoned, Kelaher and another were dismissed from the force, and the sixth was reprimanded and transferred. Barry Cox, John Shirley, and Martin Short, *The Fall of Scotland Yard* (Harmondsworth: Penguin, 1977), 126–9.

38 Peter Kellner and Christopher Hitchens, *Callaghan, The Road to Number Ten* (London: Cassell, 1976), 83.

39 Christie Davis, *Permissive Britain: Social Change in the Sixties and Seventies* (London: Sir Isaac Pitman and Sons, 1975), 47.

40 Richard Crossman, *Diaries of a Cabinet Minister. Vol. 2: Lord President of the Council*

and Leader of the House of Commons, 1966–1968 (London: Hamish Hamilton & Jonathan Cape, 1976), 220.

41 *Guardian*, 1.

42 *Sunday Times*, 20 July 1969.

43 One example is that Conservative Peter Fry won the seat for Wellingborough with a 9.7% swing in a December 1969 by-election. He made attacks on the Permissive Society a part of his campaign, and once elected brought forward a motion in the Commons that 'That this House views with grave concern the continuing decline of moral standards and the increases of violence, hooliganism, drug taking and obscenity and the consequent undermining of family life.' *Guardian*, 5 December 1969. See also Fry, House of Commons, 4 May 1970, Parliamentary Debates, vol. 801, col. 38.

44 Callaghan, House of Commons, 27 January 1969, Parliamentary Debates, vol. 776, col. 961.

45 *Ibid.*, 959. Sir Edward Wayne (chairman of the Advisory Committee) and Lady Wootton wrote a joint letter to the *Times* saying that they regarded the Home Secretary's 'statement as offensive to our distinguished colleagues and to ourselves, and particularly to the eminent medical men who signed our Report, and we particularly deprecate the implication of the emotive word 'lobby' in this context'. *Times*, 5 February 1969.

46 *Sunday Times*, 23 February 1969.

47 Crossman described her as 'a brilliant, hard-headed, immensely able, difficult, pugnacious, eccentric woman'. Richard Crossman, *Diaries of a Cabinet Minister. Vol. 3: Secretary of State for Social Services, 1968–1970* (London: Hamish Hamilton & Jonathan Cape, 1977), 615.

48 *Ibid.* Even though Crossman supported Callaghan's position on cannabis, he supported Wootton's contention that his department should have oversight on drugs. Looking into the matter, he discovered that Callaghan had intervened to prevent Health and Social Services from having that authority.

49 The headline read: 'DRUG LAW SHOCK – Jim Changes his Mind. Penalties for 'pot' smokers to be cut'. *Sunday Mirror*, 1 February 1970.

50 Tony Benn, *Office Without Power: Diaries, 1968–72* (London: Hutchinson, 1988), 243.

51 Memorandum by the Secretary of State for the Home Department, 24 February 1970, C (70) 34. (PRO, CAB129/148.)

52 *Ibid.*

53 Cabinet Conclusions, 26 February 1970, CC10 (70). (PRO, CAB128/45.)

54 Crossman, *Vol. 3*, 837.

55 *Ibid.*

56 *Misuse of Drugs Bill* (London: Her Majesty's Stationary Office, 1970), 38–9. It was presented by Callaghan, Crossman, Secretary of State for Scotland William Ross, Secretary of State for Wales George Thomas, Dick Taverne, Elystan Morgan, and Attorney General Elwyn Jones.

57 In cabinet discussion, it was decided that since the bill's 'broad principles and objec-

tives had been generally endorsed by all Parties', it should be immediately reintroduced to 'give a clear indication of their determination to deal promptly with a grave
social problem'. Cabinet Conclusions, 7 July 1970, CM4 (70). (PRO, CAB128/47.)

58 The Criminal Law Act 1977 reduced the possible jail time for summary conviction of cannabis possession to three months, even less than the term recommended
by the Wootton Sub-Committee. Roy Jenkins, who was again serving as Wilson's
Home Secretary, brought the bill forward in 1976.

59 One of the reasons why some in the counterculture considered this bill a defeat,
other than the harsh new sentences for dealing, was that the maximum penalty for
possession of LSD, the other underground drug of choice, increased from two to
seven years.

60 St. John-Stevas, House of Commons, 25 March 1970, Parliamentary Debates, vol.
798, col. 1477.

61 *SOMA* disbanded and *Release* became less vocal in its support for decriminalisation.
This role was taken over by the *Cannabis Action Reform Organization* (CARO) in
1973, which was then superseded by the *Legalise Cannabis Campaign* in 1978.

62 *Guardian*, 28 March 1982. It was a speech to the Conservative Central Council.

63 *Guardian*, 10 April 1986.

64 *Woman's Own*, 31 October 1987.

65 Margaret Thatcher, *Speech to the Central Council at Scarborough on Saturday 18 May
1989* (London: Conservative Central Office, 1989), 10–1.

66 Margaret Thatcher, *Report of the World Ministerial Summit to Reduce Demand for
Drugs and to Combat the Cocaine Threat* (London: HMSO, 1990).

67 Dominic Sandbrook commented, 'it was easy to imagine that the Prime Minister
had spent most of the 1960s practising guitar licks and stage moves with his good
friends Paul and Mick – now Sir Paul and Sir Mick – so keen were his advisers to sell
him as a child of that decade'. *New Statesman*, 21 March 2005.

68 *Independent*, 30 October 1995.

69 The full attack line was 'high on tax and soft on drugs'. The Lib-Dem candidate,
Chris Davies, won the Littleborough and Saddleworth seat despite these attacks,
and was later elected a MEP. *Independent*, 27 July and 30 October 1995, and 15
November 1996.

70 Robert Reiner, *The Politics of the Police*, 3rd edn (Oxford University Press, 2000), 74.

71 *Independent*, 19 July 2004. This prompted Joan Bakewell to ask, 'Which punitive
measure of the Fifties would Tony Blair like to reintroduce?' *Independent*, 20 July
2004.

72 Office of the Prime Minister, 'Speech by the Prime Minister, The Right Honour-
able Tony Blair MP at Cardiff City Hall – The Callaghan Memorial Lecture.' Press
Release, 11 April 2007.

73 This was in spite of the rapid growth of the medical marijuana movement in the
1990s. As Howard Parker and his colleagues noted, 'the current "war on drugs"
discourse [was] developed by consecutive Conservative governments but accepted
and maintained by Labour.' Howard Parker, Judith Aldridge and Fiona Measham,
Illegal Leisure: The Normalization of Adolescent Recreational Drug Use (New York:

Routledge, 1998), 152.

74 Deedes, House of Commons, 25 March 1970, *Parliamentary Debates*, vol. 798, col. 1463.

75 *The Conquest of Cool: Business Culture, Counterculture and the Rise of Hip Consumerism* by Thomas Frank (Chicago, IL: University of Chicago Press, 1998), although about this process in the United States, is the best work on this theme. For Britain, see Leon Hunt, *British Low Culture: From Safari Suits to Sexploitation* (London: Routledge, 1998).

76 Martin Booth, *Cannabis: A History* (London: Doubleday, 2003), 274.

77 See Howard Becker, *The Outsiders: Studies in the Sociology of Deviance* (New York: The Free Press, 1963).

78 *New Society*, 19 March 1970.

79 For discussion and criticism of Howard Parker's normalisation thesis see Shane Blackman, '"See Emily Play": Youth Culture, Recreational Drug Use and Normalisation', in Mark Simpson *et al.* (eds), *Drugs in Britain: Supply, Consumption and Control* (London: Palgrave Macmillan, 2007), and Michael Shiner, *Drugs Use and Social Change: The Distortion of History* (London: Palgrave Macmillan, 2009).

80 *Times*, 24 July 1992. This statement is from a full-page advertisement calling for decriminalisation released on the twenty-fifth anniversary of the original *SOMA* advertisement. Although it was accompanied by a *Times* editorial calling for decriminalisation, the 1967 advertisement included two MPs in its sixty-five signatories, while the 1992 advertisement had only one MP among 209 signatories. Howard Parker, Fiona Measham and Judith Aldridge, *Drugs Futures: Changing Patterns of Drug Use Amongst English Youth* (London: ISDD, 1995), 25.

81 Reiner, *The Politics of the Police*, 121–2. The Police Federation had been unhappy with liberalising trends in penal and social policy and with the Labour Party's ties to increasingly militant trade unions. It began a 'law and order' lobbying campaign in 1975 and openly supported the Conservative Party in the 1979 election. See also p. 72.

82 The 'sus' law – which came from the Vagrancy Act of 1824 – was repealed in 1981 as a result of Lord Scarman's report on the causes of the riots. Les Johnson, 'Street Crime in England and Wales', in Ian K. MacKenzie (ed.), *Law, Power, and Justice in England and Wales* (Westport, CT: Praeger, 1998), 24.

83 In 1977, forty-four per cent of those arrested on 'sus' were of Afro-Caribbean ethnicity. *Times*, 14 March 1980.

84 Riots occurred, among other places, in the St Paul's district in Bristol (1980), Brixton (1981 and 1985), the Chapeltown district of Leeds (1981), the Moss Side area of Manchester (1981), the Toxteth area of Liverpool (1981), the Handsworth area of Birmingham (1981 and 1985), and Broadwater Farm in Tottenham (1985). See Michael Keith, *Race, Riots and Policing: Lore and Disorder in a Multi-Racist Society* (London: UCL Press, 1993) for an interpretation of the riots, and Michael Rowe, *The Racialisation of Disorder in Twentieth Century Britain* (Aldershot: Ashgate, 1998) for an attempt to place them in a broader historical context.

85 By the mid-1980s, police annually seized ten times as much heroin as they had in

the late 1970s. Whereas Britain was previously a transit place for the drug, heroin now arrived for domestic consumption. Ben Whitaker, *The Global Connection: The Crisis of Drug Addiction* (London: Jonathan Cape, 1987), xx–xxi.

86 *Guardian*, 9 November 1991. The number was 97,200 offenders in 1998. *Independent*, 17 February 2000.

87 *Guardian*, 9 November 1991. In 1998, the seventeen-year-old son of the Home Secretary Jack Straw was cautioned by police for selling cannabis to an undercover journalist. *Guardian*, 3 January 1998; *Independent*, 13 January 1998.

88 *Independent*, 12 October 1995.

89 Keith, 133.

90 Andrew Fraser and Michael George, 'Cautions for Cannabis', *Policing* 8, no. 2 (1992): 88. Most of these officers had friends who were cannabis users.

91 Tiggey May, Hamish Warburton, Paul J. Turnbull and Mike Hough, *Times They Are A-Changing: Policing of Cannabis* (Layerthorpe: Joseph Rowntree Foundation, 2002), 26. One officer commented, 'I never nick anyone for cannabis, and never will, unless it's a vanload.'

92 See the Advisory Council on the Misuse of Drugs, *A Review of the Classifications of Controlled Drugs and of Penalties under Schedules 2 and 4 of the Misuse of Drugs Act 1971* (London: HMSO, 1979) and *Report of the Expert Group on the Effects of Cannabis Use* (London: HMSO, 1982).

93 Judge Peter Crawford, QC, *Drugs and the Law – A Report for Justice* (London: Justice, 1991) and Police Foundation, *Drugs and the Law: Report of the Independent Inquiry Into the Misuse of Drugs Act 1971* (London: Police Foundation, 2000).

94 The Blair government was unwilling to decriminalise cannabis for medicinal use, despite the fact that 102 MPs, including eight Tories, signed a Commons motion supporting such a move in 1999. *Guardian*, 16 August 1999.

95 *Guardian*, 4 September and 23 November 1999. Another report showed that cigarette and alcohol use was declining among British teenagers at the same time as cannabis use was increasing. *Guardian*, 15 October 1999.

96 *Guardian*, 18 March 2001.

97 *Guardian*, 4 October 2000.

98 *Guardian*, 5 and 9 October 2000, and *Times*, 18 June 2002.

99 *Times*, 18 June 2002.

100 Advisory Council on the Misuse of Drugs, *The Classification of Cannabis under the Misuse of Drugs Act 1971* (London: HMSO, 2002). Blair ordered a further study by the ACMD to give himself political cover on the issue during the 2005 election. The result was: *Further Consideration of the Classification of Cannabis under the Misuse of Drugs Act 1971* (London: HMSO, 2005).

101 *Guardian*, 7 May 2008.

102 *Guardian*, 30 October 2009. At least five other members of the 31-person body resigned in protest (*Guardian*, 10 November 2009). As Parker, Aldridge and Measham pointed out in 1998, 'the process of normalisation demands regulation and *management*. However, the political moment has not yet been reached when the State will accept responsibility for this.' Parker, Aldridge and Measham, *Illegal*

Leisure, 152.

103 *Times*, 27 January 2009.

104 *Daily Mail*, 20 February 2010.

105 At the 1970 debate over the Misuse of Drugs Bill, the point was made that a penalty of seven years imprisonment for cannabis possession was unwise because 'it was most unlikely that the court would in fact deal so harshly with an offence of this kind, [and as a result] the law itself would be liable to fall into disuse and disrepute'. In many ways, this is what happened. The definition of what legal penalties were too harsh changed considerably as cannabis use became normalised. Eventually the police as well as the courts refused to vigorously enforce the law. Cabinet Conclusions, 26 February 1970, CC 10 (70). (PRO, CAB 128/45.)

106 *Guardian*, 9 November 1991.

107 In 2009, thirty-three per cent of the adult population of England and Wales had used illegal drugs, and almost ten million had used cannabis. *Guardian*, 22 September 2009.

108 Paul Trynka (ed.), *The Beatles: Ten Years That Shook The World* (London: Dorling Kindersley, 2004), 181.

109 An act, it is worth pointing out, that may not have actually happened. John Lennon claimed it did. George Harrison says it did not. Regardless, the image of the four mop tops toking away in the palace lavatory is a cherished rock myth.

110 *Observer*, 13 January 2002.

111 'The revelation that Harry last year dabbled in soft drugs may ironically be the best evidence that he is a truly normal wayward teenager.' *Sunday Express*, 13 January 2002.

112 *Guardian*, 17 August 1999.

113 As Marek Kohn of the Guardian pointed out, 'belief in reefer madness was a casualty of the Sixties'. *Guardian*, 9 November 1991.

8

Women and leisure in Britain: a socio-historical approach to twentieth-century trends

CÉCILE DOUSTALY

R etracing women's leisure in twentieth-century Britain links history with
sociology, the public sphere with the private one, and collective empow-
erment with individual aspirations. Women's leisure therefore stands at the
nexus of the social sciences. It provides a new lens through which to assess the
impact of socio-cultural change on women's lives, including greater opportunities in the professional and public spheres and more varied gender identities
and family structures. The complexity of defining leisure has been due in part
to the individuality of experiences, though these experiences often demonstrate
strong patterns of continuity. The universality of some leisure constraints frequently conditioning women's leisure often reflects the pleasure and frustration common to their experiences. Throughout the twentieth century, women's
widening opportunities in leisure were hampered by persistent stereotypes associating women with domesticity, as they were in other economic, social and
cultural fields. As Zweiniger-Bargielowska concluded, 'Women in 2000 have
many more choices and opportunities than women in 1900 but genuine equal-
ity between men and women remains elusive.'[1]

Trying to pinpoint how leisure evolved over more than a century naturally
leads to studying how research has gradually redefined the concept of leisure
and opened up new perspectives as a result of a sometimes tense dialogue
between history and other disciplines. As a sub-field, the study of women's
leisure followed the classic periodisation of leisure, but it also challenged historical orthodoxies such as the positive impact of the 'society of leisure', in
which women were often invisible. Historians advocating a long periodisation

based on women's broadening leisure opportunities have identified three stages for the eighteenth, nineteenth and twentieth centuries, noting an emphasis on community, nation and the world, respectively.[2] In the twentieth century, the main landmarks affecting women's leisure were the First and Second World Wars and Britain's 'permissive society' in the 1960s.

Quantitative surveys often overestimated or underestimated the amount of women's leisure and hidden its intricacies. Staunch debate within leisure research gradually opened the way for a more inclusive definition of leisure. Originally equated with free time, the notion of 'leisure time' was separated and then advanced, allowing more attention to be paid to economic, social and cultural constraints. Leisure is now recognised not only as a matter of personal preference but also as constructed within an individual context made up of external influences that generally weigh more heavily on women than on men. Women's leisure forms deserve to be studied not just individually as experiences but also for their collective dimensions. The study of leisure activities, which represents only a part of leisure time, should rest on this acknowledgment.

Drawing upon reference studies and statistics which highlight the complexity of investigating women's leisure, this paper aims to discuss concepts, facts and analysis. To understand the main trends in twentieth-century women's leisure, it is necessary to draw from research across disciplinary and national boundaries, including history, sociology and gender studies. This socio-historiographical survey casts new light on the main transformations in British women's leisure pursuits and on the context and meanings surrounding them. I also critically evaluate statistical trends to pinpoint areas of continuity and change. The first section analyses the major contributions to the study of women's leisure, while subsequent sections provide a brief survey of activities and patterns. As will be shown in the final section, British leisure idiosyncrasies comprise a long-lasting female affection for bingo and male appreciation of sports and pubs – forms of leisure which, while they have become less gendered, have been replaced by newer kinds of gendered practices.

Studying women's leisure

Leisure, as a diverse object of research, prompted varied responses from generations of social scientists. While most historians initially concentrated on pre-Edwardian activities, historians in the 1990s, including Hargreaves, Langhamer and Parrat, extended their analyses to the 1960s and helped women's leisure become an academically respected subject. These historical works certainly informed future studies, in part by recognising the 1960s as a watershed, but were preceded by the three major contributions to women's leisure histories outlined below.[3]

The American economist and sociologist Thorstein Veblen's *Theory of the Leisure Class* opened the way for investigations into the relationship between paid labour and leisure as early as 1899.[4] But the British historiography of leisure, first developed in the 1960s, and the first set of key studies of women's leisure, identified the industrial revolution as the turning point from a communal and seasonal kind of leisure to urban forms of leisure stratified by class and respectability, often opposing rational recreation to vice or idleness. In the 1970s, Bailey, Burke and Cunningham's works on popular culture furthered this approach by better recognising women's leisure.[5] However, the conclusion that leisure was defined in relation to work – as all things free, unmonitored and disconnected from labour – tended to exclude some women and their recreations.[6] The first major contributions to British leisure research therefore hardly recognised gender differences and neglected the contemporary period: attention focused on industrial, institutionalised and visible leisure activities which were predominantly a male preserve.[7]

Though French historiography on leisure, the second major set of contributions, was sparse and little read in Britain, collaborations with American social scientists explain the early attention paid to gender in a contemporary context. Joffre Dumazedier, in his 1962 *Towards a Society of Leisure*, drew on history and sociology to argue that in the 'three eight-hour shifts … household chores are treated as if they didn't exist. This is astonishing, since recent studies of housework show that it takes up an impressive amount of time of a given country's labour'. Although Dumazedier was criticised for his functionalism, his pioneering study of leisure as a mass activity distanced itself from dominant class analysis to account for women's experiences. This led him to pinpoint the limitations of time–budget studies which added periods of time indiscriminately: 'Can you still call leisure time a length of time obtained by the addition of often slack moments split up along the day?' Dumazedier recommended marking out degrees of constraint and levels of work/leisure overlap to avoid overestimating leisure time and to take into account the subjective and elastic dimension of activities such as sewing, knitting or gardening, which are not always experienced as chores. His concept of *semi-leisure (semi-loisir)* aptly described these largely self-imposed activities which are still particularly numerous in the lives of women.[8]

French studies of leisure originated from sociologists and social historians who also identified the internalisation process resulting from dominant social and family norms, and the increasing role of leisure activities in the construction of people's identities, particularly as occupational identification waned and free time increased.[9] Veblen had already isolated the function of leisure in social status, but in the 1960s Pierre Bourdieu, in *Distinction: A Social Critique of the Judgement of Taste,* theorised cultural activities as strategic means of distinguishing oneself socially from others.[10] 'Distinction' can be social but also gendered, so that an interest in the social meanings and values attached to leisure has demonstrated how individual leisure patterns stem from what is accessible to individuals in their specific culture, making gender, location, status or ethnicity essential variables. From the 1990s onwards in France, sociological contributions from Elias or Bourdieu were critically integrated to discuss leisure and culture in 'micro-history'[11] or 'socio-history'[12], which, like the approach favoured by the Centre for Research on Socio-Cultural Change (CRESC, the University of Manchester / Open University) successfully implemented interdisciplinary empirical and theoretical methods to evaluate historical change.

The third major series of contributions, from feminist historians and sociologists, challenged the very frameworks of leisure research from the 1980s onwards. Feminist studies underlined both the oppressive and consumerist dimensions of leisure and noted that the field was peopled by male researchers who took male leisure as the norm. They also pointed out that previous historical monographs on women tended to concentrate on paid or domestic work.[13] Feminist researchers followed the classical periodisation of leisure historians but challenged the dominant assumption that the shift to a 'society of leisure' had been necessarily beneficial to all. The development of leisure statistics in the 1970s demonstrated this further. Their very limitations – the lack of understanding of women's tastes and motivations – proved the need for qualitative scrutiny. Feminist research attempted to fill the vast gaps in existing literature using new methodologies based on a transversal approach to redefining leisure so as to render women's experiences visible. The results of two surveys carried out for the Sports Council in 1985 and the provocative title of the subsequent reference book *Women's Leisure, What Leisure?,* presented women's leisure as a contradiction in terms in order to trigger debate.[14] In *All Work and No Play*, the sociologist Rosemary Deem concluded that not only social scientists but also women generally were 'sceptical about whether the concept [was] a meaningful one'.[15] Since 1990, the American researcher Karla Henderson has produced four extremely useful longitudinal reviews of research about women and leisure publications around the world. Most of the tendencies she noted fit with the

British context. The 'commonality' with which she reproached 1980s feminist writers – excessive attention paid to shared constraints – applied less to the British case, where it was counterbalanced by early attempts at producing a definition of leisure that would integrate women's particular experiences and the very relativity of some of these constraints.[16] Deem was one of the first to identify characteristics of leisure which are still relevant today. Women's leisure:

- includes some choice within constraints that are more numerous for women;
- is not necessarily an activity (rest), a clearly separated period of time, or a specific place;
- is an enjoyable moment;
- is an experience where enjoyment is derived not necessarily from the activity itself but from the quality of the experience (socialisation);
- is often associated with notions of well-being and health.[17]

Kay praised these groundbreaking works which, whatever their limitations, used mixed methodologies to allow women to describe their individual experiences of leisure, and included some historical background to assert that the distinctiveness of women's leisure resulted from patriarchy.[18] They in turn influenced the way historical research, discussed in the second part of this chapter, was shaped by considerations of domesticity and family in most twentieth-century contexts. Evidence was overwhelming that when one parent was in charge of the house and the children, the mother often had no salary, no timetable and no predefined budget or time for leisure. Leisure time was often an extension of domestic duties. For example, ironing could be considered leisure if done while listening to the radio. Similarly, a mother's visit to the park or the library, typically classified as leisure, could be considered less recreative when carried out purely in the interest of her children. The difference between activities chosen willingly and those which were compulsory was blurred when the moment, the place and the nature of leisure were identical to those of work. This atemporal dimension of domestic work left mothers the freedom to organise their days, but a lot of unplanned events tended to interfere: caring for a sick child, for example, could not be restricted to an eight-hour day. These women often had the feeling of always being on duty ('a woman's work is never done'), and moments of respite were often spent simply resting. Definitions of leisure should therefore not be limited to constructive activities. If informal leisure is included, women's leisure often has a more domestic pattern than that of men. Research on the twentieth century has demonstrated that, contrary to the idealised vision of the home as a place to relax, protected from external constraints, or conducive to socialising, home and family could sometimes be at the very core of inequalities, notably leisure ones.[19] Until the 2000s, however, apart from the specific literature about women, analysts kept defining concepts in a gendered way and failed to apply critical analysis to understandings of women's leisure and domestic work. Current definitions of women's leisure better reflect its complexity: they include free time, leisure time, informal or organised activities, social interaction and expressions of liberty.[20]

After redefining the concept, a second phase of British research on women's leisure attempted to identify obstacles to leisure linked to constraints affecting most twentieth-century women, regardless of individual cases. Budget analyses of couples have repeatedly illustrated that women spend less on leisure even when they work, and that their leisure budget is often intertwined with domestic spending.[21] According to Deem, male control operates:

> both on an individual basis (husbands … controlling where 'their' women go) and through the fears generated in women by collective male control over female sexuality (… sexual harassment, rape and assault of women in public places) … So whereas factors such as location, social class, money and interest are likely to have the most influence on where men spend their out-of-home leisure time, for women … it is safety.[22]

Clarke and Critcher have managed a difficult synthesis of feminist and Marxist approaches, arguing that wealth created further discriminations. Even if women considered the public sphere accessible and were less restrained in their leisure choices, some suffered from dominant definitions of identity. 'Women are expected – and come themselves to expect – to participate in those leisure activities defined as appropriate for women, at those times and in those places compatible with established female roles. All these are severe enough limitations on the access to and enjoyment of leisure.' The authors identified women as victims of a capitalist system forcing them to relinquish their own leisure needs in favour of children and husbands, a form of discrimination which could be equated with others, leisure being a reward restricted to those who produce wealth. From childhood, and regardless of age and social class, '[t]he terms in which women gain access to leisure are controlled, directly and indirectly, physically and psychologically, by dominant male interests'. Their parallels between work, wealth, power and leisure distribution was a step towards explaining why women's leisure had a lower status than that of men.[23] Feminist research, realising that neither men nor women considered women's leisure as a right, adopted a binary approach to support a global overhaul of society: 'unless radical changes do take place in the organisation of the paid and unpaid work done by women and men … (and the discourse about gender underlying these forms of work), then it is likely that many women … will continue to experience their lives as more hectic, more work dominated, and less full of pleasure and enjoyment than the lives of many men.'[24] Being seen as the primary caregiver for children or relatives leads to the stigmatisation of a woman's leisure and a lack of sense of entitlement.

Feminist researchers themselves recognised having put too much emphasis on constraints, especially since women's status was improving, notably through entry in the work field.[25] Furthermore, family life could not be viewed only in terms of exploitation resulting from social pressure. Though time spent on domestic and family tasks could be an obstacle to leisure for either men or women, caring for others could be also be positive and rewarding, and family leisure could be enjoyed regardless of the added burden it implies. A few studies debunking negative prejudices against housewives also questioned the male model of strict separation between work and leisure.[26] A 1999 survey found that eighty per cent of working women choose to work part-time so as to spend more time at home and with their families.[27] Reception studies demonstrating how consumers would mix high and low culture and resist manipulation proved that whatever commodification and globalisation process leisure was undergoing, some dimension of creativity could be involved. Theories of 'glocalisation' have reinforced the idea that one culture does not fit all, that commonality and diversity often coincide. Some activities are overwhelmingly female, but few women individually have a typical female leisure profile.[28]

Although researchers tended to overlook the fact for a long time, gender must be accounted for when studying leisure. Whatever criticism and controversies feminist studies raised, their main conclusions, developed independently from the rest of the leisure field, were endorsed by subsequent research.[29] Cross, comparing Britain, the United States and France in a history of leisure consumption, declared that feminists had mitigated their views in the 1990s by acknowledging the diversity of women's desires and the fact that caring for one's family was not systematically synonymous with oppression.[30] In 2000, Rojek, after regretting that feminist research limited women to victims of male power, eventually admitted that, without succeeding in suppressing all prejudices, feminists contributed to a better understanding of women's specific leisure discrimination and managed to 'pinpoint the links between the domestic division of labour and of the general division of labour; to expose male control of public leisure space; to examine how patriarchy represses women through the family, education, the media, and popular culture. This has reversed the position of two decades ago when feminism was marginalised in the study of leisure'.[31] 'Ghettoisation' remains, however, an issue in this female-dominated field, although the increasing recognition that there are varied female identities as well as forms of feminisms means 'accepting that multiple answers can emerge' and has triggered a more inclusive debate on 'how constraints intersect with structural inequities in gendered societies'.[32]

While the literature has demonstrated how central gender is to leisure history, and that the quantity and the quality of free time was often more varied for women than men, women have never constituted a homogeneous group. Other factors should be taken into account, such as age, health, socio-cultural background and professional status (and those of the partner), family situation, ethnic origin, geographical situation, areas of interest, personality and self-confidence. Of course, these factors also often intersected to stratify leisure.[33] Since 1945, for instance, middle-class women have benefited from more leisure time and more external and varied leisure activities than working-class women.[34] In the 1980s, Smith not only failed to find the symmetrical families theorised by Young and Wilmott but realised that couples from poorer classes presented more inequalities in leisure than others.[35] Today, larger discrepancies between social background have resumed, but surveys still illustrate their impact on the quantity of leisure – more so for women than for men. The latest figures for women's sports participation fell from eighty-five per cent for independent workers to forty-two per cent for manual workers (respectively seventy-eight per cent and fifty-four per cent for men).[36]

What Langhamer concluded for the first part of the twentieth century still applies: life cycles continue to affect women's free-time patterns more than men's. Only young, single, childless, active women tend to have as many leisure activities outside the home as their male counterparts. For mothers whose children are grown up, a new stage begins, generally associated with an increased quantity of free time. Even for older housewives, change is limited by the fact that there is often little alteration in the quantity of housework carried out by partners. On the contrary, some elderly women have plenty of free time but lack leisure opportunites, since they often suffer from poverty and loneliness. They frequently survive their spouses with smaller pensions, and family members live at greater distances from one another than they did in the first half of the twentieth century.[37] Attention to context has therefore proven central to studying women's leisure.

As Proctor noted, 'Cross-pollination of the humanities and social sciences has been another way of broadening the pool of acceptable sources for historians.' Research on women's leisure has clearly benefited from the increasing recognition of the complexity of issues and methodologies. Faced with the relative lack of official written sources, social and cultural historians have emulated ethnographers and used other types of sources, such as fiction, the popular press, objects, oral histories, family archives or photographs. Much work remains to be done, since attention has focused mainly on working-class women whose use of free time, constructed as a minor version of the male 'problem of leisure', caused anxieties, and in twentieth-century Britain was often related to the supposedly detrimental influence of popular culture.[38]

Women from the 1900s to the 1960s: full members of the 'society of leisure'?

By the early twentieth century, although female freedom was judged 'unwomanly' and associated with a rejection of male company, Proctor argued that 'many middle and working-class women were trying to break free of domestic restraints, gain more independence and claim leisure time for themselves'.[39] Catriona M. Parratt's research on working women before 1914, along with other monographs, clearly demonstrated how gender affected leisure patterns in the early twentieth century.[40] But knowledge has remained patchy by comparison with the well-documented works discussing advances in women's political representation and professional inclusion.

The ambivalent consequences of industrialisation on women's leisure have now been well researched: these consequences were more varied than they were for men, since leisure was long perceived as a male worker's right. Oakley has argued that as economic growth provided more disposable income, middle-class wives were encouraged to leave paid work as well as domestic work to lead a 'life of leisure' that was proof of their husbands' social status. Their restriction to the domestic sphere, however, obviously deprived them of many leisure opportunities. Women were idealised as perfect home-makers, and expected to facilitate the family's increasingly home-based leisure.[41] Focusing on Edwardian working-class women, Davies demonstrated that although burdened by both paid and domestic work, they campaigned in favour of payment for domestic labour rather than limitation of working hours. Indeed, as heads of the domestic budget, these women were expected to display 'self sacrifice' and 'the virtue of the "good" mother' while men claimed some money to spend on beer, cigarettes and games. Even 'good husbands' disbursing moderate amounts on leisure, spent most of their free time outside the home (pub, betting shop, football club, etc.). Davies concluded:

> Gender was central to the division of leisure in working-class districts. Some of the major spheres of popular leisure, especially sport, were overwhelmingly male-dominated, and in this sense, working-class men tended to enjoy a significantly higher standard of living than their wives. None the less ... women did frequent cinemas, dance halls.[42]

Langhamer identified the period in a woman's life cycle as the most important factor in the nature and structure of her leisure, yet stated that this discontinuity was accepted as a natural counterpart of being a woman: 'Women's social lives were maintained within a framework of financial, domestic, and moral constraints' which varied according to her status. Life cycles were even more potent in shaping women's lives than in the recent past since mothers usually had more children, enjoyed a shorter lifespan and did more domestic work. Marriage clearly assigned gender roles, but most women enjoyed new-found autonomy. If, after the First World War, young women benefited from the relative freedom of going to the cinema, dance hall or music hall, it is because working-class mentalities in particular emphasised youth as a time to have fun and find a spouse.[43] Young and Wilmott as well as Davies observed that as long as they worked, young women had a similar status to that of men, since employment was associated with a right to leisure. But as soon as they got married, and if they stopped working, they were back in a woman's world characterised by scarcer, more informal and domestic types of leisure, where values such as duty and service replaced those of independence and self-fulfilment.[44]

Women's leisure stirred little public interest before the 1960s, except when it threatened respectability, especially where young women were concerned. Proctor noted the contradiction facing service clubs and religious and political organisations alike, which had become a common form of recreation: 'How could these clubs create "good mothers" and attract females looking for adventure, independence and fun?'[45] Nonetheless, from the 1940s, youth workers, educationalists and psychologists supported the creation of respectable state-funded activities for girls. Worries about young women's leisure and societal stability were interwoven with a concern for their leisure needs, however paternalistic in form, since leisure had reached a new status during the inter-war period as a social phenomenon pertaining to the birth of democratic society, a belief that intensified with the Second World War.[46] New attitudes taken up by young women serving on the home front during the conflict were widely held to have had a conclusive impact upon gender hierarchies.[47] Langhamer

questioned this orthodoxy by exploring 'contemporary and retrospective asser-
tions that increased female pub participation constituted both an expression
of, and a contribution to, women's wartime self-confidence [and] an example
of women resisting and remaking gendered leisure prescriptions' and pointed
at 'the limits placed upon such resistance'.[48]

In assessing leisure after the war, Walvin identified the social pressure
encouraging women to go back to domestic lives and largely excluding them
from the post-war leisure industries boom, except for dance and cinema-going.
Traditional forms of female leisure were also being disrupted by rehousing.[49]
Young and Wilmott's classic monograph described traditional matriarchal
communities in London's East-End, where leisure for young women revolved
around family gatherings and socialisation with other women: 'the extended
family was her trade union, organised in the main by women and for women'.
Domestic work and leisure were bound together: moments of respite were
gained from everyday routine, chatting in the street or at the local store,
sharing work in two or three houses. This organisation enabled women to
maximise the semi-leisure opportunities, Dumazedier theorised, and even to
access organised leisure. Many grandmothers would look after the children,
a support that ceased once the families were scattered in remote and anony-
mous yet more comfortable estates.[50] Tebbutt's study on the centrality of oral
communication in women's socialisation and support networks provides an
update on some of these issues and added a welcome insight into leisure/work
practices that used 'gossip' in a nobler way than its pejorative use may imply.[51]
Such major shifts question the dogma of the industrial revolution as the frontier between traditional and modern forms of leisure for working-class women.
Yet, as Brooke notes, the improvement in living standards led to exaggerated
'rumours of the death of working class consciousness' since new leisure patterns emerged from these dramatic social and economic shifts.[52] Popular leisure
remained based on the traditional activities discussed above until consumerism and television revolutionised home-based leisure in the 1950s and 1960s.
Women were increasingly addressed as consumers of leisure when it came to
the home. Domestic appliances, such as the 'leisure cooker', were presented
by industry as objects for entertaining, equating domestic work with leisure
activity.[53]

When cinema and theatre lost appeal, commercial bingo, legalised in
1960, was an immediate success, attracting six million players a year, including more than a quarter of British housewives.[54] Along with cinema-going,
bingo-playing was one of the rare activities that was both cheap and easily

accessible. This much under-researched British idiosyncrasy deserves more academic attention. Indeed, apart from Rixey and Talbot in 1982, who did not study the rise of commercial bingo as a successful part of the leisure industry, and Downs' little-known research, scant attention has been paid to bingo.[55] By retracing former traditions of playing games of chance amongst the working-class female public, Downs recently debunked assumptions that bingo was 'a game rooted in the commercialisation of gambling in the 1960s [when] entrepreneurs targeted women who had never previously gambled, enticing them with a new [game]'. She also insisted on the large influence of bingo on British culture as demonstrated by the use of bingo terms in common parlance and 'the potential of bingo to cause moral panics'.[56] The game was held in contempt and seen as a negative outgrowth from the consumer-oriented society, a mindless game to occupy more affluent working-class women. Critics claimed it was opposed to more intellectually enriching or socially useful activities, in continuity with the Victorian rational recreation ethos. It turned out, however, to be a space for resistance, since 'neither the periodic moral panics over women supposedly gambling away the housekeeping nor the dismissal of the game itself as "mindless" by the uninitiated served to diminish its popularity'.[57] Indeed, bingo clubs played a crucial social role in combating boredom and loneliness for working-class women who lacked respectable places to convene without risking their partner's or neighbourhood's criticism, and also managed to recreate traditional forms of neighbourhood socialisation that characterised their pre-war communities.[58]

Due to marketing and commercial techniques, bingo halls remained popular throughout the post-war period. As Dawn's study of Mecca's group demonstrates, the commodification process of cultural and leisure practices over the second part of the twentieth century affected bingo as well. Mecca managed to become the leaders of the industry by first associating bingo with glamour to attract its usual customers. However, commercial gambling became less desirable through the influence of the Churches' Council on Gambling and the Labour government elected in 1964. As a result, bingo halls were primarily marketed as places for socialising, with gambling as an optional activity.[59]

Another change heralded by the 1960s, the Women's Liberation Movement, never fought on the front of leisure, but its calls against the double workday and for free childcare were intended to allow women moments of freedom. The conjunction of the extension of life expectancy with a fall in birth rate related to the introduction of birth control, modified women's life cycles with a proportionally smaller number of years devoted to children. Married and middle-class women's perceived right to leisure was improved by their increased inclusion on the work market. Access to leisure, however, was another matter since these structural and demographic changes were counterbalanced by the increasingly home-based leisure patterns stemming from increased domestic comfort and an idealised vision of family life. The seeming *right* to leisure and *access* to it were not always compatible. With the advent of the affluent society, this privatisation of leisure affected all socio-economic backgrounds, since a majority of British people gained access to home-ownership (the number doubled between 1951 and 1972). Domestic leisure spending rose when the portion of the budget devoted to cinema, theatre and dance dropped sharply. Television symbolised this 'revolution of leisure': the ratio of homes equipped with a television set rocketed from 1:15 in 1951 to 2:3 in 1960.[60] However, since family leisure moments for some can become synonymous with work for those who make them happen, many mothers' lives were burdened by a new set of tasks. As Clarke and Critcher stated, 'The expanding involvement of the family unit in creating leisure often depends on the hidden labour of the woman.'[61]

Trends in women's leisure practices since the 1970s

A 1984 opinion poll reported that half of the respondents believed a man had to provide for the family financially while the woman should be responsible for the home and family, even if she worked. However, renegotiated division of labour in post-industrial society has meant that women have entered the public economy and men have increasingly taken part in domestic life, as illustrated by the growing popularity of 'do-it-yourself' activities.[62] Today, even though it is rare to find couples where home and family tasks are divided equally, men are more willing to stay at home with children so that mothers can take part in a leisure activity.[63]

Time–budget studies have been used since the 1970s to prove how gendered the ratio of work to leisure still is, and they have also shed light on how experiences vary according to professional and family contexts. This ratio also varies more widely among women: for instance, women having young children reduces access to both paid work and leisure.[64] Still, a major change is that the proportion of working women has doubled since the 1940s and that of working mothers with children under seven has doubled in thirty years. The effect of motherhood on employment still exists, albeit reduced: in 2008 when a similar employment rate of over 70 per cent was found for both men and women with no dependent children, it fell to 57 per cent for mothers of children under

Activity	Weekday		Weekend	
	Men	**Women**	**Men**	**Women**
Television, video and radio	2:02	1:39	2:52	2:13
Socialising	0:34	0:45	1:24	1:33
Reading	0:15	0:16	0:24	0:27
Games, hobbies and computing	0:14	0:07	0:22	0:12
Sport and exercise	0:11	0:09	0:26	0:15
Arts and cultural events	0:05	0:06	0:17	0:13
Total	**3:21**	**3:02**	**5:45**	**4:53**

1   Time spent on selected free-time activities by full-time workers aged sixteen and over in the United Kingdom in 2000–1 (hours and minutes per day)

five. Women in the age range 25–34 are most affected when their children are five to ten years old, and overall for this age group 68 per cent of mothers work and 73 per cent of women without children do. But going back to work often means working part-time for a poor salary. The choice of working part-time is twice as often made by mothers as by other women. Altogether, almost half of women work part-time as compared with 20 per cent of men. Flexible working hours and time off during school holidays are enjoyed by 30 per cent of employed women as opposed to 20 per cent of employed men. The *2000 Time Use Survey* underlined that in total about the same amount of time was used by men as by women for the following responsibilities: paid work, household and family care and childcare, with the difference that women's time was more evenly divided between those activities, and thus their days were less consistent. The biggest inequalities in free time affected couples with children where both parents worked full-time, because mothers tended to still take on more family and home responsibilities (see Figure 1).

Qualitative studies have nevertheless proven that contemporary working mothers use their free time in a more autonomous way than housewives, since a personally earned income grants them more freedom. The discontinuity in women's careers, often accompanied by a loss in perceived qualifications and a lower income, reduces entitlement to leisure, both socially and internally. As Kay underlined, more than thirty years after Dumazedier, one has to be cautious as to how free time totals are structured, since 'pervasive domestic responsibility' means that fragmented free time is difficult to predict, can therefore be limited in use and is generally spent at home.[65]

Free time should be differentiated from leisure activities: statistics gathered from 1976 to 1996 with a consistent methodology suggest that women took

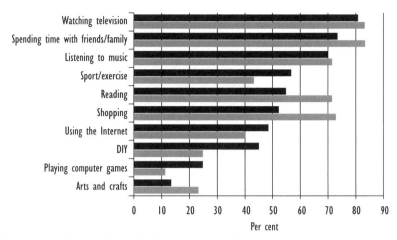

Selected activities performed in free time by men (*upper, black bars*) and women
(*lower, grey bars*) in England in 2006–7

2

part in fewer leisure activities than men and that these were less varied and
more home-based and family-oriented. While the most popular activities like
watching television or listening to the radio were appreciated by both sexes
alike, other leisure pursuits at home were gendered. Sewing and knitting have
greatly decreased as female 'leisure', and although these are still a minority activity with men, almost twice as many men were sewing and knitting in 1996.
Some very traditionally gendered activities, like do-it-yourself, have been taken
up by women. As with housework, though, these are typical activities which
may derive from perceived necessity. In twenty years, women book readers
have become more and more numerous (from 57 to 71 per cent), and the
amount of male readers has also increased slightly (from 52 to 58 per cent).[66]
But the figure reflects a male preference for press reading as opposed to fiction,
and recent time-usage surveys note that women in full employment devote
just a slightly longer amount of time to reading (see Figure 1). The Office for
National Statistics (ONS) leisure studies after 1996 have used a new methodology preventing longitudinal comparisons and asked questions for the last
year instead of the last four weeks, which tends to elide gender differences. The
new method, however, has allowed an updated list of pastimes which include
new technologies favoured by both sexes, but used more by men (see Figure 2).

The places that women frequent for leisure have become more varied since
the 1970s. Among the few that are not gendered are restaurants and live
arts venues.[67] Pub-going has become more mixed: the male to female ratio
went from 71:29 in 1990 to 60:40 in 2000, mainly because new types of

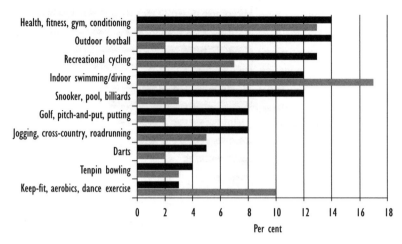

3   Selected sports, games and physical activities practised by men (*upper, black bars*) and women (*lower, grey bars*) in England in 2006–7

pubs appeared in the 1990s, characterised by large window screens with open views onto the street, followed by the more recently instituted 'gastropubs'.[68] Modes of socialising differ according to age. For the younger generation, 'binge drinking' can be a leisure in itself. Questions about drinking patterns were first asked by the General Household Survey in 1978, and it has since recorded a stable consumption among men but a sharp increase among women: 10 per cent drank more than the recommended weekly benchmark of 14 units a week in 1988 and 17 per cent in 2002. Those aged 16 to 24 were most numerous in this group and almost doubled between 1992 and 2002. Young women were instrumental in balancing out pub-going figures, notably through the developing popularity of same-sex nights out. At some of these, the 'ladettes' adopted forms of lad-like behaviour, in which alcohol abuse, loudness and provocative dress indicated a refusal to adhere to social conventions. Social disapproval allied with public campaigns concerned with sexual risks, health, weight and beauty seem to have had some effect, since the years following 2002 show a clear downward trend in heavy drinking among young women.[69] Nevertheless, there are more men than women who take part in out-of-the-home activities – consisting mainly of drinking, betting, practising a sport or watching one (see Figure 3).

Statistics referring to sports practice do not tell the whole story, notably the reasons for engaging in the pursuit. In 2002, in answer to the question, 'Which leisure activities do you enjoy?', 47 per cent of men listed a sport as opposed to only 28 per cent of women, who more often took part because of health or aes-thetic concerns.[70] Sport, as a typically gendered leisure activity where the body is exposed and sexual stereotypes are confirmed, has attracted a vast amount of research, most of which has concluded that sport remains associated with such values as a 'fighting spirit' or strength embodied in the dominant char-acteristics of male identity.[71] Increased female participation in sports since the 1980s is mainly due to the boom in gym use and in yoga classes, which along with swimming are the only predominantly female sports. Women are less well-represented in team sports and competitions. Hargreaves demonstrated that women's sports today are still the ones which fit with the social percep-tions of femininity (i.e. grace and balance) and do not challenge the traditional gender divide. Because sport is a very segregated leisure area, it is no surprise that professional female sport became a place where stereotypes were contested. Through improved female political representation, public policies have also become more aware of specific needs or expectations.[72]

Bingo participation has declined from the mid-1970s, notably because of the economic crisis and the ageing of its more devoted players. Nonetheless, the first national report on the game in 1978 underlined that it was still the main out-of-the-house leisure activity for 73 per cent of women. The first scholarly monograph on bingo's social role was published in 1982, at which time 83 per cent of the players belonged to the working class, leading to the conclusion that the game was more a class-discriminated activity than a gender-discriminated one: 'bingo excludes the middle-class more effectively, as a working class pastime, than it excludes men as a female pastime.'[73]

Today, bingo playing has remained popular and has emerged as a less gen-dered practice: the players are younger (71 per cent are less than 55 years old and 35 per cent less than 35 years old) and a third of them are now male. Meanwhile, pubs are no longer regarded as male bastions by working-class women. Bingo clubs have had to compete and have marketed their evenings as parties to rival pubs and nightclubs. They started imitating Las Vegas game rooms, to attract thirty-somethings who go there 'dress[ed] to impress', to have fun, or to find romance. This evolution has been supported by the industry's deregulation, which has allowed 500 networked clubs to raise their maximum prize to £2 million. Bingo is also the second most popular online game after the National Lottery.[74]

In 2007, bingo halls again came under threat because of competition with other games, the effect of the Gambling Act (2005)[75] and the introduction the smoking ban (70 per cent of players were smokers). A number of smaller clubs have closed as a result. Drawing on real and constructed popular memories, the Bingo Association launched a national campaign and online petition under the heading 'Stop Destroying My Bingo', led by 'bingo playing star' Linda Robson. The campaign appealed to the state to save what Robson described as an enjoyable popular cultural practice that had the rare social advantage of binding communities together: 'Closing clubs will have a devastating effect on community spirit nationwide. Tell me another activity where three different generations can go out together and have an equal amount of enjoyment, excitement and success.'[76]

The other predominantly female out-of-the-home activities are minority ones advocated by less than 5 per cent of British people. They are mainly cultural, such as church-going, attending opera or ballet performances, taking part in a visual arts, theatre, or music group, or participating in arts and crafts workshops. It took only twenty years for adult classes to become markedly more feminised (they attracted 6 and 8 per cent of women versus 4 per cent of men in 1976 and 1996 respectively).[77] These activities, theorised by Bourdieu as allowing 'distinction', can be traced back to Victorian middle-class involvement in charity work, since respectable wives had to devote their time to others or spend time in an 'improving way'. Statistics, however useful, should be handled with caution since they only give a partial view. Thus, recent questionnaires asking what activity the person has performed in the last year amount to treating regular and occasional activity in the same way, and have tended to overestimate female sporting practice and male cultural activities.[78] Likewise, activities practised with a partner from the opposite sex rarely reflect a common wish. For instance, roughly as many men as women statistically take part in cultural outings when only 39 per cent of men would describe a night at the theatre as enjoyable as opposed to 49 per cent of women.[79]

Differences in the shape, duration and location of women's leisure therefore do not amount to a limited version of men's leisure, but reflect an altogether different qualitative and quantitative pattern.[80] Recent trends in women's leisure stem from the growing independence of young women who live on their own and the increasing number of women living alone at all ages: 6 per cent of British people under pensionable age lived alone in 1971, compared with 15 per cent in 2001.[81] The long-term effects this could have on the social construction of female identity have yet to be researched, but they may be conducive to greater entitlement to leisure even if a woman later lives with a partner and/or children.

Conclusions

Conclusions on women's leisure today can only be equivocal, rendering historical and sociological approaches essential to pinpointing areas of change and continuity in women's leisure. During the twentieth century sweeping social change affected women's lives, allowing for more varied definitions of femininity and acceptable *leisure practices*. At the same time, there has been a lesser shift in the traditional causes of gender inequalities in *access to leisure* and in the amount of effective *leisure time* enjoyed by women as compared with men. Gender stereotypes, male partners and families, domestic and family tasks, or working conditions still reduce women's opportunities, while increased mobility and family atomisation have deprived mothers of traditional forms of support. The persistence of these obstacles, in a country that has experienced so many transformations, corroborates the importance of gender in society and the need to rethink the impact of social change on set habits. Though perhaps slightly overstated, Scott, Crompton and Lyonette's recent volume warned: 'There are grounds for scepticism about the extent to which individual "agency" and capacities for "self construction" have replaced structural constraints.'[82] Leisure does not simply reflect gender divisions, it validates them. However, the examples discussed in this chapter prove that twentieth-century women have found areas of freedom and opposition. The slow pace of societal evolution in favour of women was noted by the 2007 *Equalities Review*: 'We set out data showing that at the present rate of progress it may take some decades to achieve parity in employment or education for some groups; over 75 years in the case of women's political representation and equal pay.'[83]

Until recently, research on women's leisure was dominated by approaches dating from the 1980s which both challenged existing orthodoxies and isolated gender as an essential variable when studying leisure, but left out many grey areas. The field has now successfully incorporated alternative sources that allow more complex analysis of leisure trends and what they entail. A fruitful dialogue between the humanities and social sciences articulating gender with socio-cultural background, work, or ethnicity shed light on disparities between women as well. If the wealthy and the young are the least impacted by gender differences, inequalities in leisure tend to affect those women who suffer from other types of discrimination. More inter-country comparisons would be beneficial since there remains a tendency amongst British scholars to concentrate on the socio-economic dimension of leisure and amongst the French to focus on cultural and institutional factors.[84]

State intervention in leisure, inherited from Victorian society, originally targeted working-class men and women whom it tried to divert from vice and idleness. This utilitarian vision coloured subsequent policies towards a public judged at risk.[85] Feminist research has noted that leisure policies long ignored women's needs and that the complexity of women's everyday lives were and are still linked to the contradictory dimension of binaries such as work/leisure and family/leisure, concretising the axiom that employment and family policies nearly always have a direct influence on women's leisure. The interventionist turn that gender and leisure policies have taken during Labour administrations from 1997 to 2010 will therefore offer researchers opportunities to discuss women's leisure in a new light.[86]

Notes

1 I. Zweiniger-Bargielowska (ed.), *Women in Twentieth Century Britain: Economic, Social and Cultural Change* (Harlow: Pearson Education, 2001), 1.

2 T. M. Proctor, 'Home and Away, Popular Culture and Leisure', in D. Simonton (ed.), *The Routledge History of Women in Europe since 1700* (London: Routledge, 2006), 299–340.

3 One has to note, however, that they focused mostly on England. A. Davies, *Leisure, Gender and Poverty: Working Class Culture in Salford and Manchester, 1900–1939* (Oxford: Oxford University Press, 1992); J. Hargreaves, *Sporting Females, Critical Issues in the History and Sociology of Women's Sports* (London: Routledge, 1994); C. Langhamer, *Women's Leisure in England, 1920–60* (Manchester: Manchester University Press, 2000); C. M. Parratt, *'More than Mere Amusement': Working Class Women's Leisure in England, 1750–1914* (Boston, MA: Northeastern University Press, 2002).

4 T. Veblen, *The Theory of the Leisure Class*, (1899; repr., London: Penguin, 1994).

5 To cite a few, P. Bailey, *Leisure and Class in Victorian England: Rational Recreation and the Contest for Control 1830–1885* (London: Routledge, 1978); P. Burke, *Popular Culture in Early Modern Europe* (London: Temple Smith, 1978); H. Cunningham, *Leisure in the Industrial Revolution, 1780–1880* (London: Croom Helm, 1980). For a discussion on women, rational recreation and sport, see C. M. Parratt, 'Making leisure work: Women and rational recreation in Late Victorian and Edwardian England', *Journal of Sport History* 26 (1999): 471–8.

6 J. Walvin, *Leisure and Society 1830–1950* (London: Longman, 1978); N. Elias, *Time: An Essay* (1984; repr., Oxford: Blackwell, 1991); A. Corbin, ed., *L'Avènement des loisirs 1850–1960* (Paris: Flammarion, 1995); C. Doustaly, 'La genèse du soutien public aux beaux-arts à Londres aux XVIIIe et XIXe siècles', in J. Carré (ed.), *Londres 1700–1900: naissance d'une capitale culturelle* (Paris: Presses Universitaires de Paris-Sorbonne, 2010), 207–29.

7 A. Davies, *Leisure, Gender and Poverty: Working Class Culture in Salford and Manchester, 1900–1939*, 55.

8 J. Dumazedier, *Toward a Society of Leisure* (1962; repr., New York: Free Press, 1967), 91 and 101–3.

9 D. Wynne, *Leisure, Lifestyle and the New Middle Class: A Case Study* (London: Routledge, 1998), 28.

10 P. Bourdieu, *Distinction: A Social Critique of the Judgement of Taste* (1979, repr., Cambridge, Mass.: Harvard University Press, 1984).

11 Corbin, *L'Avènement des loisirs 1850–1960*.

12 G. Noiriel, *Introduction à la socio-histoire* (Paris: La Découverte, 2006); V. Dubois., *Institutions et politiques culturelles locales: éléments pour une recherche socio-historique* (Paris: Documentation Française, 1996).

13 R. Deem, *All Work and No Play, The Sociology of Women and Leisure* (Oxford: Oxford University Press, 1986), 8–17; C. Aitchison, 'Gender and Leisure Research: The "Codification of Knowledge",' *Leisure Sciences*, no. 23 (2001): 1–19. Rosemary Deem is Professor and Dean of History and Social Sciences at Royal Holloway, University of London.

14 E. Green, S. Hebron and D. Woodward, *Women's Leisure, What Leisure?* (London: Macmillan, 1990), 38–41. See also R. Dixey, M. Talbot, *Women, Leisure and Bingo* (Leeds: Trinity and All Saints College, 1982); J. Smith, 'Men and Women at Play: Gender, Life-cycle, and Leisure', in J. Horne, D. Jary and A. Tomlinson (eds), *Leisure and Social Relations* (London: Routledge, 1987), 51–85.

15 Deem, *All Work and No Play*, 17.

16 K. A. Henderson and B. Hickerson, 'Women and Leisure: Premises and Performances Uncovered in an Integrative Review', *Journal of Leisure Research* 39, no. 4 (2007): 591–610, esp. 592.

17 Adapted from Deem, *All Work and No Play,* 17–19.

18 T. Kay, 'Women's Leisure and the Family in Contemporary Britain', in N. Samuel (ed.), *Women, Leisure and the Family, A Multinational Perspective* (Wallingford: CAB International, 1996), 143–59.

19 J. Clarke and C. Critcher, *The Devil Makes Work: Leisure in Capitalist Britain* (London: Macmillan, 1985), 159–60; Green *et al.*, *Women's Leisure*, 6 and 86–7.

20 R. Deem, 'Time for a Change?: Engendered Work and Leisure in the 1990s', in G. McFee, W. Murphy and G. Whannel (eds), *Leisure Cultures, Values, Gender, Lifestyles* (Brighton: LSA, 1995), 3–22; Aitchison, *Gender and Leisure*, 41–3.

21 Aitchison, *Gender and Leisure*, 52; Kay, 'Women's Leisure and the Family', 152.

22 Deem, *All Work and No Play,* 7 and 63.

23 Clarke and Critcher, *The Devil Makes Work*, 160, 177 and 203.

24 R. Deem, 'Time for a Change?', 3.

25 Henderson and Hickerson, 'Women and Leisure', 591–610.

26 Kay, 'Women's Leisure and the Family', 155.

27 Office for National Statistics, *Labour Force Survey 1999: Social Trends 30* (2000), 70.

28 G. S. Cross, *Time and Money: the Making of Consumer Culture* (London: Routledge, 1993); Henderson and Hickerson, 'Women and Leisure', 605.

29 R. Deem, 'How do we get out of the ghetto? Strategies for research on gender and leisure', *Leisure Studies* no. 18 (1999): 161–77; B. Wearing, *Leisure and Feminist*

Theory (London: Sage, 1998).

30 G. S. Cross, *Time and Money.*

31 C. Rojek, *Leisure and Culture* (London: Macmillan, 2000), 111.

32 Henderson and Hickerson, 'Women and Leisure', 603–6.

33 'Introduction', in J. Scott, R. Crompton, and C. Lyonette (eds), *Gender Inequalities in the 21st Century: New Barriers and Continuing Constraints* (London: Edward Elgar, 2010), 11.

34 Kay, 'Women's Leisure and the Family', 156.

35 She cross-examined leisure participation, gender and socio-economic groups. See Smith, 'Men and Women at Play.' See also M. Young and P. Wilmott, *The Symmetrical Family: A Study of Work and Leisure in the London Region* (London, Routledge, 1973).

36 Office for National Statistics, *General Household Survey 1996* in *Social Trends* 32 (2002), 223.

37 Deem, *All Work and No Play*, 117–33; Clarke and Critcher, *The Devil Makes Work,* 154–5.

38 Proctor, 'Home and Away', 299 and 303.

39 Proctor, 'Home and Away', 327.

40 C. M. Parratt, *'More than Mere Amusemen': Working Class Women's Leisure in England, 1750–1914* (Boston, MA: Northeastern, 2001).

41 A. Oakley, *The Sociology of Housework* (London: Blackwell, 1974); J. Walvin, *Leisure and Society 1830–1950.*

42 Davies, *Leisure, Gender and Poverty,* 55. See also E. Roberts, *Women and Families: An Oral History, 1940–1970* (Oxford: Blackwell, 1995); A. H. Halsey, *Change in British Society* (Oxford: Oxford University Press, 1978), 124–5.

43 C. Langhamer, *Women's Leisure in England, 1920–60,* 49–51, 58–70, 144–5; E. Roberts, *Women and Families,* 151.

44 M. Young and P. Wilmott, *Family and Kinship in East London* (London: Penguin, 1957), 61; Davies, *Leisure, Gender and Poverty,* 56.

45 Proctor, 'Home and Away', 327–9.

46 P. Tinkler, 'Cause for Concern: Young Women and Leisure, 1930–50', *Women's History Review* 12, no. 2 (June 2003): 233–62.

47 Green, Hebron and Woodward, *Women's Leisure, What Leisure?,* 52.

48 C. Langhamer '"A Public House is for All Classes, Men and Women Alike": Women, Leisure and Drink in Second World War England', *Women's History Review* 12, no. 3 (2003): 423–43.

49 Walvin, *Leisure and Society,* 148–50.

50 Young and Wilmott, *Family and Kinship in East London,* 189–91, and see 47, 117.

51 M. Tebbutt, *Women's Talk? A Social History of Gossip in Working Class Neighbourhoods, 1880–1960* (Aldershot: Scolar Press, 1995).

52 S. Brooke, 'Gender and Working Class Identity in Britain during the 1950s', *Journal of Social History* 34, no. 4 (2001): 773–95, quote from 773.

53 Green, Hebron and Woodward, *Women's Leisure, What Leisure?,* 53–4.

54 J. Margolis, 'Call the Wild Night', *The Times,* 30 January 1994.

55 C. Downs, 'Mecca and the Birth of Commercial Bingo 1958–70: A Case Study', *Business History* 52, no. 7 (2010): 1086–106.

56 C. Downs, *Social, Economic and Cultural History of Bingo (1906–2005): The Role of Gambling in the Lives of Working Women* (Berlin: VDM Verlag, 2009).

57 Green, Hebron and Woodward, *Women's Leisure, What Leisure?*, 54; Downs, *History of Bingo*.

58 Clarke and Critcher, *The Devil Makes Work,* 87; and the monograph carried out in Armley (Leeds), R. Dixey and M. Talbot, *Women, Leisure and Bingo* (Leeds: Trinity and All Saints College, 1982), 15 and 162–5.

59 C. Downs, 'Mecca and the Birth of Commercial Bingo.'

60 Walvin, *Leisure and Society,* 152; F. Bédarida, *La Société anglaise, du milieu du XIXème à nos jours,* (Paris: Seuil, 1990), 355–9 and 380–2.

61 Clarke and Critcher, *The Devil Makes Work,* 225. Green, Hebron and Woodward, *Women's Leisure, What Leisure?*, 49–50.

62 Halsey, *Change in British Society*, 125 and 136–7; Young and Wilmott, *The Symmetrical Family.*

63 A survey carried out by the author on twenty amateur art groups showed that mothers, mostly middle-class ones, invariably answered the question 'Does your partner take care of the children to allow you to come here?' with 'Oh yes, I'm very lucky', revealing that it was neither obvious nor always the case that husbands provided care for wives seeking leisure.

64 Deem, *All Work and No Play,* 7–8; R. Berthoud and M. Blekesaune, *Persistent Employment Disadvantage: Report for the Equalities Review,* 2007.

65 Kay, 'Women's Leisure', 145 and 154–5.

66 Office for National Statistics, *General Household Survey 1996,* 228; *General Household Survey 1977* in *Social Trends* 9 (1979), 177.

67 Arts Council of England, *Artstats: Digest of Arts Statistics and Trends in the UK, 1986–87/1997–98,* (London: ACE, 2000), 104.

68 C. Courtes, *L'Evolution du pub en Angleterre de 1960 à nos jours* (Paris: Université de la Sorbonne Nouvelle, 2002), 260.

69 Office for National Statistics, General Household Surveys 1978 to 2002, in *General Household Survey 2007*, 42–4.

70 Market Review 2002, 18.

71 Green, Hebron and Woodward, *Women's Leisure, What Leisure?*, 45–6.

72 J. Hargreaves, *Sporting Females, Critical issues in the History and Sociology of Women's Sports*, 207–8; M. Polley, *Moving the Goalposts, a History of Sport and Society since 1945* (London: Routledge, 1998), 103–4; F. Collins, I. Henry, B. Houlihan and J. Buller for Department for Culture, Media and Sport (DCMS), *Sport and Social Exclusion* (Loughborough: Institute of Sport and Leisure Policies, 1999) 36.

73 Royal Commission on Gambling, *1978 Report* (London: RCOG, 1978), 341. Dixey and Talbot, *Women, Leisure and Bingo*, 5, 119 and 140.

74 See the 2002 Gaming Act. See also BBC, 'Find out why Bingo is Becoming Trendier than Clubbing', 23 September 2003.

75 C. Downs, 'The Changing Face of Gambling: the Gambling Act (2005) and

Working Class Gambling Cultures', in J. Caudwell, S. Redhead and A. Tomlinson (eds), *Relocating the Leisure Society: media, consumption and spaces,* LSA publication 101 (2008).

76 Bingo Association, 'Stop destroying Bingo' says Linda Robson – Britain's 3 million regular players called to act now', Press Release, 5 March 2007.

77 Office for National Statistics, *General Household Survey 1977,* 177; *General Household Survey 1996,* 114. Policy Studies Institute (PSI), *Amateur Arts in the UK, the PSI Survey of Amateur Arts and Crafts in the UK* (London: PSI, 1991), 26.

78 C. Doustaly and C. Gray, 'Labour and the Arts, Managing Transformation?', *Observatoire de la société britannique,* no. 8 (January 2010), 319–38.

79 Market Review 2000, 30.

80 Green, Hebron and Woodward, *Women's Leisure, What Leisure?,* 19–23.

81 Kay, 'Women's Leisure and the Family', 156; Office for National Statistics, *Census 2001,* in *Social Trends 33* (2003), 42.

82 Scott, Crompton and Lyonette, *Gender Inequalities in the 21st Century,* 2.

83 Equalities Review, *Fairness and Freedom* (London: HMSO, 2007), 5.

84 C. Hodak, 'L'histoire des loisirs ou le renouvellement de l'histoire sociale et culturelle anglaise', in F. Lachaud, I. Lescent-Gilles, F. Ruggiu (eds), *Tendances récentes de l'historiographie britannique* (Paris: Presses Universitaires de Paris Sorbonne, 2001), 207–26.

85 C. Doustaly, 'La genèse du soutien public aux beaux-arts', 207–29.

86 See the chapter 'Gender and Leisure Policy' in Aitchison, *Gender and Leisure,* 90–117; Scott, Crompton and Lyonette, *Gender Inequalities in the 21st Century,* 2, 4, and 10. See also numerous articles in the review *Leisure Studies.*

Index